Acknowledgments

We are indebted to a considerable number of people without whom this book would never have been written. It is not possible to thank them all without writing another book, but some names do stand out.

Over a decade before we lived in France, Professor Charles Taylor of McGill University taught both of us a method of thinking that allowed us to decode the French in record time, and that is very much at the origin of this book (though Charles Taylor has no doubt long forgotten both of us). Daniel Roux, Professor Thierry Leterre, Jean-Jacques Fraenkel, and Gustave (who we hope will recognize himself) shed invaluable light on the workings of the French mind and taught us many unexpected lessons. Miranda de Toulouse-Lautrec, David Hapgood, and Judson Gooding acted as sounding boards for our ideas many times over. Our agent Ed Knappman and our editor Hillel Black both went to bat for us and told us to be bold.

Finally, Peter Martin, director of the Institute of Current World Affairs, trusted us enough to pay our bills for two years in France and taught us to cultivate our first impressions. Lu Martin has been a constant source of support and encouragement to both of us.

To all we've named, and to the many friends and relatives who have given us inspiration, ideas, and support along the way, we would like to extend a big bear hug.

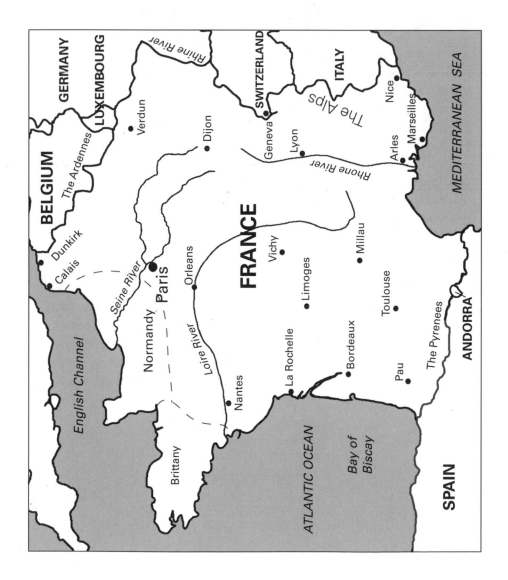

Sixty Million Frenchmen Can't Be Wrong

(why we love france, but not the french)

**Jean-Benoît Nadeau
& Julie Barlow**

SOURCEBOOKS, INC.®
NAPERVILLE, ILLINOIS

This publication is designed to provide accurate and authoritative information in
regard to the subject matter covered. It is sold with the understanding that the publisher is not engaged in rendering legal, accounting, or other professional service. If
legal advice or other expert assistance is required, the services of a competent professional person should be sought.—*From a Declaration of Principles Jointly Adopted by a
Committee of the American Bar Association and a Committee of Publishers and Associations*

Published by Sourcebooks, Inc.
P.O. Box 4410, Naperville, Illinois 60567-4410
(630) 961-3900
FAX: (630) 961-2168
www.sourcebooks.com

Library of Congress Cataloging-in-Publication Data

Nadeau, Jean-Benoît.
    Sixty Million Frenchmen can't be wrong : why we love France but not the French
/ By Jean-Benoît Nadeau and Julie Barlow.
    p. cm.
ISBN 1-4022-0045-5 (alk. paper)
1. National characteristics, French. 2. France—Social life and customs.
I. Title: 60 million Frenchmen can't be wrong. II. Barlow, Julie. III. Title.

DC34 .N33 2003
305.8'00944—dc21

                                2002153446

Printed and bound in the United States of America
                    VP   10   9   8

Table of Contents

Introduction

Imagine a country where people work thirty-five-hour weeks, take seven weeks of paid holidays per year, take an hour and a half for lunch, have the longest life expectancy in the world, and eat the richest food on the planet. A people who keep alive their mom-and-pop merchant class, who love nothing better than going to the public market on Sundays, and who finance the best health-care system in the world. A people whose companies are the least unionized and most productive among modern countries, and whose post-industrial consumer society ranks among the most prosperous in the world.

You are now in France.

Now imagine a country whose citizens have so little civic sense that it never crosses their minds to pick up after their dogs or give to charity. Where people expect the State to do everything because they pay so much in taxes. Where service is rude. Where the State is among the most centralized and pervasive in the world, and where the civil-servant class amounts to no less than a quarter of the working population. Where citizens tolerate no form of initiative or self-rule, where unions are so pervasive that they virtually dictate the course of government and even run French ministries.

You are still in France.

That was the riddle we faced when we arrived in Paris in January 1999, for a two-year stay. As we explored the country and reflected on our experiences there we would stumble upon even more mysteries. There was the famous "French Paradox," of course. Dieticians have never understood how the French smoke, drink, and eat more fat than anyone in the world, yet live longer, and have almost no obesity and fewer heart problems than Americans. We saw it firsthand, and we didn't understand it either.

But we also saw another kind of French Paradox that was equally puzzling. In spite of high taxes, a bloated civil service, a huge national debt, an over-regulated economy, over-the-top red tape, double-digit unemployment, and low incentives for entrepreneurs, France at the turn of the third millennium had the world's highest productivity index per hours worked, ranked as the number three exporter, was the world's fourth-biggest economic power, and had become Europe's powerhouse. How could this be? we wondered. France apparently wasn't meeting any of the criteria for growth according to the economic orthodoxy of the day. In case we forgot, influential publications like *The Economist, The Wall Street Journal,* and *Fortune* reminded us on a daily or weekly basis. *The New York Times* journalist Thomas Friedman published *The Lexus and the Olive Tree,* his bestseller on how globalization was changing the world (and how the world would have to change for globalization). His verdict on France was damning: "If France was a stock, I'd sell it," he wrote.

Among the many critical opinions of France, Thomas Friedman's held a special weight for us. In fact, among the many books we read on France written by American or British authors, his inspired us the most, or spurred us on, anyway. We had come to France as correspondents for the New Hampshire–based Institute of Current World Affairs. Jean-Benoît's project was to study why the French were resisting globalization. Julie was writing magazine articles on globalization-related topics. She interviewed the farmers who destroyed a McDonald's in southern France just before the World Trade Organization's ill-fated Seattle conference in December 1999. Then she talked to the director general of the World Trade Organization about the Seattle protests.

Globalization was certainly on everyone's minds when we arrived in France. But it wasn't the only issue the French were grappling with. It didn't take us long to see that France was a society in flux. The European Union had rolled in the euro eight days before we arrived, and the days of the franc were numbered. Socialist Prime Minister Lionel Jospin was privatizing government-owned French companies at a rate greater than Britain in the 1980s. Judges were beginning to launch serious investigations into embezzlement scandals, corruption, and influence trafficking among politicians. France's political class was reeling. It was not the same country we had visited as tourists seven years earlier.

It also didn't take us long to see that Thomas Friedman was wrong; his predictions hadn't come true, anyway. France's economy was doing quite well. On a hunch, we shifted the globalization idea to the backs of our minds and decided to just explore France and French thinking.

Thousands of elating and frustrating experiences reinforced or contradicted our ideas about the French over our first six months. We weren't just studying France; we were trying to make a life for ourselves. Anyone who has ever moved away from their own country knows about the unforeseeable problems that pop up every day, thwarting your effort to get comfortable in a foreign land. We decided to look at these problems as learning experiences, and they were. The process of opening a bank account, finding and furnishing an apartment, and making friends taught us many unexpected lessons.

After several months in France, it was pretty clear to us that the French were not really resisting globalization. Like just about everyone else on the planet, they were speculating about how *la mondialisation* would change their country. French companies, meanwhile, were proving to be serious players in the globalizing marketplace. Aerospace giant Airbus was already giving Boeing a beating. French car manufacturer Renault was taking control of Nissan. The French food distributor Carrefour had risen to number two after Wal-Mart.

So much for Jean-Benoît's fellowship topic.

Many things Thomas Friedman said about France in *The Lexus and the Olive Tree* were true. Yet we had the impression we were observing two countries in one. France was both rigidly authoritarian and incredibly inventive. It was a country that had barely any clout left on the international stage, but was still incredibly influential—a country at once traditional, if not archaic, and modern to the extreme. Clippings piled up in our filing cabinets, and notes accumulated in our journals. We had a paradoxical picture of France.

It took us nearly a year to realize that all these contradictions, or paradoxes, pointed to one conclusion: France was "something else" that could not be understood in the terms used in *The New York Times* or *Fortune* Magazine. Why the French were resisting globalization was the wrong question about the right topic. The French were globalizing in their own way. But France needed to be understood in its own terms. We thought of the joke that camels are horses designed by a committee. It's funny if you imagine someone trying to do dressage on a camel. But in the desert, the camel performs its required functions very well. There are reasons it looks the way it does, and all you have to do is see it in operation to understand.

Fortunately for us, the Institute of Current World Affairs allowed, and actually encouraged, Jean-Benoît to change his question. Instead of globalization, we decided to study France for what it is, to understand why it works the way it does.

At the same time that we were dealing with those paradoxes, we had to deal with the problem of sources, because it seemed that we could trust neither foreigners nor the French themselves on many issues. France has a peculiar charisma that drives people on both sides of the Atlantic to take firm positions on it—especially Americans and the French themselves, who seem locked in a perpetual spiritual rivalry, in spite of the United States' clear military and economic superiority. There is no shortage of anti-American sentiment in France, sprouting as it does from deep-seated Anglophobia, former Sovietphilia, and true cultural domination. Likewise, Americans who disparage France, say, for its huge government and mind-boggling bureaucracy, still tend to admire its culture. Yet the rivalry pushes opinion-makers to constantly hone definitive national traits and characteristics from mere news items. In France, this becomes clear every time a hot topic like anti-globalization, racism, or France's far-right party makes the international news.

The old joke that you can't see the forest for the trees is true about the French, who are in the middle of the forest. They were convinced, for example, that their trains were never on time and that the national rail service was going down the tubes. But it doesn't take much traveling in other countries to see how outstanding French train service is. French train conductors apologize if the Paris-Lyon is five minutes behind schedule. The French also complain bitterly about their health service, which is outstanding. At one point, we realized that if the French got away with making such outrageous generalizations, we just couldn't take their opinions about democracy, globalization, and racism as articles of faith.

In all cultural comparisons, there is a great temptation to turn to hard facts and numbers for firm conclusions. But in France, numbers and statistics have, at best, an illustrative value, especially for the purpose of comparison. Take one objective figure: 19 percent of the French population voted for the extreme right during the 2002 presidential elections. The way commentators ranted about it, it sounded like the consummation of a profound increase in racist sentiment in France—and it was a significant rise. Yet the figure was comparable to what you get in countries like Italy, Austria, Belgium, and the Netherlands for parties with a comparable program. Notwithstanding the 80 percent of electors who voted against the extreme right, many North Americans still felt justified in criticizing France. Yet the real issue may not be what it seems. There is probably a good 15 percent of the population in the United States or Canada that is also xenophobic, isolationist, and who would gladly vote for a law-and-order party if there was one. And for whom do American racists vote? No one knows because there is no single far-right party to tell us. But it doesn't mean that Americans or Canadians are any saner.

During our two and a half years in France, we kept ourselves very busy cutting through the slash of opinions coming from both sides of the Atlantic. This book is the sum of our findings, some of which challenge many long-held assumptions about France.

One of the basic assumptions we challenge is that France doesn't work, that it can't work. That's where Thomas Friedman inspired us, inversely. France clearly does work. Globalization will not spell France's demise. France has and will have political and economic problems like any other country. But it works. What makes it work is the harmony between the spirit of the French and the structures they have given themselves, structures that are genuinely theirs. This is what we describe in the first two parts of the book: Spirit and Structure.

We scratched our heads for many months wondering whether Spirit or Structure should come first in the book. Does the French mind-set determine the way they govern themselves, or is it the other way around? We decided that Spirit should come first because the roots of the French mind-set go back hundreds or even thousands of years, long before the modern French State even existed. The traditions of the French, their peculiar understanding of privacy, their love for *grandeur* and rhetoric, and their peculiar brand of political intolerance are the founding pillars of their society. We

xii   sixty million frenchmen can't be wrong

also included in this section two chapters on two traumatic episodes of recent history—World War II and the War of Algeria—that forced both a redefinition of structures and values in modern-day France.

The way we came to see it, the way the French think is like a landscape on which they built their structures. Different things move the French—as if they had different ropes, gears, and springs inside them. Oddly, Anglo-Americans can see that the Japanese, the Chinese, and the Indians are different, and that these fundamental differences shape national characters and the way things are done in those societies. Why can't we do this with the French? For some reason, we judge the French according to our own models, whether we're observing French business practices or social customs. In fact, the French have political and social reflexes that are absolutely alien to North Americans; their structures are built to suit those reflexes.

Paris being Paris, we must have received seventy-five guests at our home in the two and a half years we lived there. All of them were North Americans. Some knew France well, most had come more than once, and many were newcomers. Yet they had remarkably similar reactions. North Americans admire French culture, but when it comes to service in stores and other mysterious French ways, they really wonder why the French just can't be like them. Some of our visitors could see that French society worked on different gears and ropes, but they still thought, "It can't work." The most standard criticism we heard about the French was that the government was too big and the State too pervasive. Both observations are true.

Yet France does work. How? Our theory is that the structure of France is consistent with the spirit of the French. From how the government works with the State, to how France handles social programs, to the place of the local community and the social function of business, the French have the system the French need. It all holds together—and this book shows how.

The third section of this book deals with changes. It would be a mistake to be categorical about French spirit and structures. Neither is carved in stone. France has transformed itself many times during its history, and its present form and nature is only one more stage in the life of a very old people. So this last section explains the forces that are transforming France. We do address globalization, but briefly. Globalization is having less of an impact on France than other factors like immigration, sustained peace in Western Europe, democracy, and the European Union.

Part of what made this book possible was the freedom provided by the Institute of Current World Affairs to change our course of study when we wanted to. But two other factors allowed us to read the French in record time.

First, we felt authorized to take on the project of deciphering the French because, as a couple, we both had a foot in French and English cultures. Jean-Benoît Nadeau is a French-speaking Quebecker and Julie Barlow is an English-speaking Canadian from Ontario. At home, we speak both languages. We alternated weekly or monthly for ten years (with great discipline) and now, we regret to say, mix the two indiscriminately. For twelve years, before moving to France, we lived in Montreal, a city that is a hyphen between the English and French worlds. Even before getting to Europe, we were used to playing the biases of one culture against the other. Together we have published hundreds of magazine articles in French and in English. Personally and professionally, our lives have been about arbitrating two cultures for each other, our friends, our families, our colleagues, and our readers. Without really thinking about it, we trained ourselves as observers of cross-cultural differences.

The other factor that made this book possible was our method of studying France. Although we are both trained journalists, we decided to work like ethnologists when we got to France. Journalists report on what's new, try to get the meaning, and see how it fits in the big picture. Speed is the essence of their work, and to achieve this they use a number of tricks, like anecdotes or quotes and opinions from high-profile personalities. Ethnologists work more slowly. They can rely on news for information, but they don't produce news. They look for the big picture, examining each piece of the puzzle to understand how it fits. In that light, everything is significant: a remark, an article, a declaration, the small episodes of life, both pleasant and unpleasant. In spite of our training as journalists, this book is not "newsy": we did observe some important current events, like the 2002 presidential elections, but our approach has been to go beyond the news. We hope it will be used to understand the news about France: past, present, and future.

Contrary to journalists, who have to work quickly, we had the leisure to spend more than two years making up our minds about the French. And we did take our time. Like anthropologists landing in a tribe in the middle of the Amazon, we started by getting ourselves accepted there. Jean-Benoît joined a hiking club. Julie traveled in Europe, the Middle East, and North Africa. We ate and drank with friends, invited them for dinner, tried new restaurants, helped them move into new houses, supported them through job losses and personal crises, cycled, hiked, and shopped with them. Our friends were Holocaust survivors, *élite* civil servants, single-mother nurses, auto mechanics, accountants, lawyers, architects, graduate students, hospital employees, engineers, and more.

Our own neighborhood in mixed, working-class Paris was also an endless source of learning. In spite of its glamorous appearance, Paris is a hidden, private city. You only get to see inside when Parisians decide to let you in. And they only let you in when they know who you are. That was easier for us than for many expatriates because we lived and worked in the same apartment and spent most of our time in the square mile that made up our neighborhood in the eighteenth *arrondissement*. The locals all got to know our daily routines, which greatly increased our status in the neighborhood and opened many doors. When we weren't within our square mile, we traveled extensively across France to get as wide a feel of the country as possible. On our first trip we found ourselves in the middle of a comic book festival (a major local form of art) in Angoulême. We attended an agriculture salon that turned out to be a window to French food. We rowed in the canals of the Marais Poitevin, near La Rochelle, and ski trekked across the Alps. We listened to Franco-Arabic *rai* music in Marseilles and watched European-made helicopters making loops at the Le Bourget air show.

This, it turned out, was just what we needed to make sense of this unfamiliar, immense territory: the mind of the French.

We would like to make a couple of cautionary notes at this stage.

First, the reader will have to pardon our use of many French terms like *jacobin*, *Département*, *paritarisme*, *lycée*, and more. We've done our best to explain them, but many don't translate well, if at all. And that, in itself, is a sign that France really runs on a distinct model. The country can only be explained in its own terms.

Some readers familiar with other parts of Europe may think that a number of the things we write about the French also apply to other Europeans, especially in the case of our first three topics: time, land, and privacy. They're right, but this only proves that France did not evolve in a vacuum. The French share many of the fundamental characteristics of all Western European cultures, though they put their own spin on them.

The title, borrowed from a Cole Porter musical—*Fifty Million Frenchmen Can't Be Wrong*—is not meant to be taken literally. It merely reflects our sympathy, and our goal to challenge assumptions about France. It is easy to pass judgment on the French, but much harder to examine them in their own terms and on their own turf—hence the title. (We recognize that it is fundamentally sexist, but Cole Porter and his era are to blame for that).

Although we frequently refer to history, this book is not a history of France. Neither is it a specialized study of sociology, demography, political theory, or economics. Our book is a study of France.

And in case there are any misconceptions, we did not move to France to renovate a house in Provence. What we are trying to do is renovate some ideas.

PART ONE:

spirit

chapter 1

Meet the Aborigines

When we arrived in Paris at the beginning of Jean-Benoît's fellowship, it was only the second time we had set foot in France. We were tourists, and at the outset we looked at France through the eyes of vacationers. Whenever we could squeeze some free time out of the jumble of immigration, housing, and banking predicaments that monopolized our first few months in Paris, we strolled the streets in awe. The city and its monuments seemed ancient beyond belief. We visited a park in the Latin Quarter that was the site of a Roman arena from the first century A.D. In the very place we were observing smartly dressed, well-behaved little French children chasing balls under the watchful gaze of their nannies, ten thousand citizens of the Roman Empire once watched gladiator combats. The idea made us giddy. Everywhere we went we saw remnants of a past we could hardly imagine. We scrutinized rows of fifteenth-century houses on the left bank whose facades still slanted backward according to medieval construction techniques. The proud owner of a restaurant next to the Paris city hall led us down to his basement to show us the building's thirteenth-century foundation.

But one of our most acute time-warp sensations came months later, after a hike along the Seine river that ended in La Roche Guyon, a small town built on a bend of the river twenty miles west of Paris. The founders of La Roche Guyon chose a spectacular location for their village, nestling it between the river and a four hundred–foot cliff of white chalk. The more we looked around, the more La Roche Guyon impressed us with its historical layers. On the highest spur, right over the town of La Roche Guyon, there was a twelfth-century dungeon. At the base of the dungeon there was a Renaissance castle. In the cliff behind the castle, we saw the bunker where the German Marshal Erwin Rommel (1891–1944) defended Normandy against the Allies in World War II (the way he saw it, anyway). Then, as we walked across the town, we noticed several dozen houses dug straight into the cliff. The houses had neat French facades and Peugeots parked in front of them. We asked the nearby shopkeepers about them and were told that the houses were actually ancient cave dwellings, updated with modern amenities, and still inhabited.

Like many North Americans, who live on a slate wiped clean of history, we never got over the thrill of carrying out our modern lives among Roman ruins and medieval churches. Even though a lot of the monuments and structures we saw predated the founding of America, they were just part of people's daily lives in modern France. Sometimes we found them in completely unsuspecting places. East of La Rochelle, the utterly uninspiring city of Angoulême boasts nothing less than a Gothic city hall. In Provence, Avignon's massive Palace of the Popes, built in the fourteenth century, sits smack in the middle of the city's bustling downtown. To top off this effect of strange historical juxtapositions, we noticed that in many French cities, modern and ancient structures were built out of stone the same color as the gravel in the alleys. In other words, French cities looked like they had gradually grown out of the soil over the centuries, or in some cases, the millennia. Paris's Notre Dame Cathedral (the part they've cleaned, anyway) is the beige color of the city's native stone, and so is the Louvre, the Versailles palace, and even twentieth-century apartment buildings.

Later, this helped us make one of our first breakthroughs in understanding France: it is impossible to disassociate the past from the present. There is no clear line to divide ancient from modern in France, and what goes for architecture, goes for the people, too. As a society, they slowly grew out of the soil. It's as if they live in the past and the present at the same time. Yet it took us a while to figure out what that actually meant.

Our first impression of the French was that they were busy living modern lives. When we got to France, people were starting to moan about the troubles the new euro would cause them. Life didn't look that different from what we were used to in North America. People drove their Renaults to work and heated up frozen lasagna from *Picard* for supper. Even while we were starstruck by castles, churches, and dungeons, many things about the country struck us as incredibly modern. "Smart cards"—cards with microprocessor chips that carry personal information and an ID code—made modern commerce feel space age to us.

At the same time, there were moments when we felt like we were living in the past. Smart cards worked well in automated machines, but when we went to the bank in person, the clerks could not use them to access our accounts. We had to give them our name and account number (which we learned to carry around on a little slip of paper in our wallets). In restaurants, waiters tallied our bill and processed our payment with little remote-control microwave radios—very advanced technology. However, when we asked for the directions to the rest rooms, they sometimes showed us to an outdoor Turkish toilet, essentially a glorified hole in the ground.

Other mind-boggling customs left us scratching our heads as we were impatiently tapping our toes. Our baker individually wrapped every pastry she sold no matter how many people were waiting behind us to place their orders. Our dry cleaner meticulously (and slowly) wrapped each article in paper, gingerly, as if our shirts were *St-Honoré* cakes. At the grocery store in our neighborhood, people still paid by check, even for five-dollar purchases. We got the finishing touch when we rented our apartment and the rental agent handed us a set of oversize keys straight out of *The Count of Monte Cristo*. Just what era do the French live in, anyway? we wondered.

We started to get the answer to this question nine months after our arrival, during a visit to the Périgord region, east of the city of Bordeaux. Périgord is the destination of choice for the world's gourmands. It's the land of *foie gras*, truffles, and duck *confit*. The area's most beautiful city, Sarlat, is a jewel of preservation with its narrow, winding, cobblestone streets, perfectly restored medieval houses, and stunning collage of Romanesque, Gothic, neoclassical, and Renaissance architecture. But preservation is perhaps too strong a word. Until the 1960s, the residents of Sarlat actually *lived* in medieval conditions, with no electricity or running water. It was the Minister of Culture of the time, André Malraux, who saved them. In 1962 he created a law for the preservation of historical monuments and Sarlat, a twenty-year renovation project, was his several-hundred-million-dollar guinea pig.

There is no museum in Sarlat: Sarlat is the museum. Several houses in the city still have original roofs made of *lauze* (flat stones piled on top of one another). We arrived at the tail end of the tourist season and made the most amazing discovery of all: Sarlat is also a regular town, where regular people lead regular lives in spite of the historical splendor. Three steps out of the historical quarter we ran into the shiny facade of a Monoprix drugstore.

On the same trip, we visited the town of Les Eyzies, along the river Vézère, a tributary of the Dordogne. Once again, we confronted this clash of modern and ancient lives, except this time the history went much farther back. Les Eyzies is where archaeologists identified the first specimen of the Cro Magnon man of the Paleolithic age, a couple of ice ages ago. The term Cro Magnon is Occitan, one of the dialects spoken widely in southern France until one hundred years ago. Cro Magnon just means Mr. Magnon's Hole. Mr. Magnon was the nineteenth-century Frenchmen who owned the barn built over the rock shelter right where the first known Frenchman was discovered—he was buried there some twenty-two thousand years ago. There are dozens of other prehistoric sites along the river Vézère, including the cave paintings of Lascaux that are more than twenty thousand years old.

We were aware of France's ancient past before visiting Périgord, but we hadn't tried to fit space-age modernity and ancient civilizations into one frame. We didn't see a single picture, only a confused patchwork.

Then, all of a sudden, as the French would say, the mayonnaise took.

It occurred to us that the French are really the aborigines of France. The word aborigines is usually associated with primitive peoples now, but it really just means "original." The ancestors of the French go back several ice ages. They are not a people who, like North Americans, arrived in the midst of a primitive culture, erased it, and started over. They have always been there. There was plenty of upheaval throughout French history, but no definitive break with the past. In America, the parallel would be something like this: the Indians won, not the cowboys, and the Aztecs went on to create a country that sent rockets into orbit and delivered the mail twice a day, but still celebrated human sacrifice on the stairs of pyramids.

For North Americans, the past and the present are two categories. We of the New World associate modernity with something novel that arrived on a ship and pushed aside every tradition that stood in its way so it could build something new. We may try to convince ourselves otherwise, but when we want to build something new, instinct tells us to first get rid of the old. In the relative wilderness that was North America even one hundred years ago, getting rid of the old was not even necessary most of the time.

It would be a mistake to suggest that the French have always glorified their past. On the contrary, they have tried to rid themselves of their past many times during their history. Cathedrals, châteaux, and entire cities in France have been razed during wars and invasions (or, in the case of Paris, because of a mix of hygienic necessity and grand urban ambitions). But the past was never erased, probably because there's just too much of it. Everything in France is built on layers of other things that existed before. The present in France is only a compromise between the past and the present.

And so it is with the French themselves.

In 1830, while he was doing the research for his groundbreaking work *Democracy in America*, French writer Alexis de Tocqueville was struck by how new the New World was. "America is the only country where we can clearly see the point of departure," he wrote—which makes America more the exception than the rule. Tocqueville identified one of the fundamental differences in American and European thinking and culture and it still holds. Americans have no past, while Europeans are loaded down by ancient customs, habits, and prejudices that shape their behavior.

French history is so long and complicated that it's impossible to define when France actually became a country. We could recount a different version of France's origins for each chapter of this book and not repeat ourselves. There is no clear beginning. Depending on what point a historian wants to prove, it might have started with the Gaulish chief Vercingetorix

(72–46 B.C.) who resisted the Romans, or with Frankish King Clovis (466–511 A.D.) who first unified the country into a kingdom, or with Frankish emperor Charlemagne (742–814 A.D.) who created the first empire. Or with King Louis VI the Big (1108-37), who first consolidated the king's power in the Paris area. Or with any of their sixty-four kings— and that's not counting characters like Napoleon, Richelieu, and Charles de Gaulle, or institutions like the *Académie Française* of the *Conseil d'État*, all of which to some extent defined modern France.

So on one hand, it's impossible to say where France started. But on the other hand, there has never been a clear break between all these rulers and empires and the modern country of France. The French are their own native peoples.

The term aborigine, of course, does not designate a single ethnicity. There is no such thing as an "ethnic" French person. No matter how far back you trace the country's evolution, it's impossible to establish a shared ethnicity across France, and the nearer you get to the present, the more mixed it becomes. France is a hodgepodge. There were the Gauls (though nobody knows what they were), who adopted the Roman culture and language quite willingly. Saxon, Viking, Moorish, and English invaders came and went after that. Only centuries later did national identities start to emerge in Europe. The people you meet in France are really descendants of all the tribes and races that ever invaded France, and all the immigrants that ever flocked there from other countries.

In present-day France, one-third of the population has grandparents that were born outside of France. Waves of European immigration in France in the early twentieth century were quickly absorbed. After a generation or two, sometimes less, they took on the French spirit and became indistinguishable among citizens in speech, manners, or taste. One of France's greatest prime ministers, Mazarin, was Italian. Marie Antoinette was Austrian. Napoleon was Corsican. Alexandre Dumas, author of *The Three Musketeers*, was mulatto. At our home in Paris, no more than one-third of the plaques on the mailboxes had traditional old-stock French names. Most of the Ben Jelils, Ben Hammoudas, Johnsons, and Lopezes were no less French than the Ledoux, Sutras, and Nadeaus. And if they were, they wouldn't be for more than a generation or two. It is not race, or a myth of common origin, that binds the French. The French are French because of the culture they share.

And that culture is a native one. This idea profoundly affected our way of thinking about them. It broke down an important division that we, as North Americans, spontaneously make about the modern and the old. We understood that when we tapped our toes at the bakery and sighed and rolled our eyes at the dry cleaners, the problem was us, not them. We were holding the French up to New World standards. The French are modern. But they're no more New World than the Japanese.

The typical traveler to Japan, China, or Africa is more open-minded than the typical traveler to France. The fascinating rites of the Chinese, Japanese, or Zulus may cause travelers considerable discomfort and inconvenience, but travelers in these countries tend to accept the obstacles stoically, reasoning (rightly) that things are just done differently in foreign cultures. For some reason, when it comes to the French, North Americans drop this reflex. We lodged dozens of North American friends and family members during our stay in Paris, and we saw this syndrome unfold over and over. When North Americans, or more broadly, "Anglo-Saxons," (in chapter 20 we explain what the French mean by this term) are faced with France's peculiar way of doing things, they do not reason that they are dealing with an ancient people who have their own way of doing things. Actually, they accuse the French of being inefficient, overly bureaucratic, unhygienic, and stuck in their ways. And they take it personally.

We tried this aborigine concept out on a number of our French friends to see how it would go over. It didn't go over. They thought we were equating France to an underdeveloped nation. But aboriginal doesn't actually mean underdeveloped, backward, or primitive. As we noted earlier, it means original, the first ones there.

What our French friends didn't understand was that we chose the word "aboriginal" to show humility, something North Americans are hard-pressed to remember when they're faced with French bureaucracy, "rude" service, or "arrogant" behavior. Everyone admires Paris's cathedrals, cobbled streets, monuments, statues, and gold-plated obelisks, yet the more we examined the country, spoke to the French, and read their magazines and newspapers, the more it became obvious to us that the people were as ancient as their castles. French culture is a Noah's ark of atavisms, customs, temperaments, and attitudes that took shape over dozens of centuries of history. And when you look closely at the facts of everyday life in France, the intricate links between past and present rise to the surface. This chapter only touches on these links, but it is a theme that recurs in almost every topic we discuss in this book. There are always reasons things work the way they do in France, whether you look at France through a political, sociological, anthropological, or other lens. France is a modern country, but new technologies are adapted to old mentalities and the old mentalities endure. Why would it be otherwise?

Despite what North Americans and Anglo-Saxons think, there's really no contradiction between being resolutely modern and ferociously archaic at the same time. The French are the proof that it can work. The French invented the metric system, the Civil Code, high-speed trains, and the Concorde. But they also relish traditions, native and borrowed. They still produce blue cheese like Roquefort according to a technique that dates back twelve centuries and play medieval Italian card games like Tarot. Napoleon modernized contractual law and created the Civil Code, which is now used by most European countries. Yet French criminal law still applies principles that date back to the Inquisition. At the same time as President Charles de Gaulle (1944–46, 1958–69) was creating French astronautics, he was so old-fashioned that he refused to answer a telephone and toyed with the idea of reestablishing the monarchy. Traces of the past are evident in everyday language. When the French speak of ministries of war, diplomacy, finance, and the interior, they refer to these as the *regalian* ("the king's") powers.

But the real lessons about how the past and the present coexist are there in the day-to-day life of the country. A week or so before our departure from Montreal, a French friend in Montreal congratulated us for choosing our dates so wisely. We didn't know it when we left, but mid-January to mid-February is the period of *Les Soldes* (The Sales) in France. For a month, almost all the stores throughout the country put their merchandise on sale. Theoretically, we could have furnished our apartment for a song. (In reality, we were too busy weeding through bureaucratic problems that month to go shopping, and we felt like we were stuck in the middle of a permanent Boxing Day sale.)

Les Soldes is not a custom. The police set the dates and supervise the sales across the country: stores are only allowed to have sales from mid-January to mid-February and from mid-June to mid-July. To hold a sale outside that period, merchants have to obtain special approval from the police. The rest of the year, small shops and big retailers can't so much as offer a rebate without facing the wrath of the law.

We decided to look into this "tradition" and learned that it dates back to practices of the merchants' guilds in the Middle Ages. At that time, guilds had two functions: they settled disputes among tradesmen of one town and protected the tradesmen against competition from other towns. Guilds set the standards for quality and pricing—they made rules along the lines of "bread can't contain more than 10 percent sand" (thankfully standards have evolved). Guilds guaranteed social protection to their members and, starting in the thirteenth century, even managed their members' retirement funds. But if individuals failed to abide by the rules set by the guild, a medieval cop known as the Provost broke their legs. Provosts evolved into police officers (though many French would dispute the claim that they evolved at all), but the system of policing prices and sales continues in the form of *Les Soldes*. And the practice or regulating sales predates the discovery of America by at least three hundred years.

In architecture and urban planning, remnants of the past shape the present in ways that might even surprise a lot of French. Strolling along the swanky avenue Deaumesnil one afternoon, we popped into a boutique where a Paris map from the 1730s had caught our eye. At the time the map was drawn, Paris was about a quarter of its present size, but the future boundaries of the modern city were visible in the ring of farmland and hunting domains around the city. The present-day *Place de l'Étoile*—where the *Arc de Triomphe* stands—is visible on the map. In 1730 it was in the middle of a forest. Up until that moment we had assumed that *places*, where streets converge in roundabouts, were the result of the city-wide renovations that transformed Paris in the middle of the nineteenth century.

Clearly it wasn't so. The *Place de l'Étoile* existed before it was absorbed by Paris. As it turns out, many roundabouts in Paris are vestiges of an old hunting custom. Hunters used to clear crossroads of forest paths in order to be able to spot animals when they came out of the bush. By increasing the number of paths that converged on crossroads, hunters increased their chances of spotting game. When the city encroached on these hunting grounds, it simply absorbed the crossroads that were already there (along with the names, apparently).

The French, like the rest of the world, have only held onto their history when it suited their needs or adhered to the fashions of a given time. Notre Dame Cathedral was used as a saltpeter plant during the French Revolution. It had fallen into such neglect by the middle of the nineteenth century that authorities considered demolishing it and using the stones to build bridges. Determined to save the decaying monument, French author Victor Hugo wrote the novel *Notre Dame de Paris* in the hopes of getting French authorities to take an interest in it (it worked). Likewise, we now gaze at Gothic architecture in admiration. But at the time of Louis XIV, it was regarded as passé and torn down wherever people could afford to replace it.

The French have an old expression: *un passé qui ne passe pas* (a past that doesn't pass), which denotes the ambiguous relationship they have with their own history. It is not always easy to live with the weight of ancient traditions, and at times, France has been shaken with very violent attempts to get rid of them. The French Revolution is a good example. Some innovations introduced during the revolution, like the decimal calendar, never took root. But others, like the *préfet*, the administrative head of the French departments, still endure. France has been through other violent ruptures, like the period of 1870 to 1900, when the State waged a battle against the Catholic Church, to the point of closing three thousand religious establishments in 1902. Between 1936 and 1945 French society was subject to extremely violent tensions that resulted in a new constitution and mass nationalization of industry. France at the turn of the third millennium is the sum of what was preserved and what was discarded throughout the country, for as many reasons as there are French men and women.

By calling French culture "native" we aren't suggesting it is permanent or unchanging. We're just calling attention to the fact that old mentalities persist within new customs. The globalizers of the world would do well to remember this.

On Halloween of 1999, sitting in a café overlooking the port of Honfleur, in Normandy, we had this thought as we watched a bizarre exercise of cultural cross-fertilization unfold before our eyes. Halloween is only a few years old in France. It's not an easy custom to adapt, partly because French urban structures don't lend themselves well to trick or treating. Kids would need to know the four-number *digicode* of many buildings just to get through the door to ring doorbells, and there aren't many front porches for people to decorate. In Honfleur, local authorities found a way to surmount these logistical obstacles. They organized a Halloween parade so local children could trick or treat *en masse* in the cafés and shops along the port.

People, of course, draw on the models they already have—Halloween in Honfleur looked and sounded more like a labor strike than the traditional children's ritual we were accustomed to. The Honfleur children marched in a crowd between police cruisers, their little fists raised, chanting, "We want candies! We want candies!" And what did they do as they proceeded along the port? They actually stormed all the restaurants and boutiques in their path ordering merchants to hand over the goods. We were stunned to see this hostile pack of rampaging ghosts and ghouls (they were having fun, though) but even more surprised to see the grown-up French going along with it.

But when we thought about it, it made sense. Begging for candy—even pretend begging—isn't very noble, especially in a country where there's no tradition of philanthropy. People draw on the models they have. Demanding candy via a legally recognized, police-escorted *manifestation* made more sense to the French, even when they were just having fun.

So much for trying to teach an old country new tricks.

chapter 2

The Land on Their Mind

Late in the morning of August 12, 1999, a rag-tag procession of French sheep farmers' families gathered in Renaults and Citroens on the edge of the Larzac Plateau in Southern France. Idling behind four tractor-trailers, they rolled down the slope of the plateau toward Millau, a town of twenty-five thousand dug deep in the Tarn River Canyon. About halfway down the hill, the procession turned off the highway into a parking lot where a half-built, nondescript, brown edifice stood locked behind a chain-link fence. Two yellow and red flags fluttering over the parking lot revealed the building's future vocation as a McDonald's restaurant. The farmers had definitely not come for the food. They were about to perform what they called a "symbolic dismantling."

No one who had been warned about the event knew what a "symbolic dismantling" was, yet nothing at the time suggested it would be anything more than a run-of-the-mill French demonstration. The Larzac farmers said they were demonstrating to protest a grab bag of issues: the 100 percent surtax the U.S. government had recently slapped on Roquefort cheese, the World Trade Organization, multinational corporations, genetically modified food, and fast food. There were a few local TV reporters standing by, smoking distractedly while the farmers poured onto the asphalt in front of the McDonald's. Four policemen had shown up to make sure nothing got out of control.

The farmers drove their tractor-trailers straight through the fence. One protester broke open the McDonald's door, while several others jumped from the trucks onto the restaurant's roof to begin painting their slogan on the brown tiles: "Out with McDo, Protect our Roquefort" (the famous blue cheese).

The rest of the farmers proceeded to strip off roof tiles, paneling, pipes, and every other removable part of the restaurant they could find, and started piling the McDonald's remains onto their trucks. While the farmers joyfully sacked the restaurant, their wives handed out chunks of blue-rippled Roquefort cheese on French baguette bread to bystanders. After an hour and a half, the restaurant was stripped clean and only four walls, the windows, and a foundation remained. The farmers drove the debris to the prefecture of police and deposited it on its front step, then headed home to tend to their sheep.

Little did the authorities know that this McDonald's was about to become one of the most famous in the world. The man who had come up with the idea of the "symbolic dismantling," José Bové, was also about to become one of the most famous Frenchman in the world and a household name in his homeland.

We had been living in France for six months at the time, and were used to seeing demonstrations almost everywhere we traveled, but this was the first time we'd heard about a group protesting globalization—or so it seemed. August is a slow month in France's newsrooms since the whole country takes the month off for holidays, so the Paris media relished the opportunity to report on a colorful, provocative event that had an international angle. Within a few days, the story of the McDonald's protest virtually monopolized the French media. The police arrested four of the farmers' leaders, but couldn't find the ring leader, José Bové. They declared him a fugitive. When Bové turned himself in (he had been vacationing in Bordeaux), all the national papers and television stations were there to document his surrender. When French authorities saw the story was getting blown out of proportion, they decided to release the farmers, but Bové refused to pay his bail, *à la Gandhi*. The sympathetic farmer, with his droopy mustache and shackled wrists, was back in the headlines. And the story grew.

In the next two weeks eighteen European deputies, from greens and communists to the extreme right, demanded Bové's release—including socialist prime minister Lionel Jospin. There were scores of demonstrations by unions and farmers across the country. Messages of support flowed in from as far away as Amazonia and *The New York Times* ran an article portraying Bové as France's new "anti-globalization hero."

Since we had moved to France six months earlier to study why they were resisting globalization, we thought we had struck gold. Talk of the World Trade Organization's upcoming Seattle conference was in the air and anti-American sentiment had been intensifying since the beginning of the NATO bombings in Kosovo. Bové's story seemed to be the culmination of all of this.

But his incredible popularity left us a bit mystified. After his release from prison, Julie decided to shadow Bové for a few months, following him to conferences and protests to try to put her finger on why the French had turned him into an icon. Later that fall, we visited Larzac and met the other farmers who were jailed after the McDonald's sacking. The fastest route to Larzac is a good ten hours from Paris, but it turned out to be time very well spent because in Larzac we discovered that Bové's protest and growing personality cult were less about globalization than they were about the peculiar relationship the French have with their land.

In Larzac, farmers carry out their business pretty much the way it's always been done, on family farms of a couple hundred sheep each, feeding their stock mainly what they grow on their own land. As we would soon see, innovation is not a particularly popular concept there. The farmers we met were far more likely to wax on about what they were feeding their sheep at the moment, scooping up handfuls of grass and grain and explaining the proportion and provenance of the different grains and grasses. José Bové is one among twenty-five hundred farmers in the one hundred–mile radius of the town of Roquefort-sur-Soulzon who raise sheep mainly for milk used in the famous blue Roquefort cheese. On his farm in the hamlet of Montredon, he and his two associates at the time were raising 550 sheep, forty pigs, and seven cows, both for meat and milk, and producing their own salty cheese, *la Tomme*, which they sold directly on the market.

Roquefort cheese is a two hundred million dollar per year business. About 80 percent of the fifteen thousand tons produced each year are bought by the French, who pay more than thirty dollars a kilo for the delicacy. Roquefort cheese can only be produced in the caves of the town of Roquefort-sur-Soulzon because it is aged using a particular bacteria that reproduces there. It was the first non-wine produce in France to be granted the AOC label (*Appellation of d'Origine Contrôlée*). According to the standards of this centrally controlled quality assurance stamp, cheese can only be called Roquefort if it meets three conditions: the milk used to make it must come from the sheep of the twenty-five hundred sheep producers who operate in a radius of about one hundred miles of the town; three-quarters of what those sheep eat has to come from the ground of that same one hundred–mile radius; and the cheese must be aged in the Roquefort caves. (It's the same logic that applies to the labels of champagne. Champagne comes from the region of Champagne, and Bordeaux come from around Bordeaux.) AOCs are a kind of non-moveable trademark recognized by both the European Union and the World Trade Organization. The owners of the Roquefort caves, the Besnier Group (who purchased the whole deal from Nestlé and Perrier), can only make as much cheese as the ground in the designated radius of Roquefort can produce: the area supports about seven hundred thousand sheep.

Such restrictions obviously limit the production. Farmers get good prices by limiting the quantity of milk they produce and increasing its quality as much as possible. Because of those restrictions, there will never be big sheep farming operations in the Larzac area, nor big fortunes to make. However, the sheep farmers never go broke either, and the French get their cheese. The AOC system also applies to wine and other high-quality products like nuts, green lentils, and even onions. Call it subsidies, call it protectionism, but it sounds logical to most French men and women, even if they do indulge in fast food from time to time. (The Bové anecdotes will recur in chapters 5, 10, 16, 17, and 20.) Trade deregulation of the kind the World Trade Organization promotes does indeed threaten this kind of production—so it's no surprise that the French react suspiciously to the World Trade Organization and its agenda. José Bové became a hero for deciding to take on the WTO himself.

A lot of the peculiarities of French society, including their obsession with food, can be traced back to the relationship the French have with their land. During our first week in France, we stayed with two very friendly, helpful women who operated a bed and breakfast out of the second floor of their apartment. Josée was a retired teacher who volunteered for an association to assist victims of crime. Anne was a professor of microbiology at a Paris university. They were a modern and worldly lesbian couple who read *Le Monde* and kept up to date on cultural events in the city. For a few days we were sure we were in the presence of true *Parisiennes*.

We weren't. Like most people who live in Paris, our hosts told us they were *de la province* (the expression, borrowed from ancient Rome, means "anywhere outside of the capital"). "*Mon pays c'est l'Angevin*" (My country is the Anjou region) Josée informed us. Anne picked up the cue, and reported, "*Mon pays c'est le Dijonnais.*"(My country is the Dijon region). We were puzzled. We thought their country was France.

The French word *pays* (pay-ee) doesn't translate. Literally, it means country. But inside France, it refers to areas that are recognized as distinct, though they aren't delineated by legal or administrative boundaries. Over the two years we spent in Paris we only made two friends who were true Parisians, meaning fourth or fifth generation. The rest told us they came from some *pays* or another, including *le Périgord* (east of Bordeaux), *le Trégor* (in Brittany), *le Dauphinais* (next to the Alps), or Larzac.

There are hundreds of *pays* in France. If you ask the French where they were born, they'll give you the name of their *pays*, certainly not the number of their *Département* (the ninety-nine administrative units of the French territory). *Pays* are the spiritual countries of origin of the French— some are former kingdoms or duchies from hundreds of years ago, others are just regions around France's major cities.

The first thing we noticed about *pays* was how intricately linked they are to regional cuisine. During a hike, a friend of Jean-Benoît's took a picture of him leaning against a road post that read: Rozay-en-Brie 12 km, Coulommiers 32 km, Chaumes 5 km. Brie, Coulommiers, and Chaumes are best known as famous cheeses, but first, they are three distinct *pays* east of Paris. Beaujolais is not first a wine, but a *pays* north of Lyon. Roquefort and Châteauneuf-du-Pape are other *pays* in the south of France.

The French are obsessed with their land, its geography, its history, and the traditions that sprung from it, and no matter where they end up living, their *pays* stays with them. These geographical origins occupy a much bigger place in individuals' identities than even "home towns" do in North Americans'. Cuisine is extremely varied among France's different *pays* and the French hang on to their regional tastes with a fervor bordering on national pride. Eating with friends can feel like a flag-waving session.

Over our three years in France, we understood that the French attachment to their land went well beyond the dinner table. It is often said that the relative paucity of the British Isles and their isolation contributed to their British character, making them defiant of the rest of Europe, and pushing them to seek elsewhere what their land could not provide. The opposite conditions in France seem to have created the opposite result. France's land is rich and varied. And if anything, that has pushed them to constantly look inward.

Nature has blessed France with a combination of physical characteristics that gave it a natural head start when it comes to gastronomy. The first is a moderate climate. France isn't quite as big as Texas, and it enjoys about the same climate. The only instances of cold, even polar, weather are found in the south, in the high mountain ranges of the Alps and the Pyrenees. France can thank the Gulf Stream for its mild weather, but also the fact that there are no mountain ranges in the west, which means trade winds sprinkle rainwater evenly over the country. France is also a peninsula, which means two seas, west and south, regulate its climate. It suffers few continental weather swings simply because the continent lies far to the east—down from the trade winds.

Geographically, France is spectacularly varied, although it is smaller than Texas. Every fifty miles or so the climate and the landscape change, from permanent snow and glaciers in the Alps to active volcanoes and lake areas in the center of the country, to rain forests in the Basque area, long fishing shores down the west coast, and finally, arid plateaus north of the Mediterranean. Very long and quiet rivers drain the territory, the longest being the Loire River, which flows just south of Paris. Around Paris vast plains provide land suitable for highly productive agriculture, and everywhere else in the country distinct soil types make it possible to grow almost anything. Only Italy's land comes close to matching the exceptional diversity and generosity of the French land. But the Germans declared the winner in the rivalry long ago with their expression *Leben wie Gott in Frankreich*: "Living like God in France."

France's geography also has built-in protection from outside threats. The French refer to their country as the Hexagon because it has roughly six sides. France's borders were not delineated by treaties or geometric conventions like parallels and meridians. The Atlantic Ocean and the Mediterranean make up three sides. The border with Spain, an impregnable barrier of mountains, is the fourth. To the east, the Alps and the Rhine make the fifth side. The sixth side, France's only real open border, is shared with Belgium, Luxembourg, and Germany, and a part of that is the Ardennes, a series of plateaus and deep canyons that are difficult to pass.

The most obvious characteristic the French share with their geography is diversity. In a famous interview with *Newsweek* in 1961, President Charles de Gaulle (1944–46, 1958–69) asked, "How can anyone govern a country that has 246 kinds of cheese?" What he meant was, "How can anyone be expected to govern 246 different kinds of French?" France has miraculously and curiously projected an image of cultural uniformity to the outside world. Inside, French men and women cherish their regional identities as if they were ethnic origins—and they often are.

Until the French Revolution, France was a divided patchwork of nationalities similar to the present-day Balkans. There was hardly any relationship between the Alsatians, the Flemish, the Bretons, the Basques, the Occitans, the Burgundians, the Lyonnais, the Bordelais, the Provençaux, the Corsicans, and the Savoyards. They all spoke different languages, lived in distinct geographical areas, and, of course, ate different food. Even one hundred years ago a lot of the French still spoke regional languages. More than once in our travels in France we met people whose parents or grandparents had never spoken a word of French, although their families had inhabited the territory for hundreds of years. France didn't end up like the Balkans because Paris effectively bulldozed regional differences after the Revolution to create a common French identity. Still, many regional differences subsisted, in a subdued way.

Cuisine is one of them. For an article he was writing on decentralization, Jean-Benoît interviewed Jean-Claude Jandin, a high-ranking civil servant who ran a nonprofit organization networking cities around Orléans. Jandin lived in Paris and worked in Orléans. His *pays* was *la Lorraine*, not far from the German border. He replied to Jean-Benoît's observation by saying *"Ach so!"* instead of *"Ah oui."* A keen observer of present-day regionalisms in France, Jandin believed cuisine became important to the French precisely because it was one of the few modes of expression of local cultures that the French State didn't eliminate in the centuries of centralization following the Revolution. Sometimes the nuances became quite elaborate. In an Orléans restaurant, over a plate of beef cheek, Jandin explained that although everyone ate red cabbage in his *pays*, Catholics ate it cold and Protestants ate it hot.

Wine drinkers familiar with French or Italian wines will know the expression *terroir*. In the case of wine, *terroir* refers to the particular traces of flavor left by specific soils. The term also refers to the specific local foods of any country. In France, *terroir* is divided into the specific foods produced in each geographical region of the country. France is obviously not the only country with a *terroir*, but it probably spends the most energy thinking about regional specialties, with the possible exception of Italy. Partly because of climactic diversity, France has as many *terroirs* as it does *pays*—and even inside *pays* food production is again divided up into sub-categories of *terroir*. Everyone in France knows what grows in each *pays*.

Most French *terroirs* go back so far in history no one really remembers who invented certain dishes or drinks. In the Alps, we discovered a popular drink called *génépi*, made from a medicinal plant of the *alpages* (high-grazing grounds) that are barely accessible. It's consumed mostly as a *digestif*. Nobody actually knows who made the first *génépi*, or what its original purpose may have been. The same goes for *foie gras*. Nobody knows who figured out that force-feeding geese and ducks makes their livers taste delicious. The identity of the first Frenchman to produce non-pasteurized cheese covered with mold has also been forgotten (though not the recipe).

We started to understand what *terroir* means to the French at the *Salon de l'Agriculture* (agricultural exhibition) held every March in Paris. At first we were surprised that France's agricultural show was even held in Paris, not somewhere "in the provinces." But of course Paris is located the middle of France's richest farmlands, which were themselves the source of Paris's early might. With the *Salon*, Paris once again flexes its muscles for the rest of the country to see. Each year the president, the prime minister, and half of the cabinet members do the rounds at the *Salon de l'Agriculture*, shake hands with farmers, squat down and milk a few cows, and pet prize piglets. Their moves are carefully documented by the press. However, it's more of a test than a choreographed photo op. All French politicians are expected to know about farm animals and produce. President Jacques Chirac gets rave reviews every year for deftly handling lambs and enthusiastically slapping cows' rears. But reputations can also be tainted by poor performance at the *Salon*. Former Prime Minister Édouard Balladur made a fool of himself with his poor handling techniques when a lamb relieved itself on his suit jacket, and the incident has remained on his record.

We arrived at the *Salon* expecting to visit a traditional American farm fair, indoors. We thought there would be cows, pigs, and maybe horses in one section, and tractors and machinery in another, with hot dogs stands somewhere in the middle. To our great surprise, there was no machinery. Tractors were being exhibited in an obscure hall in a suburb of Paris. There were no hot dogs, either. The Paris show was about animals and cuisine— and the French were not shy about mixing these themes. Cattle pens were decorated with huge posters of raw steaks and sausages. There was a stand with live ducks right beside another one selling their livers in jars. The tight juxtaposition of live animals and meat ruined our appetite at first, but once we got used to it, we nearly made ourselves sick tasting *cidre*, wine, cheese, *saucisson*, and *tartiflette* (a savory Savoy potato stew boiled in cream and gratinéed with Reblochon cheese).

By the end of the evening we understood that the point of the *Salon de l'Agriculture* is not just to celebrate the extraordinary gastronomic garden known as France, where olives, basil, and wheat grow next to deer, boars, and bulls. The *Salon* is a celebration of the dialogue between nature and culture. The way the French look at it, cooking is not a detached process of transforming food. It's an extension of the land itself, a natural prolongation, a system of value-adding where the end product is an extention of the dirt where it started. The French are profoundly land attached, or, as they say, *terrien*.

As we would discover, though the French cling to their rural identity through this glorification of *terroir*, that identity is essentially a myth. Only 2 percent of the French live off of the land. French agro-business is the most aggressive, the most productive, and the most mechanized in the world. France is the world's second-biggest agricultural producer after the United States. In 2000, the U.S. exported sixty-six billion dollars worth of produce; France exported forty billion dollars in produce from a territory fifteen times smaller. In spite of their attachment to *terroir*, the French are modern food consumers like the rest of the industrialized world. There are McDonald's restaurants in every city and McCain's food in every grocery store. Judging by the shelves in those stores, it's fair to guess that the French eat as much sliced bread, canned food, and industrial cookies as any other developed country.

Still, spiritually, the French remain rural. France is the only developed country where the term "peasant" isn't pejorative. On the contrary— French farmers *prefer* to be called peasants, even the ones who drive half-million dollar tractors. The term denotes an attachment to the land that all the French share, whether they're urban or rural. For that matter, features of country life persist in the cities. There are chain supermarkets in every neighborhood in Paris, but there are still bakeries, cheese shops, and butchers everywhere. Even if the French don't shop traditionally all the time, they know how to, and menus in all good restaurants change regularly, adapting to what's in season. The French insist on being reminded where their food comes from. Ideally, cheese made from cow's milk should taste like a cow, and cheese made from goat milk should taste like a goat. This nuance seemed beyond us until we tasted *andouillette*, a specialty sausage made out of pig's intestines, at *Salon de l'Agriculture*. It really did taste like a pig. A French politician is famous for having said that *andouillette*, like politics, is better with a wiff of shit.

A week after the *Salon de l'Agriculture* it was Julie's birthday, and we celebrated in Paris's Marais neighborhood at a fancy restaurant called *Le Dôme*. The menu was small and inventive, offering refined but robust cuisine. One of the six courses intrigued us: *pigeonneau* (young pigeon). We were new to France and we had had some surprises at the *Salon de l'Agriculture*, so before ordering it we wanted to make sure we wouldn't be eating the street variety of the species.

"*Pigeonneau* is game, right?" we asked the waiter.

"Yes," he said, gauging our reaction with a wry smile.

"Where does it come from?"

He looked to the ceiling, lifted his arm, flexed his thumb and forefinger to mimic a pistol and pointed up. "*Ça vole... Poc! Dans l'assiette* [It flies... Bang! Straight into the plate]."

This waiter was obviously making fun of our ignorance. Still, no waiter in a fancy restaurant in North America would dare suggest a relationship between live animals and the contents of a plate—let alone act out the slaughter before his patrons' eyes. But for the French, there's nothing distasteful in the thought that what they eat once lived and breathed. On the contrary, they love the idea. Their steak bleeds; they eat oysters live; they buy chickens that still have claws; and rabbit is sold (and cooked) with the head. Our butcher often showed us pictures of the cow being cut into pieces that day. Customers seem to find it reassuring to be that much closer to the moment of death; to them, it's natural. There is no sanitized vocabulary in French to separate animals from meat. In English we eat beef, not cows; we eat pork, not pigs. *Boeuf* in French is the generic word for cattle, whether in fields or on dinner plates. *Porc* and *cochon* are generic terms for pigs, whether in piggeries or sausage. *Veau* means calf and veal. And when the French order *escargots*, they're calling a snail a snail.

The *terrien* mentality in France applies to a lot more than attitudes toward farming and cuisine. France is a modern, post-industrial country, but in everything from regional development to foreign policy, it still shows a distinct *terrien* reflex.

France didn't urbanize massively until after the Second World War. In 1945, 40 percent of the population lived directly off of the land—a proportion eight times higher than Britain's and three times higher than Germany's—but throughout the process of urbanization, farmers retained a strong voice in public affairs. During World War II, the French government created the *Chambres d'Agriculture*, special chambers of commerce for farmers that gave them direct input into the government's agricultural and regional policy. French farmers' influence on regional development is hard to miss. We spent our second Christmas holiday in Le Grand Bornand, a quaint Savoy town less than an hour from Geneva that boasts two thousand inhabitants and two thousand cows. On our afternoon walks we saw small hamlets on the outskirts where producers sold Reblochon cheese and mountain spirits made out of herbs from miniature farms that literally hung off the mountain slopes—totally inaccessible to machinery. Such inefficient, *artisanal* production exists thanks to direct and indirect subsidies from the government, like funds for converting part of a farmhouse into a bed-and-breakfast.

The French are *terrien* enough to be willing to pay a lot of money to preserve the countryside—even if they only use it during their seven weeks of holidays. Most French live in cities and work in either industry or the service sector. Their link to the land is more fantasy than reality, but they still cling to it. We met more than one middle-aged or retired couple who owned two, three, and even four houses in different corners of the country, houses they had inherited over the years. They hang on to them rather than sell them to keep a link with their *pays*. The countryside remains quaint and attractive because it enjoys generous government subsidies of all kinds designed to maintain it for the consumption of tourists, both French and foreigners.

Hunting is another *terrien* fantasy the French hang on to. Six months after our arrival, in June 1999, the European elections were held. One of the big election surprises was the appearance of a new party: "Hunting Fishing Nature and Tradition." At first we thought the party was a joke. We wondered how there could be enough hunters in France to form a club, let alone a political party, and couldn't believe there was anything to hunt in this country so small, so densely populated, and so void of what any North American would call "nature." Well, the joke was on us. It turns out that there are 1.5 million hunters in France. The party was formed to protest a 1997 directive by the European Commission to regulate hunting practices, and they obtained 7 percent of the vote, or 1.2 million voters, which means there were three hundred thousand hunters and fisherman out there who voted something else!

Hunting rights have always touched a raw nerve in France. Prior to the French Revolution, hunting was a privilege reserved for the aristocracy. If French peasants were caught trying to supplement their diet of roots and oatmeal with some game, they were put in the stocks. As we all know, French peasants eventually came to resent this treatment. Shortly after the populace stormed the Bastille in 1789, France's newly formed *Assemblée Nationale*—the parliament—abolished all aristocratic privileges, starting with hunting. Commoners took to hunting with a vengeance, literally, exercising their newly won privilege first on a few thousand French aristocrats. Hunting remained a potent symbol. When the monarchy was reinstalled in 1815, the first thing the new king did was give the aristocrats their hunting privileges back. From one revolution to the next, hunting rights shifted from the people to the nobles and back, until the right to hunt became universal once and for all under the Third Republic, in 1871.

Being *terrien*, the French have never cared much about maritime issues. Throughout the sixteenth, seventeenth, and eighteenth centuries, France neglected its navy and its colonies for the benefit of a primarily continental policy. While Britain was stretching its influence to the Americas, France was focused on controlling Italy and the Mediterranean. By the time Napoleon took control of Italy in the late 1700s, France had lost America. In the 160 years of the colony of New France (1608–1763), France only sent ten thousand colonists. Britain's population was three times smaller, but it managed to send fifteen times more people to America in the same period. By 1763, one English subject in six lived in America, compared to one French in three hundred. After France lost the Seven

Years' War in 1763, Britain gave it the choice of keeping either New France or the "Sugar Islands" (Guadeloupe and Martinique), and France chose the Sugar Islands.

The French are the only European society that never migrated *en masse* to America at some point in history. The only massive French migration was some three hundred thousand Protestants called Huguenots who were kicked out of the country in the last decades of the seventeenth century. Being no less French than the Catholics, most Huguenots decided to move to other European cities rather than migrate to the New World.

French *terrien* thinking may even explain an enigma of French human geography that has puzzled two generations of historians since World War II. For some reason, the birth rate in France stagnated between 1750 and 1945. Up until then, France's population was far greater than that of other European countries, thanks to the richness of the land. Historians estimate that in 1300 France's population was between thirteen and twenty million, four times that of Britain. The population rose and fell through epidemics and famines, but by 1740 it had reached twenty-five million, still twice the population of Britain at the time. Then, during the next two centuries, until 1940, France's population reached a plateau of forty million while countries many times smaller caught up with or even surpassed it. Britain's population rose to fifty million and Germany's rose to sixty-five million (eighty million when Austria and Czechoslovakia were annexed).

An English economist named Robert Malthus formulated a theory in 1798 that probably explains this phenomenon. His idea, put simply, was that the population grew faster than food production—a paradox he thought explained not only famines, but also wars and even epidemics. All agrarian societies had to make choices about how to deal with food shortages. One solution was to upgrade the entire production system with all the social changes this would entail—such as breaking up the feudal system. That was the choice of the Germans, the British, and particularly the Dutch. Throughout the eighteenth and nineteenth centuries, these countries went through radical modernization processes, establishing trading economies, importing food, breaking down feudal ties between landlords and serfs, and allowing vast numbers of people to move to cities and overseas.

While its European neighbors chose the path of unrestricted growth, France adopted a policy of restriction. It's impossible to establish a cause-and-effect relationship, but French peasantry during the same period resisted changes in agricultural practices, and yields increased more slowly. Because France was so slow in modernizing its modes of agricultural production, it couldn't accommodate drastic population growth so somehow, somewhere, birth control was introduced—some historians suspect it was as early as the mid-sixteenth century, a century earlier than anywhere else. The French married late and had four or five children at two-year intervals, and since life expectancy was no higher in France than elsewhere in Europe, the population stagnated. In the nineteenth century the French government actually became alarmed by the slow population growth. Politicians and the clergy implored the population to make babies. But the reflex for restriction was already in place, and nothing could be done.

Whether the conservative agrarian mode of production or the introduction of birth control came first in France is a chicken-or-egg question. What's clear is that both phenomena worked together to preserve the population from famines and epidemics. The result was that France never faced the kind of population explosion that led its neighbors to pursue aggressive colonial policies and industrialization.

The French just wanted to stick to the land.

chapter 3

Private Space

Montignac is a sleepy town in the southwest corner of the country and the picture postcard of a French *commune*. It boasts a fourteenth-century castle, ancient houses with red tile roofs, and a surprisingly dense urban life for a population of three thousand. Smack in the middle of *le Périgord*, the *pays* east of Bordeaux renowned for *foie gras*, *confit*, and *cassoulet*, it is the closest town to the prehistoric site of Lascaux, a cave where twenty-two-thousand-year-old paintings of horses, buffalo, and deer cover the walls. But we will remember the town for a lesson we learned about privacy there.

In the company of Jean-Benoît's parents, we were wandering the streets in the upper reaches of the town, grumbling because we hadn't been able to visit the town's castle, which was private property. Walking back to the town's center, Julie and her mother-in-law stopped to inspect a tree that had two dozen CDs hanging from its branches. On closer inspection, we saw that it was a fruit tree and the CDs were there to scare away birds. Whether the plum-size fruits were figs or quinces, we didn't know, but before we could decide, the owner of the garden emerged from a grove of bamboo and banana trees in the back of the yard.

Without introducing himself, he settled the question of the fruit. It was indeed a fig tree. We told him we were surprised to find figs growing in France in October, and the conversation got rolling. The man told us the history of the village, explained the contents of his garden, and mentioned that he had built his house himself. He even gave us some juicy details about local politics. ("There are lots of Dutch who buy houses here," he said, "but locals don't like them because they never spend their money at local restaurants.") We asked him about the famous Lascaux caves, and he told us it was a childhood friend of his who had discovered them in 1940. After listening to us rave about the figs, he went inside to get us a jar of his wife's homemade fig jam. His wife came back with him, and the six of us chatted for half an hour over the wooden fence, at which point he invited us inside for *l'apéro* (a drink).

The man was a perfect casual host. He was not finicky about his own appearance—we had caught him gardening, after all—and graciously presented us with a platter of peanuts, pretzels, and *pastis*. He had traveled a lot and was curious to find out what we thought of France and the French.

We had been in the country long enough by this time to know some rules about conversation. Questions North Americans consider polite, to the point of being banal, are sometimes considered rude in France—especially, "What do you do?" or, "What's your name?" We had learned that you should extract names and occupations indirectly by talking about other things like politics, culture, arts, or anything related to food. So when it was time to leave, we got ready to say, "We are very sorry to end this conversation and hope we can pursue it on another occasion," a technique that had often produced the desired result. There are other ways to get people's names. Though it sounds precious and formal to North American ears, you can ask, "What should I do to have the pleasure of speaking to you again?"

Though he'd traveled in France before, Jean-Benoît's father, a businessman, had no idea there were different rules of conversation about being too direct in these circumstances.

As he shook hands with our host before leaving, he asked, "So, what's your name?"

There was an awkward pause. Our host looked puzzled—not shocked, just perplexed, as if he didn't see the point. He pulled out a card and handed it to Jean-Benoît's father.

Mr. H.L. Brossard, *pour vous servir* (at your service).

Mr. Brossard and Jean-Benoît's father, both kind men, would not have admitted they had actually rubbed each other the wrong way. Mr. Brossard had given us a tour of his garden, taken us into his home, opened up his bar for us, and showed us pictures of his children without telling us his name. Mr. Nadeau had listened all the while wondering why our host didn't have the good manners to introduce himself. We'd been through this ourselves when we were visiting the Beaujolais (the *pays* north of Lyon) with parents of a close friend. A sports physician we met invited us into his renovated thirteenth-century castle and even took us to a private wine tasting in his village, but never told us his name or asked ours. (We slyly read it on an envelope on the dining room table). Another time, a friendly couple we met in a neighborhood restaurant in Paris actually offered us the use of their car if we ever needed it, but never told us who they were.

This reticence to offer names may be one reason the French are so often accused of being aloof. Yet these incidents had nothing to do with lack of hospitality. Perfect strangers had invited us into their homes, spent entire afternoons entertaining us, and offered us the use of their cars. The misunderstanding over introductions comes from different notions of privacy. Americans and the French simply have entirely different ideas about what information you share with strangers, and what information you don't share. Conflicting notions of privacy make the behavior of one seem inappropriate to the other.

By privacy, we don't mean the issue of legally protecting personal information. We're not even talking about ideas of personal space, though the French are clearly less finicky than North Americans are about physical proximity to strangers. By privacy here we mean each culture's intuitive sense of what's intimate, and what's public. For instance, North Americans freely discuss names and occupations in public, but these things are considered extremely private matters in France. The French freely kiss and argue in public, while North Americans consider it more appropriate to do these things in private. And that's just the beginning

We tend to think of communication as verbal, but a lot of it (anthropologists say, most) is actually nonverbal. Even before we open our mouths, others assess dozens of things about us. In a split second they determine whether we are dangerous or not, put us in categories, and decide whether they want to speak to us, even before a word has been uttered. Privacy is a part of this nonverbal system of communication. Or as author Polly Platt so aptly describes it in *French or Foe?*, her guidebook to French manners and more, people walk around inside a series of concentric bubbles that define what's public, what's private, what's personal, and what's intimate. Each of these bubbles can be penetrated without creating hostility if you know the codes. But if you don't know the codes, there will be trouble, and words won't save you.

Such difficulties have nothing to do with language: Jean-Benoît is perfectly fluent in French, but he still got hostile reactions from the French when he inadvertently entered the private sphere without knowing it. For a long time, when the French acted snobby, hostile, or aloof with us, we thought we were just dealing with some difficult individual characters. But eventually we understood how we were bursting privacy bubbles without knowing it. And after we understood that, we could see how different ideas of privacy explained a lot of things about the French, from the way they relate to one another and to strangers, to their attitude about money, their world view, and even their notions of political accountability.

One French custom that puzzled us was their habit of saying *bonjour* and *au revoir* every time they went in and came out of a store. It took us a while to figure out that those were the magic words in France for getting good service. You have to say *bonjour* when you enter a store (looking at the owner in the eyes) and *au revoir* when you leave, even if the owner isn't there—in which case, if it's a neighborhood store, another customer may answer for him. If you enter or leave without uttering the passwords the owner, his employees, and sometimes even the regulars will frown at you—when they're being polite. When we caught on to this behavior we, too, frowned at the rude customers who entered our regular haunts without presenting themselves.

In North America stores are extensions of the public space. Apart from large chains that force their employees to mechanically greet customers at the door, traditionally, communication in North American stores is purpose-driven. No one speaks to you except to help you find what you need. But that's not the way it works in France. The French store is considered the extension of the owner's home—in many cases, it actually is. So the French tend to treat businesses as part of the private sphere. It's up to the customer to say something nice when entering and exiting the premises. Even an open newspaper counter in a train station has an "inside" and an "outside," and the cashier might not take your money until you've said *bonjour*. This explains why it is so hard to get good service in big stores in France. Employees are notoriously aloof in these stores. There's no ritual in place to regulate their interaction with customers. If there was a way of yelling *bonjour* loud enough to be heard by all in a thirty-five-thousand-square-foot space, maybe that would help. But neglecting to say *bonjour* to a clerk when entering a department did guarantee us bad service.

The *bonjour/au revoir* ritual is one way to secure goodwill from the French. Handshaking is another. Employees of companies have to go through the routine of shaking hands with everyone at the office when they come in and when they leave. The behavior was reproduced almost exactly by the members of Jean-Benoît's hiking club. Before heading out on an expedition everyone shook hands or kissed, and they did it again before leaving. Kissing as a salutation is a complicated matter because it is an act occasionally performed on almost complete strangers. It's a prudish thing that involves a mere rubbing of cheeks most of the time and very rarely extends to anything like a hug. Still, we learned that some people in Paris expected to give four kisses, while most people outside of Paris were satisfied with two—or sometimes three. A friend of ours, Paola, an architect, told us that the best way of expressing dissatisfaction with a colleague is to skip the handshaking session for a day or two. The offending party will almost certainly know something is amiss.

In all cultures, houses are the barometer that measure where the public ends and the private begins. In Amsterdam, Julie was amazed to see that the Dutch don't put curtains in their enormous front windows. She could see them eating their dinner as she walked down the street. The message appears to be: nothing to hide. In rural Mexico, where we also traveled, many houses had no front doors, and if they did, they were open all the time, making the line between public and private pretty subtle. What a shock when you compare these countries to France. The French house is a categorical affirmation of its owners' privacy. You never see the inside of people's homes from the street. Houses in Paris actually turn their backs on the street; the facade is rarely as interesting as the inside courtyard. On the street side, windows have thick curtains or shutters that block out the world. In the countryside and suburbs, houses are often in the middle of gardens that are usually fenced in.

The window shutter in France was an ongoing source of fascination to us. In North America, window shutters are decorative planks fastened to the outsides of houses, but the French *use* them, almost religiously. In every household we visited, in every part of France, summer or winter, our hosts went through the same morning and evening ritual of opening all the windows, opening or closing the shutters, and then closing the windows. Thanks to this custom, whole streets in French cities and villages are blacked out at night. We were certainly the only apartment dwellers on our street who never drew a curtain or closed a shutter during the two-and-a-half years we lived there.

Like the *bonjour/au revoir* routine in stores, the custom of shutters puzzled us for a long time. Everywhere we stayed we asked our hosts why they opened and closed the shutters every day, and each time we got a different answer. One fellow said it was to block out light so he could sleep better, though that didn't explain why he closed the shutters on *all* openings of the entire apartment. Another person said the shutters helped him save on heating, but the little energy he saved with this extra insulation was certainly lost opening and closing all the windows of the house twice a day. Another host said shutters were a good replacement for curtains, but most French homes have shutters *and* curtains.

We concluded that the shutter reflex, like a lot of things in France, was probably an ancient atavism. Shutters did protect windows from destruction, or replace them in times of war and riot, which wasn't that long ago in France. But we did find another explanation: the traditional tax collection scheme called *la taille* (the cut). France did not tax its nobles for many centuries. To tax city dwellers and peasants, they needed a system for evaluating what they were worth. Starting four centuries ago, the government contracted *fermiers généraux* (tax "farmers") to levy a certain amount of tax money in a given area. The tax farmers subcontracted the work out to lesser tax farmers who hired local delegates to spy on their neighbors and figure out how much they had in their houses. Rates of taxation were based on "apparent" wealth, judged at eyeshot by looking through people's windows. So the shutter was a tax evasion scheme, and even when France started taxing aristocrats after the Revolution, the reflex remained. The French are still staunchly defensive about the privacy of their homes.

Money is also considered part of the private sphere in France. Even though France is the world capital of luxury goods, the French often come across as hating money. It's not mere pretense. The French have an uneasy relation with the idea of money. They don't actually hate it, but it is considered a vulgar topic of conversation. No class in France earns more general disdain than the one that dwells on money: the *nouveaux riches*. If the French like money for money's sake, they don't advertise it.

Salaries are very rarely discussed in public in any context. When people do discuss them, they claim to earn less than they actually do. Although civil servants' salaries are theoretically public, the system is so riddled with perks and bonuses that it's impossible to actually know what any civil servant earns. By the same token, French tax offices have always had difficulty assessing how much money there is in the country. The switch to the euro brought a lot of cash back into the system because an estimated 80 percent of all five hundred–franc bills were said to be stashed in mattresses and pillows across the country. When French protesters demonstrate, they never openly ask for money; they wrap it in another demand like better working conditions.

The French consider money base. In his book *Le Mal Français* (*The French Disease*), former minister Alain Peyrefitte recounts a mind-boggling anecdote that illustrates how far this attitude goes. During a reception for a French Nobel Prize winner in physics, one of Peyrefitte's assistants deplored the fact that the professor had never patented his discovery and that others (Americans) had gotten rich on his invention. One science student vehemently disagreed. "At least the French man was honest!" he said. It's as if talking about money tarnishes things.

What goes on in the French bedroom is also considered private—even where politics are concerned. We were lucky enough to be in France during the Monica Lewinsky affair that rocked the second term of Bill Clinton's presidency and watched the French relish the chance to sneer at Americans for their puritanical attitude about sex. But when the fun wore off, it was clear to us that the French failed to understand what all the fuss was about in the first place, or why Americans were making such a fuss about the president having an affair. The French truly consider sex a private matter. They don't think what politicians do with cigars in the intimacy of their own offices is the public's business. The French gossip about the sex lives of public figures at dinner parties, of course. But they don't have the same urge as Americans or the British to instantly go public with the details.

At the 1996 funeral of former president François Mitterrand (1981–95), the famous French gossip magazine *Paris Match* published a cover photo of Mitterrand's wife with his mistress and illegitimate daughter standing by her side. The photos surprised the nation, but it turned out that several hundred journalists and politicians had known about Mitterrand's mistress for the last twenty years. No one even thought about making it public. No one even criticized Mitterrand for keeping his mistress and illegitimate daughter in a mansion at taxpayers' expense while he was in power.

North Americans would see Mitterrand's behavior as immoral and as an abuse of power, but the French just think it's Mitterrand's business. His illegitimate daughter, Mazarine, even became something of a media personality since her "coming out" at her father's funeral. The French don't grill their politicians over their private conduct—or that of their family members—like Americans do. The assumption is that as long as no crime was committed, the bedroom is a private space. While an American might think the French are opening the door to debauchery, this attitude does have one advantage. It makes politicians a lot less subject to blackmail.

The French expect people in power to run the country, not set moral standards. As a consequence, French journalists don't investigate sex scandals—or care that much about other countries'. In 2001, when France's head of their Supreme Court, Roland Dumas, was charged in a corruption case involving his mistress, not a single French talk show asked Dumas's wife how she felt about her husband having an affair. It was a private matter. An outsider may jump to the conclusion that the French have no morals, but what they really have is a different idea of what constitutes a morally reprehensible action, and what level of scrutiny is acceptable.

But there is no doubt that they are more tolerant about extra-conjugal affairs. During our stay, the national train service ran an add showing four pairs of feet popping out from under a duvet. The text read: "Tell your spouse you're on a business trip." According to statistics, the number of Americans who admit to having committed adultery is 50 percent—the same number as in France. Adultery is a big sin in France, like elsewhere, but not the same kind. In the United States, adultery is a breach of trust, or a breach of contract. The French are primarily concerned about the impact it has on family life. The family is still pivotal in France, and ruining a family is more appalling than a breach of contract, which happens all the time.

We lived a short walk from Pigalle, which was once Paris's red-light district. The crowds we saw heading there were mostly busloads of tourists on their way to drink champagne and ogle the skimpily dressed dancers at the neighborhood's cabarets. In the mind of foreigners, especially Anglo-Americans, French is almost synonymous with sex, and many people would swear that the French are the most lecherous people in the world. The French do talk a lot about love and sex, and often in graphic detail. They have a gigantic body of poetry and writing dating back to the eleventh century that testifies to their interest in exploring new dimensions and new postures. The Marquis de Sade was French, and Nabokov, the author of *Lolita*, though Russian, was published in Paris, as was Henry Miller, author of *Tropic of Cancer*. And a great part of their film production over the last century has been dedicated to exploring the frontier between good taste and bad taste. Talking about sex graphically is acceptable behavior in public—up to a certain point—but more as an abstract idea than a testimony of one's actual conduct. Regarding this, they come out, paradoxically, as rather prudish. The French don't even have a term for French kiss, except the very vulgar *rouler une pelle* (literally, roll a shovel). And it may well be that they prefer the heroics and the talking to the actual act.

The French pay a price for being so defensive about the private lives of their leaders, though. Even for matters far more serious than sex, they are sadly neglectful about calling their politicians to accounts. Every month, the prime minister hands each of his ministers an envelope with fifteen thousand euros in cash for discretionary expenses. Ministers are not expected or required to report on what they do with this spending money. (Despite the French National Assembly's vast powers to investigate such matters, by tradition, or out of convenience, politicians are rarely made accountable for their spending. This practice was forbidden by the new prime minister, Jean Pierre Raffarin, in 2002.) Since all ministers benefit from this kind of corruption, no one has been willing to take on the system. Besides, it's no secret to the public, and they aren't doing anything about it, either.

The French media don't even seem to understand what "conflict of interest" means. Journalists often sneer at the idea of political accountability, calling it an Anglo-Saxon concept. In recent years, a generation of young French judges, who are not part of the traditional political class, have been trying to stop the systematic corruption in the political system by nailing some high-profile politicians. Their investigations into party financing scandals have revealed that all of France's political parties are involved (one political party asks for kickbacks and pays the other parties to keep quiet). Yet even as the judges unveil dozens of political scandals, the French public has been surprisingly indulgent about corruption. They tend to think that once a wrong act has been punished it turns back into a private matter. So they reelect politicians in spite of allegations of corruption, or even after some have been found guilty of fraud. The French media have not exactly been trained to hunt out corruption, and stringent privacy laws haven't helped them. In the early 1970s, the *Assemblée*

Nationale passed an anti-libel law that would make reporters guilty of libel if they *intended to harm* a plaintiff's reputation, even if the facts revealed were true!

The French are horrified by Americans' attempts to develop the Internet and the Web by allowing companies to document individuals' transactions, profile their spending habits, and trade those profiles as commodities. France's privacy laws prevent companies from using personal information of any kind either for marketing purposes or to gain credit information. In France, there is no such thing as a private company keeping records of people's credit ratings. That's the government's business, and the French are even wary of letting the government get too much information about them. It is forbidden to ask questions about ethnic origin or religion on national censuses. A landlord in Lille asked his tenants to indicate their ethnic origin on an informal survey in 1999, and it turned into a national scandal. (See chapters 15 and 21 for more on this.)

In some ways the French are more guarded than North Americans are, but in other ways they are definitely more open. We found them extremely welcoming toward strangers on the whole, though not in the way North Americans are. For instance, the French don't show guests around their homes. It's simply not part of their concept of hospitality. Guests who come to dinner or for *l'apéro* are pretty much restricted to the living room and the dining room. The doors to the rest of the rooms are usually closed. During our first Christmas season in France, we were invited by a French friend to stay at his parents' place in Pau, near the Spanish border. Our friend is married to a French-Canadian woman. The four of us slept on the second floor; his parents' room was on the first. When we got up the next morning, the doors to every room on our floor were wide open. When we went downstairs for breakfast, the doors on his parents' floor were shut, as were the shutters.

North Americans are always impressed (though not always pleased) by how much protocol and ritual still exists in France. One reason is that the French consider eating a public act. When North Americans try to imitate French meals, they come across as overly formal and uptight. They've missed the point. The French aren't formal just because they enjoy rules and decorum. Since eating is a public act, it follows clear rules everyone agrees on. Diners place their napkins on their laps as soon as they are seated. Cutlery is handled a certain way, and dishes are served in a certain order. The dining room—not the kitchen—is the most public room in the French house.

The French don't do this for show. It's an automatic reflex. They don't understand why North Americans eat at all hours and in any circumstances. (Eating is in the private sphere in North America. You do what you want, and it's nobody's business.) A Christmas shopping trip to Paris's *grands magasins* confirmed our theory. We decided to eat at the cafeteria of *Au Printemps*, one of Paris's upscale department stores, and expected the casual lawlessness one usually sees at tables in cafeterias. Instead, all the French families were sitting with their cloth napkins on their laps, holding their cutlery correctly (knife in the right hand, fork in the left), taking their time as if they were enjoying a Sunday dinner. The food on their trays was arranged in three courses: appetizer, main course, and dessert, with water or wine. Pretty civilized for last-minute Christmas shoppers. Although *Au Printemps* is an upscale store, the behavior of its clients is more the rule in France than the exception. On every road trip we ever took we saw people acting the same way at *L'Arche*, a roadside cafeteria chain.

One of the reasons the French stay skinny in spite of their eating habits is that they don't snack much. Snacking flies in the face of their definition of eating: when you snack, you're doing what you want in your own private way. For the French, it's an invasion of the private over the public sphere—a little like someone talking loudly on a cellular phone on the train. Whenever the concierge in our building saw us eating an apple, drinking a coke, or eating a sandwich on the run, he looked us in the eyes and wished us *bon appétit*. He said it with a smile, but something about his tone made it feel like a mild slap on the wrist. What is so remarkable about eating an apple in the elevator? It's an abrogation of the rules of eating.

Conceptions of private and public explain a lot about the way the French converse. During the last year of our stay, we were invited to a housewarming party of a friend of ours, Dalila, a French woman of Algerian parentage. Dalila's parties were always interesting cultural mixing pots. That night there were at least fifty guests, half English speaking and half French, the English on one side of the apartment and the French on the other. We floated back and forth between these two worlds. On the English-speaking side, people started conversations by asking our names and what we were doing in France. English conversation was like a game of handball where players just try to keep the ball in the air.

On the French side, no one ever asked our names. We were admitted into conversations when we spoke up and expressed an opinion on something, preferably with wit. French education and film policy were the topics that night. One young man argued that both were in a crisis. Another said that both were fine. Everyone else added their bit, supporting or attacking positions. No one ever came to a conclusion: it wasn't really the point. French conversation is not cooperative. It's about scoring points and proving you have something interesting to say. People that night spoke at the top of their lungs, interrupted each other, veered off onto new angles without warning, argued, sought confrontation, and didn't particularly try to resolve disagreements. And at the end, we exchanged names and a minimum of personal information, and expressed the hope of seeing each other again.

Again, it's all about different notions of private and public. At Dalila's party we had moved between two sets of privacy rules. The English freely asked personal questions that the French would consider too private to broach with a stranger. Yet the French argued—something the English definitely prefer to do in private.

Different definitions of private and public spheres also affect how couples act in public. As a bicultural couple, we had experienced this ourselves, but only realized what was going on when we read an excellent book on French-American cultural differences called *Cultural Misunderstandings*, by French ethnologist Raymonde Carroll. Carroll is herself married to an American ethnologist, which is an ethnological experiment of sorts. She says the typical American couple seeks to display harmony. American spouses rarely contradict each other in public, but instead try to show support for one another. Arguing and criticizing one another in public is regarded as distasteful, if not dysfunctional. It's something you do in private.

The French expect exactly the opposite: there's something wrong with a couple that doesn't contradict one another in public and constantly displays harmony. In their minds, a relationship should be strong enough to withstand differences, which are only normal in a couple. All the better if differences are displayed in public with wit and spirit—it makes conversation more interesting. It's not that French spouses disagree all the time and that Anglo-Americans never argue. The behavior is just restricted to different spheres.

Conversation, according to Raymonde Carroll, has a different function in both cultures. We realized this in the subway. At rush hour, the only thing distinguishing the Paris *métro* from the Tokyo subway is that nobody is paid to do the pushing. The French have a very discreet way of forcing their way into the jammed subway cars. While Americans tend to push their way forward in crowds with their elbows, the French simply turn their back and enter backwards. And then, no matter how many body parts get mingled in the crush, the French never say anything to each other. For the French, talking is a way of making contact with people, of getting to know them, and they don't want to know strangers in the subway. Americans have exactly the opposite reflex. Partly because physical proximity with strangers is so unsettling for them, they talk out of embarrassment, and as a way of marking distance from others. If an American ends up talking to a French person in this situation, the French person only tries to avoid engaging in a conversation, with the predictable consequence: each rubs the other the wrong way.

Carroll mostly writes about cultural differences that create misunderstandings in personal situations, but judging from what we observed in France, her ideas might also explain some misunderstandings that take place between countries. While we were in Europe we watched France and the United States disagree about some very serious issues: the bombings of Kosovo, different international treaties, the World Trade Organization negotiations in Seattle. During every conflict, the press and diplomatic circles reacted with Pavlovian predictability. The Americans blamed the French for disagreeing all the time, and the French criticized Americans for lacking subtlety and always thinking they were right.

Americans are definitely irked by the French habit of contesting the United States on every issue, but what really bugs the French is that the Americans seem to expect everyone to agree in every instance. We started to wonder if Raymonde Carroll's theory of couples' behavior didn't also apply to France and the United State's on the international stage. Americans want nothing more than a perfect show of harmony among allies. The French think that if the relationship is strong enough, it should be able to withstand strong differences in public.

It is very difficult for a foreign observer to define what's private and what's public in a culture, what's intimate and what's open, what you show and what you hide, what is intuitively affirmed or understated. We're hardly conscious of these rules in our own culture. Yet entire populations have things they want to show, and things they want to hide. North Americans like to hide the role of their State. It's not that the American or Canadian State is particularly small, but we don't affirm it. Business, private interests, and community life are what we like to talk about. The State has a lot to do with the way we live our lives, but we play down its importance. It's not a fundamental part of our identity.

But it is for the French. The French State is so central to their identity—and they're so proud of its accomplishments—that they often attribute to it deeds that are not the State's doing at all. For instance, most of the redistribution of wealth in France is carried out by employers and unions, not the State. Religion, local cultures, and local government are also important elements of French culture, yet the French downplay them the same way we downplay the State. The French rarely talk about the economy, even though economic success is an important part of their way of life. That doesn't mean the economy isn't there. It is just part of France's "private life."

chapter 4

Grandeur Is Better

Despite all of Paris's pleasures, in the winter the city seemed rather melancholy to snow-lovers like ourselves. At the end of our first year there, we made a weekly outing to the ice rink in front of the Paris city hall for a small fix of winter. Parisians skate exactly the way they drive cars in city streets—as if they never learned the rules—but the atmosphere amply compensated for the shortcomings of our fellow skaters. Every week we gazed in wonder at the city hall's richly ornamented facade, with its rows of statues and steeples.

That winter, Jean-Benoît befriended Daniel Roux, a civil servant who worked as a technical advisor in the mayor's cabinet, and a great gourmand with whom we would share many meals. In January 2001, Daniel invited us to a guided tour of the city hall, the *hôtel de ville*.

We weren't let down. The building's sumptuous interior definitely lived up to the promise of the elaborate exterior. Until 1871, the city hall had been an architectural collage of various wings, some of which were built five centuries ago. When it burned in 1871 after an uprising, the new third Republic decided to restore it and give Paris's city hall its former *grandeur*. As the French would say, *rien de trop beau pour la République* (nothing is too nice for the Republic). In the hour-long tour we visited a succession of offices, ballrooms, and halls, each more gigantic and ornately decorated than the last, with mirrors, statues, gold trim, velvet tapestry, enormous wall murals, oil paintings, and more. The government had evidently tackled the restoration project with all the pomp they could muster, ordering dozens of painters and sculptors to execute original works right on the walls. Unfortunately, we could see neither the mayor's office nor his ten-thousand-square-foot apartment (a quarter of an acre in prime Paris real estate). But at least we understood why all visiting heads of state make a mandatory stop at Paris's city hall for *l'apéro*.

There is hardly a city in the world that rivals Paris's splendor. Gold-plated statues adorn everything from bridges, fountains, and churches to public buildings and traffic circles. The splendid Louvre is no less than a kilometer long. The French president lives in a palace enclosed by an iron fence with gold-tipped posts. The dome roof of the church of the *Hôtel des Invalides*, which houses the tomb of Napoleon, is covered in gold leaf. And of course there is the Notre Dame Cathedral and Versailles.

The only mistake travelers might make is to assume that this love of pomp is a remnant of France's past. It's not. Love of *grandeur* is one of the fundamental characteristics of French culture. They haven't had a king for more than one hundred years, but they still yearn for the trappings of royalty. The French are willing to pay the price for it, too, no matter how much it costs to build new opera houses with marble floors or decorate public buildings with rows of oil paintings and priceless antiques. When the president invites five thousand journalists to his annual Bastille Day garden party at the Elysée Palace, he feeds them champagne and *foie gras*, and nobody complains about taxpayers footing the bill. These are the attributes of *grandeur*, and pretty much everyone in France embraces them, whether right wing or left wing, traditional or modern, old or young. Communist and socialist ministers don't hesitate to show off the Louis XV furniture and sixteenth-century Dutch tapestries in their offices any more than their right-wing rivals do.

Grandeur is a tough concept to translate. The closest equivalent, "greatness," brings to mind "eminence," "distinction," and "excellence." But *grandeur* is more than that. It evokes power, glory, and moral and intellectual elevation. Like Paris's own monuments, the idea of *grandeur* troubles our democratic spirit. But for the French, democratic ideals and *grandeur* are perfectly reconcilable. In *Democracy in America*, written at the beginning of the nineteenth century, Alexis de Tocqueville praises the United States for embracing the ideals of liberty and democracy. But he laments the disappearance of *grandeur* in the American system. The French believe in equality, but they don't embrace the lowest common denominator.

Grandeur is a socially accepted value, and is much sought after in France. The whole society cooperates to single out the great ones among them in politics, the arts, intellectual life, sports, and more. To some extent, great ones replace the French aristocracy. These days, France's nobles (anyone whose name begin with "de") have more *cachet* than actual power or money, but what really struck us was France's culture of *notables* (worthies). Notables are often owners of local castles or companies who are recognized locally as moral, intellectual, and administrative authorities (many actually do come from the aristocracy). The notables, who often form local dynasties, don't necessarily hold elected office, but they often find a place in local politics. France has thirty-six thousand *communes* and half a million city councilors, so there's plenty of room for them.

The French press helps satisfy the country's thirst for *grandeur* by singling out stars in every domain of life. French journalists have a peculiar reflex of attributing superior qualities to cultural figures and making them the incarnation of their discipline. Artists or thinkers who gain this status are referred to by their last name only ("Sartre") or by their initials (author Bernard-Henri Lévy is simply "BHL"). Sartre was an extreme example. During his lifetime the French sought his opinion on everything—even topics about which he knew very little—to the extent that Sartre actually created an intellectual void around himself. An expression took root during his life: "Better be wrong with Sartre than right with Raymond Aron" (an intellectual who held different views but turned out to be right about many things, including the future of communism).

The French find it reassuring to recognize undisputed leaders in fields, and they are constantly searching for the "great ones" of every field of scientific or intellectual endeavor. Abbé Pierre, founder of the *Disciples d'Émaüs*, is Mr. Poverty. Jacques-Yves Cousteau was Mr. Sea. Haroun Tazieff became Mr. Volcano. Spelunker Michel Siffre was Mr. Caves. Yves Saint Laurent was Mr. Fashion. Crowned princes and princesses change, but having nobody to crown really irks the French. That seems to be the case in politics right now. A lot of people say the political class has nothing to offer because there is no "great one" running it.

France has created and maintained many structures to promote and affirm *grandeur* among its citizens. The *Académie Française*, which polices the French language, is run by forty elected "Immortals" who are chosen from among the top crust of France's literati. The *Collège de France* was created to pick out the country's fifty or so top professors to deliver free lectures about their specialty. And of course, there's the *Panthéon*, the huge capitol-like dome in the center of Saint-Germain-des-Prés that holds the remains of France's greatest authors, politicians, soldiers, and scientists. The slogan above the neoclassical columns on the front of the building explains its mission: *Aux Grands Hommes la Patrie Reconnaissante* (In Recognition of the Great Men of the Country). The government decides whose ashes or body parts (often hearts) are transferred there. Only three hundred men have earned this rank. For the others there's the *Légion d'Honneur*, an award given to three thousand individuals per year, which means France has 116,000 living *légionnaires*.

Some of the greatest encounters we had in France happened because Jean-Benoît joined a hiking club in Paris. The club was a remarkable cross section of middle-class France and the members were warm, curious, and talkative. Over the course of many day hikes in the outskirts of Paris and weekend outings in the far corners of France, Jean-Benoît made friends with a sheet metal worker, an engineer, several accountants, various civil servants, a nurse, teachers, and a physiotherapist—and our friend Daniel from city hall.

One of the first hikers Jean-Benoît befriended will be named Gustave at his own request. He was a remarkable man, sharp-witted and fluent in German. Gustave quickly understood what Jean-Benoît was doing in France. He had a thorough understanding of the French administration and enthusiastically explained the functioning of the State from the first day they met. By the end of the day, Jean-Benoît had learned that Gustave was a graduate of *ÉNA–École Nationale d'Administration* (National School of Administration), the famous training school for top civil servants and government utilities.

ÉNA is the most famous of France's five hundred or so *grandes écoles* (great schools), all of which have the explicit function of training France's caste of political, managerial, and intellectual leaders. Since its creation in 1945, six thousand people have attended *ÉNA*'s classes, and 80 percent of its graduates have occupied top functions in the French administration. Half of the ministers in any cabinet, six of the last nine prime ministers, and two of the last three presidents studied at *ÉNA*.

Foreigners often criticize the *grandes écoles* system for being elitist, but creating an *élite* is the school's very purpose. The *grandes écoles* supply the *élite* to run virtually every human activity in France: engineering, chemistry, teaching, business administration, law, history, the penal system, and more. In France, no university degree can match the luster of a diploma from *École Polytechnique* (for engineers), *les Hautes Études Commerciales* (business administration), or *École Normale Supérieure* (for professors).

The real question, perhaps, is why the French feel they need to deliberately "create" an *élite* at all. The idea makes most North Americans shudder, probably because it sounds like a caste system. North Americans have their own systems for selecting an *élite* (Ivy Leagues schools), but they don't openly affirm their *élite* quite the way the French do. One reason is that the word doesn't quite mean the same thing to the French. In France—and most of Europe as well—the term "*élite*" connotes not just privileges, but also duties. Becoming an *élite* civil servant in France means that one accepts the vocation of public service. An *ÉNA* graduate who leaves the public service to work in the private sector is referred to as a *pantouflard* (a slipper-wearer).

People in all democracies accept the idea that armies need officers of higher rank who can lead battles. The French just believe the same thing about civilians. They consider their *élite* the officer class of society. It sounds anti-democratic, but that's the way French democracy functions. The whole system is set up to find and cultivate an *élite*. To be admitted to the *grandes écoles*, students have to go through a severe selection process of written and oral examinations. It's not a pure meritocracy, since those admitted tend to come from the middle class and higher. But it's far from an aristocracy. (More is said on the *grandes écoles* in chapters 13 and 14.)

The fact that the French embrace their *élite* has never prevented them from being ferociously critical when their *élite* fails them—but that doesn't mean they want to get rid of them. Historically, when the French *élite* has broken down or failed, the French have either replaced it with another or invented institutions to renew it. Twelve years after the French Revolution, which nearly wiped out the French aristocracy, Napoleon replaced the old aristocracy with a *noblesse d'empire*, a brand-new nobility made out of high-ranking commoners. In 1871, when France suffered a severe beating at the hands of the Prussians, it created the *Fondation des Sciences Politiques* to renew the government's managerial class. In 1945, after four years of Nazi occupation, General de Gaulle created ÉNA to train high-level civil servants.

One reason the French are so open about affirming their *élite* is that they love power. Power is something you use and show in France. This realization really sunk in when we watched the fourteenth of July parade down the Champs Elysées in Paris. The parade started at ten o'clock with the horse guard, followed by the soldiers, air force troops, police officers, and firemen carrying guns and bayonets (in France, they are part of the military). After that, Mirage fighters, helicopters, and cargo planes flew overhead. Then the machinery rolled out: rocket launchers and heavy tanks, camouflage bulldozers and portable bridges. The Bastille Day Parade is really a great Republican mass, an orchestrated demonstration of France's power for the pleasure of citizens and presidents alike.

The French simply don't expect humility from powerful people, whether they are elected officials, intellectuals, or business leaders. People with power are expected to demonstrate it and use it. One of the powers the French president gets when he enters office is the right to grant amnesty to criminals, regardless of their crime. President Mitterrand set 6,233 prisoners free when he took office in 1981. Jacques Chirac declared a general amnesty on all traffic and speeding tickets. Chirac has been more selective about the type of criminals he sets free, but the French still expect their president to use these powers. They see the overt police presence in their cities as *dans l'ordre des choses* (natural) and don't bat an eyelash at the busloads of riot-squad police conspicuously parked around the government buildings of the seventh *arrondissement*.

Like all high civil servants, our friend Gustave has had to move around a lot. When he was appointed to manage health in the overseas *Département* of Guadeloupe, he had to leave with three weeks notice. Gustave was thrilled because he was bored to death by the office job he had to take between two overseas assignments. Over one last supper in Paris before he left, he told us a lot about his experiences as deputy prefect of police.

Gustave shed light on one issue in France that had deeply offended us as North Americans: the constant presence of riot police. As he explained, there is a strong element of theater policing in France. Organized protests are as much about demonstrating power as they are about making demands on the government. Groups that protest have to get permits ahead of time so authorities know more or less what's coming. They have a one-size-fits-all policy. When protests occur, troops of riot squads are called in whether the protesters are nurses, schoolteachers, farmers, or tobacco workers. The police are armed with shields and clubs and dressed in uniforms that make them look like a cross between gladiators and hockey players, though most of the time they don't do anything. We asked Gustave why the French government felt compelled to display so much force during peaceful protest, and he answered that union leaders actually *complain* if the *préfet* of police doesn't bring out riot squads for their demonstration. "It looks like the government isn't taking them seriously, and it is bad for internal union politics," he said. (More on this in chapter 17.)

The French value power and privileges, and prerogatives are considered a natural complement to it. If France seems like a democracy of aristocrats at times, that's because to some extent it is. During the Revolution, the French National Assembly stripped the aristocracy and the clergy of their privileges, but instead of abolishing privileges altogether, they just assigned them to another class: politicians. Today, the President of the Republic has virtual impunity and cannot be tried for anything during his mandate except high treason. Elected officials have so much status and power that judges usually don't dare launch investigations of corruption. And the population pretty much accepts this situation. Elected politicians get the privilege to elect other politicians. Popular voting only takes place in elections for municipal, departmental, and regional councils, members of the National Assembly, members of the European Parliament, and the president. Candidates for all executive offices, mayors for instance, are chosen by their peers.

These privileges go very far: for instance, the French government created the office of *Médiateur de la République* (Government's Ombudsmann), whose job is to settle problems between the people and the government. But interestingly, normal citizens are not allowed to file complaints directly to the *Médiateur's* office: only senators and *députés* can, on behalf of ordinary citizens!

Every *député*, every minister, and every mayor also expects to accrue some material and social benefits from his or her elected office. Some of these privileges are reasonable, like limousine services, high status, and free lodging—one extreme example is the Paris mayor's apartment. Others, though, are questionable, like politicians' practice of creating fictional jobs for friends or family members, or of lodging them in publicly owned apartments renovated at taxpayers' expense. Former prime minister Alain Juppé (1995–97) was famous for doing extensive renovations for himself and his son, on the public purse, while he worked as an assistant to the mayor of Paris in the 1980s and 1990s. In a biography on Jacques Chirac, a former *député* talks about the safe the president kept in his office when he was the mayor of Paris. It was full of five hundred–franc bills, just in case he needed some quick cash. Even though everyone knows about them, these abuses don't bring down governments in France.

Privileges and prerogatives aren't reserved exclusively for the upper echelons of power, either. In each *Département*, top bureaucrats are housed and supplied with chauffeurs, limousines, and cooks. It's also common for *gendarmes* to be lodged in the *gendarmerie*, nurses in apartments in their hospital, or teachers in their schools—all at taxpayers' expense. Because post offices in France also serve as banks, waiting lines are often long.

Certain citizens get priority cards that allow them to jump to the front of the line: not just the elderly and pregnant women, but business people as well. Journalists get free access to public buildings, including museums, just by presenting their card. People don't usually protest when someone jumps ahead in a line because they know that not all citizens are really equal.

North Americans assume that a political function is bigger than the mere person who holds the office at a given time (so "the presidency" is bigger than "the president"). As a consequence, a politician who is even suspected of having a conflict of interest may be forced to resign as a gesture of respect for his function. But in a system like France's, where *grandeur* is a prized object, individuals become the incarnation of the institutions they head and of the positions they hold, to the extent that the two become indistinguishable.

· This tendency in France shows up in the vocabulary used to talk about politics. Journalists speak of *la Jospinie, la Chiraquie,* or *la Mitterrandie* to refer to the system of government and the thinking of Prime Minister Lionel Jospin (1997–2002) and of Presidents Jacques Chirac and François Mitterrand (1981–95). Journalists could just say, "the Jospin years," but instead, they use an expression that makes Jospin sound like a philosopher king.

The French press automatically transfers this terminology to other countries, referring to President Bill Clinton's two term as *la Clintonie,* of his thinking as *le Clintonisme*—right up there with *Jospinisme, Chiraquisme,* and *Mitterrandisme.* First the French transform their politicians into veritable schools of thought, then they turn them into adjectives like *Pompidolien, Fabiusien, Giscardien, Rocardien* (after the names of former presidents Georges Pompidou and Valéry Giscard d'Estaing, and prime ministers Laurent Fabius and Michel Rocard). The best is *Malrucien,* for André Malraux, writer and Minister of Culture under de Gaulle, on par with philosopher Pierre Bourdieu, who was said to be *Bourdivine.*

The French love of *grandeur* and power unfortunately does translate into a tendency to hoard power. As noble and well-intentioned as politicians may be, they tend to treat their elected positions like personal possessions. One political tradition even allows them to stock up on elected offices: the *cumul des mandats* (literally, the accumulation of electoral mandates). No law actually forbids this practice in any liberal democracy, but politicians everywhere else refrain from it. In France, a whopping 89 percent of *députés* and 60 percent of senators hold another office at the same time. Half of them hold three!

Just imagine if the secretary of state, an appointee of the president, was also a congressman, governor of his state (or senator), mayor of his town, and head of the school board. In France, the mayor of a city like Paris can become minister or prime minister without giving up being the mayor. President Jacques Chirac was a champion of the *cumul*. While mayor of Paris from 1977 to 1995 he was also the prime minister of France, from 1984 to 1986, he was *député* for his home region of Corrèze and *député* in the European Parliament. One limit has always existed—it's never been possible to be senator and *député*. And although other limits were imposed over the years, there remains a great number of possible combinations between France's five levels of government (*Communal, Départemental*, regional, national, and European levels).

French politicians use their right to accumulate offices to its fullest. They can add up the salaries to a maximum of eight thousand dollars per month. More importantly, holding several offices makes them politically unsinkable. A *député* or senator who is mayor or president of his Regional Council (or both) has a say in most local decisions, the distribution of subsidies, the attribution of contracts, and the allocation of day-care places—putting him or her at the center of a vast patronage network. Influence at the national level also adds to the *député's* appeal as mayor. The double, triple, or quadruple mandate is the equivalent of a good insurance policy for a class of politicians who regard their function as a vocation. When we met the thirty-six-year-old mayor of Meaux, a mid-size town near Paris, the former *député* referred to being a politician as his *métier* (trade).

The *cumul* explains the resilience of French politicians who, like cats, seem to have nine lives. Some politicians literally last forever. François Mitterrand, who became president in 1981, had been Minister of Information in 1949 and Minister of War Veterans in 1947! When President Valéry Giscard d'Estaing appointed Jacques Chirac prime minister in 1974, Chirac had already been combining municipal and national politics for ten years. He was elected mayor of Paris in 1977 and prime minister from 1986 to 1988 (while remaining mayor of Paris), and used his office in Paris to launch a third unsuccessful bid for the presidency in 1988, until he finally succeeded in 1995.

The *cumulards* (those who accumulate mandates) argue that holding more than one office at a time allows *députés* and senators to keep in touch with their grassroots supporters. It's a surprising argument. In other democracies, members of parliament (or the equivalent) keep abreast of issues in their hometowns without being mayor at the same time. The main effect of piling up offices is that it creates built-in conflict of interest in the French political system. It also encourages patronage and makes renewal in the political class slow. Politicians also have less time for each of their functions. But the system is so ingrained in the French mentality that most French hardly question it. When our French friends complained about politicians who, in their opinion, had been around too long, we told them they could solve the problem by putting an end to the *cumul*. Most just looked back at us with startled expressions. Few in France have put two and two together in this matter. Still, medieval as it looks, there is at least one advantage to the *cumul*: it is one of the few ways local politicians can actually undercut some of France's centralizing policies. If a mayor has the added clout of being *député*, he or she can stand up to the powerful *préfet*. (More on this in chapter 11.)

Over the last thirty years, the *cumul* has been hotly debated and criticized in political circles, especially by the Left. Some restrictions have been put in place over the years. *Députés* are now forbidden from being senators concurrently because those positions vote together on issues like modifications to the Constitution and because senators debate laws from the National Assembly. Since 1958, the Constitution specifies that ministers must resign their seat as *députés* and that legislative and executive powers must remain separate, like in the United States. In 1985, the Left voted in a law that forbade *députés* from holding more than one other office. However, it excluded all *communes* of less than twenty thousand inhabitants from the rule—or 98 percent of them.

The problem is that as soon as the politicians who criticize the *cumul* get into power themselves, they drop the issue. Socialist Prime Minister

Lionel Jospin's government was committed to eliminating the *cumul*, but only succeeded in limiting it. In 1997, newly elected Jospin ordered his ministers to resign their city hall functions. But it was a private party initiative, not a law, and it was never fully applied. Jospin's government tried to get a law against the *cumul* passed in 1998. However, with the ensuing two-year tug-of-war with the right-dominated senate, the text of the proposed law was watered down to limit the number of mandates to two or three depending whether they are local or national. Like the French love of *grandeur*, the unabashed love of power is simply part of how the system functions. Jospin was leading a noble mission, but he was up against a reflex as old and solid as France's ancient cathedrals.

Grandeur has its advantages—it's grand—but it has drawbacks as well. For one, it has perpetuated a political culture of privileges and entrenchment in France. This applies not only to politicians, but to all people with power—bureaucrats, scholars, and managers of all types in associations, government position, and unions. A complicated set of mechanisms and values allow the French to literally lock themselves in their position and stay there forever. This pattern, in turn, makes it difficult for any marginal group to enter power—whether socialists in the past, or immigrants and women in the present.

Sexism and machismo among French politicians don't help this situation. When female representatives become too vocal in their demands, male representatives often slam them by decrying *le concert des vagins* (the vagina concert). The French were slow to grant women the right to vote (1944) and women are entering the upper echelons of French politics, business, and research much more slowly than their North American counterparts. On the other hand, North Americans tend to be deceptively positive about the situation of women in the United States. While French women hold only 10 percent of the seats in Parliament, compared to 20 percent in the United States, the U.S. rate is not brilliant when one compares it to Scandinavian countries, where women generally hold 50 percent of the political offices. The difference in the balance of gender representation in politics between France and North America is a matter of degrees, not quantum leaps.

France was among the first countries to create a parity law for wages and recruitment in executive positions, but the makers of the law admit they made mistakes by not including in the law any possibility of punishment for breaking it. Furthermore, contrary to what happened in the wage parity battles in Canada and Scandinavian countries, French unions did not take up the cause.

But things in France are definitely set to change. In 2000, a law was passed requiring that all political parties present equal numbers of female and male candidates. At the 2001 municipal elections, the number of female candidates was almost equal to that of men. As a result of the elections, female representation in city councils increased from 20 to 33 percent.

French women do not look at the issue of rights or representation with the same eyes as their North American peers. When French women got the vote, their involvement in political organizations soared to 5 percent, but then melted down to as low as 2 percent. Is simple machismo at the root of this? Maybe, but Jean-Benoît spoke to some elected representatives and they told him that French women simply prefer more discreet forms of political involvement, like associations. Furthermore, French feminists and non-feminists alike have never rejected their physical attributes as part of their discourse. When French women are complimented on their beauty and their dress, they do not regard it as harassment.

Things are changing, but they have a long way to go. During the two years we spent in France, we must have been invited to dine with friends one hundred times in a total of forty or fifty different households. In all, only two men actually did the cooking—even among young couples in their twenties and thirties. This corresponds to the proportion of household chores done by French men. There is no doubt that militant feminism in France remains marginal, certainly because the nuclear family is very strong in France, and fathers have kept until recently an intensely paternalistic function—doing very few chores. According to many women with whom we discussed this custom, a change has been taking place in the last ten years and men are actually starting to take care of children.

It will no doubt take a couple of generations for women to bump the grumpy old men out of France's power ring.

chapter 5

The Art of Eloquence

We had been in France for more than a year when we had a memorable discussion about politics with our friend Daniel Roux, a technical advisor to the mayor of Paris. It began when we told him how much trouble foreigners have understanding the nuances of French politics. The French speak of the Right and the Left like two distinct camps, but as far as we could tell, each camp had at least four subdivisions feuding amongst themselves. The greens and the socialists fought as bitterly as the socialists, and the Gaullists were split into two factions that disagreed about everything except their mutual rejection of the far Right. All this was complicated by the fact that, historically, the Right had conducted left-wing policies like creating social security and nationalizing companies, while the Left had privatized state-owned companies that the Right had nationalized in the first place.

"So, what exactly is the difference between Right and Left?" we finally asked Daniel.

He rubbed his chin. "How interesting. I never looked at it that way before. You mean, how do the Right and Left in France differ exactly? Interesting."

Julie saw the ploy. "Everyone in this country does that!"

"Does what?"

"Everyone repeats the question they've been asked. Then they put it in new terms. A lot of times they just rephrase it and never answer it, but they always put it in their own words."

Daniel rubbed his chin again. "You're right. It's a rhetorical strategy. We all learn to do that in school. How interesting."

The art of rhetoric is so alien to North American culture that few people even understand what it is. But rhetoric is the treasured art of the French, much the way that theater is for the British, singing is for the Italians, and violin is for the Germans. Rhetoric is not the mere science of persuasion and oratory. It is the art of eloquence, whether in writing or in speech.

The French learn to value and practice eloquence from a young age. Almost from day one, students are taught to produce plans for their compositions, and are graded on them. The structures change with fashions. Youngsters were once taught to express a progression of ideas. Now they follow a dialectic model of thesis-antithesis-synthesis. If you listen carefully to the French arguing about any topic, they all follow this model closely: they present an idea, explain possible objections to it, and then sum up their conclusions. Just for fun, we tried applying the thesis-antithesis-synthesis model to our own daily topics of discussion—everything from constitutional reform to the status of domestic animals—and, sure enough, it made it possible to talk about a single issue for hours.

This analytical mode of reasoning is integrated into the entire school corpus. History books for twelve-year-old children contain summaries of events in point form with references to the original historical texts. In one text, there is a section on Romanesque architecture that is divided into the following sections: the origins of the style, the layout of Romanesque churches, technical problems encountered in building, and Romanesque art and decor. French students study philosophy in grade twelve and learn to analyze problems by using categories and systems of classes, even before they enter university. Obviously, not all students turn out to be brilliant writers and orators, but they are all exposed to the same high standards. Students who pursue social sciences in university are subjected to rigorous rhetorical drills. Students at the *Institut d'Études Politiques* (Institute of Political Studies, a type of *grande école*) even have to reconstruct original press releases by reading articles on an event written in different papers. The excellent students shine, but even the average students learn to listen and express themselves very well.

There is a built-in incentive for becoming eloquent: the French *concours*, competitive examinations that candidates must pass to enter the civil service. Even the most menial government job requires candidates to pass exams that test both their knowledge of the position and their general culture. There can even be questions about French poetry on these exams. Higher up the ladder, candidates for the civil service take an oral exam before a jury of three to five people.

At the Grand Oral Examination of the *École Nationale d'Administration*, the most prestigious school in France, candidates are bombarded with fifty to one hundred questions on any aspect of public administration, which they must answer in forty-five minutes. Some of the questions are notoriously unfair, and examiners interrupt candidates in mid-sentence with other questions just to see how they will recover. One former ÉNA student told us she was asked the price of a vacuum cleaner while she was answering a question about family allowances. Good recoveries are the stuff of legend in France, like the story of the candidate who was asked the depth of the Danube River and replied: "Under what bridge, sir?" Maybe it's an urban myth, but that's the kind of brilliance the French expect from their civil servants. (For more on this topic, see chapters 13 and 14 on ÉNA.)

The emphasis on rhetorical skill shows up in every level of society in France. Even the beggars in the Paris subway do their best to be eloquent, each almost ritualistically following the same order of ideas. When they enter the subway car, they excuse themselves for disturbing the other passengers. They then carefully explain how they arrived in their present conditions, laying the basis for the request that follows. We even heard beggars deliver these speeches in rhyming couplets. It can take two, three, or even four *métro* stops to get through them, and much of their original audience is gone by the time they wrap up, but they rarely cut corners. They always sum up their request the same way, by explaining they need money to "eat, drink, and stay clean." Then they thank the passengers for listening to them and wish them a good day as they collect any handouts before exiting the car. North Americans couldn't expect that kind of eloquence from a politician.

But of course, the French love talking—we saw a literary talk show prolonged for fifteen minutes because the quality of the debate was so good. Several months after our arrival we went to see a film called *Rien sur Robert* (Nothing about Robert) that was all about talk. There really was nothing about Robert. It was a two-hour story of the I-love-you-me-neither variety of love affairs the French are so famous for. It even ended *en queue de poisson* (in a fish tail—inconclusively). In North America, moviegoers stranded in a production like that would gaze at the screen trying to understand the *meaning* of it all. But the reaction of the French crowd—they laughed the whole way through—taught us that the film was about verbal jousting, no more. The story *had* no point. The only interest was the *esprit* of the central characters. What they said didn't matter. *How* it was said was the point. The film was just great dialogue with pictures—the concept hardly even translates into English.

The French like the level of discussion to be as high as possible. Whether friendly or hostile, conversations are always competitive, steered toward someone getting the upper hand, demonstrating wit, or otherwise making an impression. This style can come across as aggressive to Anglo-Americans because when we enter into conversation we instinctively seek complicity and understanding. The French seek wit and intelligence, qualities born of confrontation. Conversation is a game, an invitation to go head to head with someone. There are surprisingly few rules. It's not impolite to start a second, or third, conversation in a group before the first one has ended. It's not even impolite to interrupt someone in mid-sentence. Interrupting shows you're in the game. Rambling on about yourself and work was the only thing we could see that was truly unacceptable, because it's boring. People don't want to hear about your problems. They want to see what you have to say.

Esprit is the French word for the highest degree of conversational brilliance. *Esprit* is never self-deprecating, the way English humor tends to be. To practice *esprit*, one usually needs a target. During our first week in Paris, we attended the famous one-man show of French actor Fabrice Luchini, which was a mind-boggling demonstration of *esprit*. The night we saw him, Luchini stood alone on the stage of the *Théâtre de Paris* reading classic French literature. After the readings were over, he spent at least another hour talking and joking with the audience, on stage. Luchini never laughed at himself. He just made fun of different spectators—real and imaginary, past and present—weaving in and out of different subjects to find new ammunition. The audience loved it (we thought they had paid a lot of money to be laughed at). The French certainly have a sense of humor; they laugh at the same jokes we do. But there is a side of them that prefers this combative form of humor, fueled by ridicule and mockery.

The French also value precision in language use. The term for speaking well is *une langue châtiée*, which literally means a "punished tongue." And that's not far off the method used to make children express themselves in a refined and polished manner. Even before they go to school, children are drilled in grammar and rhetoric. After years of that treatment the grown-up French don't hesitate to correct each other, and especially foreigners like us. Sometimes they repeated whole sentences to make sure we had understood our "errors." The word "*si*" was a constant problem for us. Dictionaries often translate *si* as yes, but this is missing the point. The term is the affirmative answer to a negative question:

"*Tu ne viens pas?*" (Aren't you coming?)

"*Si.*" (Yes I am).

Quebeckers no longer use the *si*. Friends and strangers constantly corrected us when we said, "*Oui, oui,*" as Quebeckers do, instead of "*si.*" This driving compulsion to be precise often struck us as affected, verging on pedantic, but of course, it's just the product of a good education in France. In the daily newspaper *Libération*, a journalist once wrote *exeunt les politiciens* (out with the politicians), not *exit les politiciens* (exit is a Latin word, so the proper plural form is *exeunt*). In 1992, the National Assembly wanted to modify the Constitution to include the phrase "French is the language of the Republic." Parliament debated the issue for several days and finally concluded that the sentence should be, "The language of the Republic is French." (The term "Republic" had to be in the subject clause of the sentence, instead of the object, because everything in France must proceed from the *République*.)

In the summer of 1999, we attended a colloquium at the Canadian embassy where Lloyd Axworthy, the Canadian Minister of Foreign Affairs, presented his proposal for an international treaty on "human security." Axworthy, whose efforts contributed to the success of the international land-mine treaty, argued that international treaties should consider the economic, social, and environmental welfare of the peoples, not just of the states, a very Canadian idea. Canadians in the audience mainly asked questions about how such a treaty could be applied. But then a cabinet director from France's Ministry of Cooperation and Francophonie stood up to speak. The Frenchman wanted to know whether Axworthy's idea was a "framework of analysis" or a "new concept." The Canadians in the audience stared at him blankly. We simply never think of speeches in such categories. Mr. Axworthy, himself, was speechless.

Everything about French society seems to raise the standards for verbal expression. One unfortunate result is that the French refuse to utter the words, "I don't know." We quickly learned to banish the expression from our language. North Americans say, "I don't know" to convey an impression of openness, ingenuity, and honesty—even when they know. But the French consider it shameful to admit to ignorance on a matter. It's considered either a mark of stupidity or, strangely, of arrogance—because it means you refuse to engage in conversation. Of course, even the well-spoken French can't know everything, so they have ritualized strategies for avoiding "I don't know." When they're stuck without an answer, they often fall back on that rhetorical trick our friend Daniel used, rephrasing questions to buy time. And sometimes, when that doesn't work they simply declare, "*Ça n'existe pas!*" (It doesn't exist!), an expression as perplexing to foreigners as it is insulting to their intelligence. At one point we decided the French were just playing a kind of intellectual "chicken" with us when they said this. We learned to reply, "*Si*" (Yes it does exist). That put the onus on them to prove that it didn't exist and we usually won the game.

One of the beauties of eloquence as a social value is its accessibility: anyone can get it, whatever their income level or status. French society really does allow anyone to shine, whatever their origin, as long as they can display verbal *savoir faire*. This eloquence was definitely one of the factors explaining José Bové's sudden rise to stardom. On one hand, the Larzac peasant benefited from a wave of antipathy toward globalization that had nothing to do with him. But on the other hand, he exploited it brilliantly by being a skillful orator. After he was jailed for questioning and French authorities tried to release him to quell the controversy, he refused by say-ing: "I will not buy back my liberty"—a snazzy line that turned out to be a ready-made photo caption.

Self-professed "peasant" though he is, Bové is a master of the spirited *réplique* (comeback). Two months after the McDonald's trashing, in October 1999, we attended an anti-globalization rally in Paris that he had helped organize. When we got there, he was already surrounded by a dozen cameras and microphones and was answering the questions of an American journalist from the FOX Network—who pronounced his name "Hosay" (rather than Josay) in some bizarre association with Latino campesinos.

"You don't actually think you can stop globalization, do you, Hosay?"

"Well, we managed to stop the Accord on Multilateral Investment in 1997," Bové replied, poker-faced, in broken English, referring to the inter-national agreement that would have given foreign investors prevalence over national laws.

"But, uh, Hosay, isn't your struggle a little like David and Goliath?" the interviewer shot back, rolling his eyes.

"Well, if we're David, that means we'll win."

The interviewer was stumped.

Given the French love of rhetoric, precise language, and *esprit*, it should come as no surprise that they expect their politicians to express themselves well, both in speech and writing. If a French president is caught reading poetry on his way to an international conference, no one accuses him of being pretentious, wasting his time, or squandering taxpayers' money. National politicians who have published a book are well regarded, and it's not uncommon to see ministers publish while they are in office. In

1976, while he was still in power, President Valéry Giscard d'Estaing even took a fifteen-day hiatus from his duties to finish his book *Démocratie Française*. And politicians are only the tenors and the sopranos in the gigantic choir of French society. Judges produce books in mid-career. While investigating a complicated maze of political and financial scandals involving the French oil company Elf, investigating magistrate Eva Joly wrote a book based on her experience. She even commented on what the suspects told her during the investigation.

The French's love of words and *esprit* creates a strange dynamic in political coverage. The words politicians choose are often the real news— not what they actually say. Nothing fascinates the French more than what they call the *petite phrase* (little sentence), or murderous verbal jab, designed to cast ridicule on political opponents. After the president's highly ritualized New Year's Greetings, the press scrutinizes his words for two weeks. Endless editorials are written on what his real intentions may have been by using a certain word or expression. Was he making a dig at the prime minister? Was he trying to send a message about the budget? In 2000, we watched the press go at this for two weeks until an oil tanker sank off the coast of Brittany and mercifully changed the topic.

Skillful politicians know how to use the fascination with the spoken word to throw powder in opinion makers' eyes. President Jacques Chirac is a master of it. His first mandate has been marred by accusations of a dozen cases of corruption, embezzlement, and kickbacks that allegedly occurred during his mandate as mayor of Paris (1977–95). Most of his former collaborators have been named in more than a dozen cases under investigation, and some have even been jailed.

In the fall of 2000, Chirac was named for the first time when it was revealed that a former fund-raiser had recorded a testimony on videotape just before his death. The fund-raiser claimed to have witnessed the exchange of a briefcase containing one million francs in Chirac's presence. The press went berserk, but a few days later, the president made a rare appearance on television and called the allegations *abracadabrantesques*. (The term, which can be translated loosely into "preposterifying," is borrowed from nineteenth-century poet Arthur Rimbaud). The ploy worked.

The press dissected the expression for two days and then forgot about the allegations.

A year later, another scandal erupted when Chirac was alleged to have paid cash for half a million francs in traveling expenses while he was mayor of Paris. During his televised Bastille Day speech, Chirac predicted that the allegations "would go *Pfsht!*" (the sound of a firecracker that flares but doesn't explode). This kind of verbal inventiveness is probably the oldest trick in the book of rhetorics, but the press was mesmerized by the president's use of this onomatopoeia, and the whole issue actually did end up going, "*Pfsht.*"

As a spin master, Chirac found a close match in Prime Minister Lionel Jospin (1997–2002). Jospin was not flamboyant, but his rhetorical acumen was proverbial, and during his term in office, he skillfully kept the press distracted by novel expressions while he implemented some very tough reforms. The expression *la gauche plurielle* (the plural left) will no doubt outlive him. It's just a fancy brand name, but one that gave a luster of virtue to a prosaic coalition government of socialists, communists, and greens. While the country marveled at the term, Jospin privatized more state-owned businesses than all of his predecessors together at a pace only equaled by Margaret Thatcher in the 1980s. All the while, Jospin spoke of "normalization" instead of "privatization." He baptized his pro-market policies *le réalisme de gauche* (realism of the left) and tough budget measures *parenthèse de rigueur* (a necessary parenthesis).

In a country where eloquence and rhetoric are prized, it should come as no surprise that authors and artists are highly regarded. As writers, we were in a good position to measure this. In North America, the first thing people ask when they hear we are writing is how we earn a living. To avoid this question we usually present ourselves as journalists. But in France, as we discovered, journalists are only of secondary interest (the French are not really interested in salaries, for that matter). When we understood this attitude, we introduced ourselves as writers, and the invitations to parties, conferences, and round tables started flowing in. Writing is simply one of the most highly respected vocations in France.

Intellectuals proliferate in such fertile grounds, and the French prize their intellectuals above all. Unlike in North America, the French intellectual is not just an expert or scholar. French intellectuals are, by definition, *engagés* (committed to a cause). They are accomplished authors who push a cause either by getting involved in politics themselves or by throwing their weight behind a polemical issue, or even by creating an issue. The poet Alphonse de Lamartine (1790–1869) was one of France's first high-profile intellectuals. He produced a fantastic body of poetry, but was also a politician who gained enough notoriety to become one of the five members of the executive council of the provisional government of the Second Republic. It was he who was chosen to proclaim the New Republic in 1848. Victor Hugo (1802–85), author of *Les Misérables* and *Notre Dame de Paris*, won a seat as *député* in the same assembly. Alexis de Tocqueville (1805–59), author of *Democracy in America*, was a *député* and Minister of Foreign Affairs. In the twentieth century, one of the most prominent intellectuals was author André Malraux (1901–69), who became Minister of Culture under de Gaulle.

It was Émile Zola (1840–1902) who set the standard of the *intellectuel engagé* with his inflammatory pamphlet, *J'Accuse,* written in 1898. Zola denounced an army conspiracy against a Jewish captain, Alfred Dreyfus, who was found guilty twice of spying for the Germans, in fixed trials, and sent to the infamous Devil's Island in French Guiana. Zola accused almost every witness and general involved in the case of lying and covering up the affair. He demanded a third trial, but ended up on trial himself, accused of defamation. He was found guilty and voluntarily went into exile in London, but the issue polarized the Right and the Left in France and snowballed into one of the most severe political crises of the Third Republic. Dreyfus was tried twice more before being released and rehabilitated as an officer in 1906. Zola died a mysterious death by carbon monoxide poisoning in 1902.

And of course there was philosopher, author, and playwright Jean-Paul Sartre (1905–80), who was never elected to any office, but whose political opinions held incredible sway in France throughout the twentieth century. In the wake of the May 1968 protests in France, Sartre founded France's first left-wing newspaper, *Libération*, which was openly Maoist.

But writers don't need to be Zolas, Hugos, or Sartres to become intellectuals. All they need to do is take on the establishment and forcefully fight an issue. Author Alexandre Jardin, who wrote the popular comic novel *Le Zèbre* and a number of other romantic comedies, became a respected intellectual by using his reputation to campaign for literacy, education, and a number of other causes.

French filmmakers, and some actors, have also earned the status of intellectuals. Their most famous accomplishment to date has been the successful campaign to sink the Mutual Accord on Investments in 1997. In 1995, the OECD proposed creating a complex treaty that would allow foreign investors to override the laws of any country. No one else in the world seemed to notice the treaty, but a group of French filmmakers and scriptwriters rallied together to publicly oppose it. Their proclamations and speeches attracted the attention of several French ministers, including the Minister of the Interior, who actually sent the police to pick up a copy of the treatise at the Playwrights Union (although he could well have gotten it from Foreign Affairs). That got French *députés* and ministers questioning the treaty and put French Foreign Affairs on the defensive. The French government finally refused to sign the treaty, which required unanimous consent from member countries, and the MAI was sunk.

During our stay in France we often heard Canadian and American friends complain about the French press. They accused French journalists of not presenting the facts and lacing their articles with too many personal opinions. In their eyes, the French journalists took too long to tell the reader what happened. French newspaper and magazine journalists often wait until the end of their article to explain actual events.

Being writers, we took a professional interest in the way articles and stories were written. When we first started reading the French press we had the same reaction as most Anglo-Americans. We thought articles were too wordy and too full of journalists' opinions. But after reading both the French and the American press on a daily basis, and comparing stories on similar topics, we changed our mind. We realized that the two presses simply operate in different rhetorical systems. The qualities generally attributed to the Anglo-American press—plainness and emphasis on facts—are themselves part of a rhetorical system. Few people in North America really think about a rhetorical system in the Anglo-American press, but it is there, shaping how our own news is written. This system has its own shortcomings, too.

Among the thousands of articles we clipped during our stay, one story from *The International Herald Tribune* caught out attention. The title was, "Versailles Stripped of Trees Again—Gift of U.S. Seedlings Sent Back for Violating European Union Regulations." *The Herald Tribune*'s story followed all the canons of the short newspaper feature. It started with the context: on December 26, 1999, two powerful windstorms toppled millions of trees in France, including ten thousand in Versailles alone, among which were two tulip poplars given by George Washington. Next, it described the events: after the storm, students of Fayette Middle School, of Fayetteville, Georgia, wanted to help the French, so they convinced the Forestry Association to donate five thousand trees to send so France could replant Versailles's gardens. Then there was the conclusion. The French returned three thousand seedlings because they failed to meet European Union regulations. Without explicitly saying so, the journalist left the reader to conclude that European Union regulations, or French bureaucrats, were the villains of the story. These bureaucrats had stamped out the goodwill of some well-meaning American kids.

The *Herald* journalist never actually stated this. The article looked like it was giving the "facts." Yet one hardly needed to read between the lines to understand the journalist's stance. The facts were organized to lead the reader to a conclusion—that European Union regulations are nasty—without ever saying so directly. The journalist reinforced his point by extensively quoting kids, teachers, school directors, and public-relations officers (the victims). He also omitted one very important "fact" that French journalists raised in a story on the same topic. In the late nineteenth century, Europe's entire wine industry was wiped out by the phylloxera parasite, which had arrived on evergreen seedlings from the United States. European regulations exist to prevent a repetition of this kind of catastrophe.

Anglo-Americans consider the *Herald Tribune* style of reporting "objective." But of course, there is no such thing as objective reporting. As journalists ourselves, we are well aware that the "facts" we provide about a story—and more importantly, those we omit—depend on the angle according to which we write the story (and that's usually decided by an editor). It's not about trying to hide information for some sinister plot. Presenting facts that lead a reader to a conclusion is simply the rhetorical style of preference in Anglo-American journalists. The goal is to make a case without having to explicitly state your purpose. To do this, journalists include some facts and ignore others. And they use understatement—a powerful tool in English-speaking cultures.

The French use an entirely different rhetorical style in their journalism. Their articles contain a lot of hard facts, but reporters are much more up-front about their opinions and impressions. The French consider attitudes and opinion to *be* facts, on par with events, numbers, quotations, or physical descriptions. So quite often, reporters give their opinions at the front of an article. Culturally, the French do not value understatement. They think it's a manipulative way to write. Many French reporters consider the Anglo-American style hypocritical and even suspicious because reporters don't make their own opinions or positions clear.

It's amazing to think that such profound incomprehension arises not from what is said, but from the *way* it is said.

chapter 6

Until-the-Bitter-End-Ism

We lived in France during the government's longest period of *cohabitation* ever. The term literally means coexistence, "living together under the same roof," and is normally reserved for unmarried couples who live together. From 1997 to 2002, it referred to a marriage of convenience between political leaders: the French president was from the Right, and the prime minister was from the Left.

The French hate this kind of political compromise, which is strange, since they bring it on themselves. When socialist president François Mitterrand (1981–95) was in power, they voted in a right-wing majority in Parliament. Mitterrand had to *cohabite* with right-wing prime ministers twice, for a total of four years of his fourteen in power. Then French electors did the same thing to right-wing president Jacques Chirac who had to live with socialist prime minister Lionel Jospin for five years. Yet during the three years we were in France, no one ever had a nice thing to say about the situation. They said *cohabitation* had made the Republic "ungovernable," politics petty, and politicians complacent. Why? Because cohabitation made it impossible to exercise power, they said.

That attitude seemed odd to us, and not just because the French brought the situation on themselves. Cohabitation didn't seem to be preventing the country from functioning. France survived a number of political crises while we were there, including battles over World Trade Organization regulations, the war in Kosovo, and various high-level corruption scandals. As far as we were concerned, *cohabitation* was representative of the political will in France. We told our friends that power-sharing was healthy, but our liberal appeals fell on deaf ears. For the French, *cohabitation* meant a permanent state of political compromise. In their view, politicians should have power and use it, so sharing power was a handicap, nothing more.

This French disdain for compromise doesn't stop at politics. As a society, they are remarkably intransigent. The tendency can be hard to discern from their love of *grandeur*, privilege, and incendiary oratory. But it is something else. The French have a penchant for being extremely divided over everything—an attitude that probably stems from their great love of power. Intransigence is like a deep centrifugal force that spreads to every corner of French society. Once we became aware of its existence, we saw it everywhere: in the news, people's conversations, history, politics, business, day-to-day life, and labor relations. In France someone always wins and someone always loses. At least on the surface, positions always look irreconcilable.

We had a hard time finding the right word to describe this attitude. "Extremism" and "*maximalisme*" are too strong, because they are now associated with communist regimes and religious fundamentalism. "Intolerance" is associated mainly with racism. But "intransigence" and "lack of restraint" didn't convey just how far the French have been willing to go to get the upper hand over their own countrymen and women. We settled on "*jusqu'au-boutisme*" (until-the-bitter-end-ism). The French use the term themselves to describe hard-liners who are willing to fight to the end, no matter what the costs, even if it means losing everything.

Except, of course, all the French are a little *jusqu'au-boutiste*. Yet France works in spite of this character flaw. In some ways, the last eight hundred years of French history have consisted of ongoing experiments to find a cure for it. The solution, ironically, was a compromise. The French have organized themselves in a way that contains it. They have a government structure that includes extremism without even really repressing it—an "absolutist" democratic government. (All of chapter 9 explains this.)

It's hard to avoid thinking of war when you're traveling in France. The spirit of aggression is everywhere, in the museums of the tiniest towns, in the mentality of the people, and in the way the French have inhabited their country. We marveled at cave dwellings when we visited Périgord, but quickly understood that the dwellings weren't built just for protection against the elements. Their locations were obviously chosen for their strategic value in case of attacks from neighbors. Entire valleys in France are peppered with castles with moats and drawbridges and fortified churches. What's left standing in France today looks quaint and charming, but most of it was built with the intention of waging war. Aggression was the common denominator in most of France's history.

The French had to deal with a considerable number of invaders: Vandal, Moor, English, Turk, Spanish, and German. But first and foremost, they had to deal with one another—their neighbors from the next village, castle, county, duchy, or *pays*. In an extremely complex agrarian society such as France, nobles and landowners constantly sought to enlarge their own property and influence. They had two methods at their disposal: marriage or war. But greed for land and power mongering were not the only reasons the French fought each other throughout their history.

The French fought over who should be king, whether the pope or the king should have supreme authority, whether there should be a king at all, whether he should be subject to the Constitution, and more. The French have fought each other for these and less important questions, sometimes with unfathomable savagery and at a human cost that is difficult to fathom.

The French have actually shown a talent for dividing themselves into opposing camps throughout most of their history. During the Hundred Years' War (1337–1453), between the French and the English, most of the "English" were actually French who regarded the king of England as their legitimate ruler. They had a point. During the Wars of Religion (1560–98) a century later, Catholics and Protestants in France killed each other off in staggering numbers and continued doing so even during the relatively peaceful seventeenth century. Until 1789, the clergy and the nobility enjoyed a lot of privileges—the most significant of which was their exemption from paying taxes. It reached a point at which revolt was the only means the lower orders of society could use to break this injustice. The French Revolution of 1789 unleashed a new brand of violence that opposed the *républicains* to the aristocrats, monarchists, and Catholics for the next century and a half.

By 1830, labor relations added a new dimension to the conflict, polarizing it into a struggle between the Right and the Left. That led to the Paris uprising of 1871 (during which twenty thousand were killed) and a quasi-civil war from 1898–1906 over the Dreyfus Affair. In the 1930s, the Right became openly violent. Nazi occupation (1940–44) ended in a low-scale civil war between members of the French Resistance and collaborators of the Vichy government. In 1958, the issue of Algeria's independence again pushed France close to a civil war. From 1789 to 1962, the French went through five democratic regimes, three monarchies, two empires, and a fascist dictatorship, all of which ended in violence (See Appendix 1).

In *Democracy in America*, de Tocqueville discussed the concept of "self-interest well understood." In his view, it was one of the main reasons American democracy worked. The absence of this concept in Europe also explained why democracy had not taken root there (he was writing in the 1830s). Self-interest well understood still describes what Americans do when they act in self-interested ways that end up being good for everyone. Americans believe in creating business empires that put people to work; they make charitable donations for tax deductions. Business leaders talk of finding "win-win" solutions to problems.

France has traditionally run on a lot of self-interest poorly understood, a tendency that leads many intelligent people to use their political liberty in ways that only serve themselves. Liberties were not tempered by a philosophy of restraint in France the way they were in North America. When the French government decided to allow freedom of the press in 1881, extreme right groups used the liberty to publish pamphlets and newspapers calling for the murder of left-wing politicians and Jews.

In traditional French thinking, problems are usually "win-lose." Disdain for compromise shows starkly in French labor relations. German union leaders are proud to announce that they've reached a compromise, or middle ground. The term is absent from French union vocabulary: they won or they lost, even if a compromise was reached in reality. On the scale of what's private and public in France, what's hidden and what's affirmed, compromise is definitely hidden.

Unions aren't the only institutions that eschew compromise. Capitalism has a bad reputation in France thanks to the open-faced greed of French capitalists throughout history. In the nineteenth century, and until the mid-twentieth century, they lacked the wisdom to share even a little bit of what they possessed, even to buy peace. In 1830, French capitalists actively supported the government of the new king Louis-Philippe d'Orléans, who granted voting rights only to France's super rich—the so-called "200 families." Workers were outraged, but the rich voting class didn't lift a finger to extend the voting rights. Capitalists' unwillingness to give up their monopoly on power over the next twenty years eventually brought on a revolt. The king reacted by forbidding political meetings of any kind. Riots broke out in Paris. The monarchy fell in three days—to be replaced by the short-lived democratic Second Republic in 1848. In the same period, the British ruling class more or less peacefully extended the voting rights to the middle and lower classes without provoking the fall of one government.

In other words, there never was a French Ford—someone who figured out that industry would perpetuate itself if workers had rights and were well paid. "Fordism" fostered the idea that if owners paid employees well, workers would buy the product they made. The aim was to create a working class affluent enough that it would lose interest in socialism and communism. It was prompted above all by the self-interest of Henry Ford himself, but it worked. The French may make equally good cars, but French capitalists never elaborated a doctrine of redistribution like Ford's. Generous social benefits and welfare perks in France are post-war phenomena. (More on this in chapter 18.)

Until World War II, the French lagged behind the British and especially the Germans, who created social peace by modernizing their labor laws, reducing the legal work week, granting holidays, and devising retirement funds. French capitalists refused to make these concessions, or applied them only begrudgingly when forced to do so. When a left-wing coalition known as *Front Populaire* was voted into power in 1936 on the promise of reducing the work week to forty hours and granting two weeks of paid holiday to all, France nearly broke into civil war—again.

The distrust employees have of employers in France is visceral. That was only too obvious from the debate we witnessed about giving employees stock options, a concept that the French had picked up while doing business with the outside world. Not surprisingly, the Left and unions openly opposed the "capitalist" practice of paying employees with potential future earnings instead of real wages. But company executives didn't want to give employees stock options anyway. As a rule, only executives and board members in France get them—perfectly fitting with France's hierarchical business mentality.

Other buzzwords from the globalizing economy, like "empowerment," were stirring controversy in France while we were there. In North America, "empowerment" usually refers to giving employees autonomy and tools to stimulate initiative that allow them to make decisions on their own, rather than wait for their orders. We knew from our conversations with both French and North American friends working in France that employees weren't interested in taking initiative. They didn't want to make decisions for their bosses. It simply wasn't part of the culture. Bosses were not interested in relinquishing authority or giving employees the information necessary to empower them. Bosses in France are used to having the last word.

This same kind of intransigence shows up in their ideas about company governance. The French don't believe that shareholders will actually act for the benefit of the company as a whole. While we were in France, the French press discovered that huge pension funds like the Scottish Widows or California Teachers had investments in French companies through their pension funds. The French were not flattered by the fact that foreigners wanted a stake in their thriving economy. Rightly or wrongly, their first reflex was to see a threat and a power struggle rather than an opportunity. The Left and Right united over the issue. "How can we let our companies be the toys of Scottish Widows?" they asked. Only time will tell if they are right or wrong about this. But as a rule, the French can detect a power struggle one hundred miles (or yards) away.

Federalism is another topic the French find universally alarming. From its early history, the United States had to deal with strong religious differences and strong community identities that rivaled the state. The solution was to create a federation that allowed communities to retain some powers, and to write a constitution that didn't mention God. The formula didn't prevent civil war, but it could have been worse. In Canada, language and religion threatened unity, so Canadians created an even looser federation leaving large powers to the provinces. Belgium was originally created as a centralized, unitary state, but when that provoked quarrels between the French and Flemish elements of the country, the Belgians switched to a federation of six overlapping jurisdictions, three territorial and three linguistic. It's odd, but it works. In the United Kingdom, the centralist government kept a semblance of decentralization by allowing the Bank of Scotland or the Bank of Ireland to issue their own notes. Faced with some minorities they never assimilated fully, like the Irish, they accepted the creation of the Irish Republic in 1922, and of regional parliaments in Scotland and Wales in 1999. Spain did the same with the Catalans. In many countries, differences are dealt with by devolving power.

Federalism is one way for countries to accommodate differences among the populations, but it is not the French way. The French solution was absolutism and centralization. Despite several attempts to create a constitutional monarchy and a federation, federalism never took root in France. Throughout French history, kings methodically stripped princes, dukes, and counts of regional powers.

The one exception was Henri IV, who signed the Edict of Nantes, granting the Protestants freedom of religion and the control of two hundred fortified cities. His successors restricted the edict until his grandson Louis XIV (1661–1715) revoked it in 1685. Until 1790, France was engaged in a kind of semi-permanent, low-level civil war between centralists and groups demanding some kind of autonomy, whether it was Cathars, Albigensians, *Bourguignons*, English, Protestants, *la Fronde*, or *Vendéens*. During the French Revolution this old fault line resurfaced as the quarrel between federalists *Girondins* and the centralist *Jacobins*. The *Jacobins* won, and federalists became the bogeymen of French politics.

Historically, British-style constitutional monarchies have worked whenever the crown was willing to submit itself to a parliament, generally composed of aristocrats and later extended to representatives of commoners. In France, the aristocracy made dozens of attempts to check the king's power but never succeeded. From 1614 to 1789 France had a form of parliament in the Estates General, whose members included appointed representatives of the clergy, aristocracy, and commoners. But French monarchs governed during this period without asking advice from this body once. And in any case, if they had, the clergy and the aristocracy would have joined together to overrule the commoners.

Attitudes about power sharing haven't changed that much. When we talked to our French friends about how things worked in the Canadian system, they said it sounded like "anarchy." That's undoubtedly what the French would get if they did try a federation. Federations work because of unwritten rules of restraint. Even if powers overlap and competing jurisdictions step into each other's turf, constituencies don't usually try to solve conflicts by taking up arms against each other. Conflicts are a normal part of the system and institutions are in place to arbitrate them. The system requires moderation and compromise, but the French are too *jusqu'au boutiste* for that.

The French opted for absolutism long before the existence of the modern French State. Their whole history pushed them in this direction. In medieval times, the king had to compete against the aristocracy and the church, and he didn't always win. Any bishop who bore a grudge against the king could excommunicate him. Gradually, power of excommunication was restricted to the pope. But by the seventeenth century, the king's authority was considered greater than that of the pope. So absolutism was born. (The word absolutism did not yet exist. It was coined in 1797, eight years after the French Revolution ousted the monarchy.) An absolute leader knows no judicial, constitutional, executive, or legislative restraint on his power. He represents the absolute good of the State. All European states tried out absolutism as a way to establish order and security—in

France absolutism held things together in relative peace for nearly two centuries until the Revolution.

After the Revolution, France went through a period of political instability that lasted until 1958, but democracy made constant progress, despite many setbacks. In 1799, Napoleon installed himself as first consul, and a form of parliamentarism existed, although the emperor-to-be decided on the ultimate good. During the various monarchical regimes that followed, Parliament subsisted, although its faith varied from king to king. Democracy was reestablished briefly in 1848, only to be replaced by the second empire in 1851.

(The second empire lasted until 1870. A sort of democratic equilibrium was reached with the so-called Third Republic, which lasted from 1870 to 1940, but even that barely survived the *jusqu'au boutiste* reflex. There was nothing written in the Constitution that said Parliament was supreme, but the tradition had taken root. When governments disagreed with it, they were either dissolved or they resigned. Between 1871 and 1940 France went through 120 governments. The situation was wholly unstable.)

The next two chapters deal with two traumatic historical episodes in French history: World War II and the War of Algeria, during which *jusqu'au-boutisme* reached new heights. Strictly speaking, the wars are events, not "characteristics" of the French mind-set. Yet no book on French culture and the French mind-set would be complete without them. Both wars forced France to create many of the institutions we describe in Part II, institutions which, in turn, shape the way France operates and the way the French think, both about themselves and the rest of the world.

chapter 7

World War II: The Unforgotten War

We were reminded of World War II almost every day we lived in France. About halfway down the quay of Guy Môquet Metro Station near our apartment, the former stationmaster's cabin had been converted into a shrine for Guy Môquet, an idealistic seventeen-year-old French youth who had died in front of a German firing squad in 1941. Inside the glass case, photos and posters documented the short life of Guy, who was jailed for protesting against German occupation just months after France was defeated and signed an armistice with Germany. Beside Guy's photo, there was an ancient orange poster written in German and French, denouncing the murder of a German officer who was killed in the same period. That poster warned that one hundred French hostages would be shot if the culprit was not turned in. Another one signed by the head of the Vichy government, World War I hero Maréchal Philippe Pétain, exhorted the French to turn in the culprit and save the lives of innocent French hostages.

Guy was one of the hostages. No one turned in the killer, and as the short text in the display explained, Guy was duly executed, along with twenty-six other hostages from his camp. In an enlarged copy of his farewell letter, Guy begs his mother to "be brave," and in a message carved into a wooden plank, he asks that "those who will die never be forgotten."

As the Guy Moquêt display attests, the hostages never were forgotten—but the real story behind their execution was. Over the course of research on the World War II persecution of Jews in France, Jean-Benoît learned that while German soldiers pulled the trigger, the French government edited the list of hostages they executed. The Germans had sent the French a list of one hundred candidates—probably a mix of protesters, resistance fighters, and black marketers—and the French Minister of the Interior removed forty names and replaced them with the names of communists and labor activists. At his trial for war crimes in 1945, the Minister would explain: "I could not let forty good Frenchmen die."

Six decades have passed since World War II, when a defeated France surrendered to Nazi Germany. Most of the main actors are dead, and as the generation of those who were children is now fading away, the war in France is finally, slowly becoming history. But it's not over yet. The French are still struggling to come to terms with what actually happened.

Up until September 1939, the French, like the British, were doing everything they could to avoid another European war and the millions of casualties it would leave. Like the British, their main fear was the Soviet Union, not Nazi Germany. Watching Germany rise in power and influence, France and Britain were both prone to compromise rather than confront it, so they stood by and watched as the Germans annexed Austria in 1938 and Czechoslovakia in 1938–39. Only in late August 1939, when Germany and the Soviet Union signed a pact of non-aggression and attacked Poland, did Britain and France declare war on Germany. And then, for a year, they did almost nothing.

France's defeat was not long coming. On May 10, 1940, the Germans launched the most brilliant military campaign of all history. The French fought savagely—130,000 died in six weeks, twice the number of American casualties during the Battle of Normandy four years later. The French had one of the biggest armies and good material, but the Franco-British effort suffered from poor coordination of their arms and poor use of modern technology. When it was clear that France was about to lose the battle, a tremendous wave of defeatism overwhelmed the political and military leaders of the country and some French leaders were ready to sign an armistice as early as May 20.

Not all the French were so quick to give up. A number of members of the government—including a certain deputy secretary of state to war named Charles de Gaulle—proposed evacuating the French government and remnants of the French army to Algeria, and continuing the fight against Germany. Though underused, France's aviation fleet at the time was still strong, and the French navy was the second most powerful in Europe.

The defeatists won, mainly thanks to the reputation of Maréchal Philippe Pétain (1856–1951), a World War I military hero and the most revered Frenchman alive at the time. Pétain was venerated in all French households as the man who had saved France from defeat in the great World War I battle of Verdun (1916–17). Pétain propelled himself to the head of the government by arguing that the French government should remain in France, not go into exile, and most French believed Pétain would be able to make the best of France's defeat and keep the Germans at arm's length.

France signed an armistice with Germany on June 22, and the Germans split the country into four zones. The Germans occupied the northern zones, including all the Atlantic shores, and annexed the zones of Alsatia and Lorraine. Along the Italian border and a southern section of France around Nice were annexed by Italy. That left about 40 percent of French territory, mostly in the south, as part of the Free Zone governed by the French. On July 10, the French Parliament scuttled the Republic and gave Pétain "dictatorial powers." Pétain moved the seat of government from Paris to Vichy, the famous spa town in the center of the country, and his government would henceforth be known by that name.

The French, unfortunately, got more than they expected from Pétain. Pétain was both authoritarian and conservative, and he believed that France's defeat to Germany had been caused by too much socialism, democracy, and parliamentarism, and too little authority. He argued that liberty, equality, and fraternity had actually weakened the fiber of French society. While he was in power, he changed France's motto to "Labor, Family, Fatherland."

For the first two years of the occupation, historians agree that most French believed that the great Pétain was playing a *double jeu* (double game) with the Germans—in other words, pretending to play into the Germans' hands while he was in fact preparing France's revenge. Pétain seems to have convinced himself that this was what he was doing.

In his *History of French Jews*, French author Pierre Bourdel recounts an anecdote where a doctor, asked to become the president of the Order of Physicians, was told he had to apply a quota on Jewish doctors. The doctor protested and Pétain replied: "If you don't do it, the Germans will. *We must not let German authority substitute French authority.*" As it turned out, Pétain was so obsessed with "asserting French sovereignty" that there was little left for the Germans to do themselves. According to some accounts, Germany sent less than thirty thousand troops to police France during the war. France, for its part, sent hundreds of thousands of men to Germany to support the war effort as voluntary and forced labor.

Pétain's government became a mere puppet regime in November 1942, when the Germans occupied the Free Zone. The French administration remained in place and administered its own rules, like everywhere in France, but was now subject to German orders. Pétain was a mere figurehead by that time; his prime minister, Pierre Laval (1940, 1942–44) really ran the government. Laval was in favor of even closer ties with Germany. Vichy became more and more aggressive, hunting down members of the French Resistance and deporting many thousands of Jews to German concentration camps. Laval is famous for having said in the summer of 1942 that he "longed for a German victory."

To this day, the French tend to see themselves as having resisted Nazi Germany, both before the armistice and during the occupation. Yet compared to Yugoslavia—where soldiers and civilians organized overnight into a guerrilla army, grounding as many as eight German divisions and successfully ousting the Germans before the Soviets arrived—the French did little to fend off German occupation. The

French actually had little fighting spirit left after their defeat in the battle of May 1940. However, nobody will ever know the precise number of
French men and women who later went on to become active members
of the French underground, known as the *Résistance*. When sixty thousand French soldiers were evacuated from Narvik and Dunkirk in July
1940, only three thousand continued the struggle, mostly under General
de Gaulle's Free French Forces based in London. Some specialists say
there were fewer than ten thousand working for the Resistance in early
1942. The numbers swelled in 1942 when the Germans imposed the
mandatory work service in Germany and occupied the French Free
Zone, but decreased in 1943 as the Gestapo, the German army, and the
French militia itself started cracking down on networks. By 1944, when
an Allied victory became more of a certainty, the Resistance counted
two hundred thousand members.

Yet the activities of resistance fighters varied greatly, as did their motivations, making it very difficult to generalize about them. Doing a research
on second-language teaching, Jean-Benoît met eighty-year-old Jean-Marie
Bressand, a language immersion specialist who was one of the few true
heroes of the Resistance. Between 1941 and 1943, working under the war
name Casino, Jean-Marie became one of the best sources of intelligence on
the German military. Yet over the course of his last interview with
Bressand, Jean-Benoît realized an uneasy truth. In 1937, at age seventeen,
Jean-Marie had fought the Spanish Civil War as a *légionnaire* of France
against the communist and the republicans. In other words, Bressand
fought *with* fascists before he fought against them. By such a standard, one
would have expected to find Bressand among France's collaborationists
and anti-Semites during the war.

Bressand's about-face shows how futile it is to try to understand
wartime France through labels, either good or bad. The seventeenth of a
family of nineteen, raised in a rigorously Catholic family that attended
mass twice a day, he grew up fearing evil and communism. When civil war
broke out in Spain, his faith drove him to join what he thought was a crusade against the anti-Catholic revolutionaries trying to overthrow the
Spanish government. But it was his faith that drove him away from fascists,

too. "It certainly wasn't Christian, the handraising salutes, the goose-stepping, the Nazi doctrine, and the weird cross," he says now.

Bressand is only too happy to poke holes in the myth that all of the French resisted the Germans. A popular belief persists to this day that on June 18, 1940, General de Gaulle rallied the country to fight the Germans over the radio. "Nobody ever entered the Resistance at de Gaulle's call, because no one ever heard him on the radio!" says Bressand, who was an officer cadet in the artillery school at the time. Not all French radios could catch messages from London, and the speech was not publicized because the French government already considered de Gaulle a traitor.

In fact, a unified "Resistance" did not even exist at the time, as Bressand's story shows only too well. After France signed the armistice with Germany, Bressand decided to "fight the Germans however he could" on his own. From his hometown of Besançon in the east he got himself a job at the local cinema, the Casino Theater. The owner, also a patriot, gave Bressand a back room he could use as a base to carry out underground activities against the Germans, but at first, anyway, Bressand wasn't too sure what to do.

Circumstances would guide him. Besançon turned out to be one of the best places possible for gathering intelligence on the German military. Located near the German and Swiss borders, and several miles from the no-man's land that divided occupied and unoccupied France, the town of fifty thousand became an important hub for battle-weary German divisions who were stationed there to rest and recuperate. The Casino Theater, next to a thermal station and a restaurant, became the German army's official enter-tainment center. As director of the soldier's cinema, Bressand had orders to find the best sweets he could for the Germans. To perform this service, he was given the papers he needed to move freely across the no-man's land.

After a series of chance meetings and introductions, Bressand found himself supplying German military intelligence to the British via the French army's second Clandestine Bureau in Lyon. Utterly untrained in the arts of espionage, he started out emptying garbage bins, documenting rail activity, and searching the pockets of the German officers' coats in cloakrooms. His activities quickly escalated as he gained experience, skill, and contacts. In 1942, he eavesdropped while German admiral Wilhelm Canaris gave a secret conference on submarine warfare at the Casino. Later, with the help of a janitor, Bressand figured out how to remove decrypted military documents from the local university's incinerator before they were burned. He even managed to steal the briefcase of the Chief Inspector of the Supply Corps and Paymaster of the Reich's army, which contained a detailed report of the state of the armies stationed on the Russian front.

While Bressand was supplying intelligence to the British, other resistance cells were getting organized across France and de Gaulle worked to unify them, partly to boost his own legitimacy as the leader of the Free French. By the winter of 1943, the Resistance was organized and active enough to attract the Gestapo's attention, and they started cracking down on the movement. In the sweep of arrests that followed, most of the officers at the second Clandestine Bureau in Lyon were captured and the Germans discovered rows and rows of secret documents labeled "Casino." Having gotten word of the arrests, Bressand tried to flee to Switzerland, but was stopped. The Germans questioned him for nineteen days before figuring out that he was "Casino." Bressand was shipped to a prisoner camp in Compiègne, northeast of Paris, but escaped and fled to Switzerland. He managed to reach North Africa, via Spain, where he joined de Gaulle's Free French Force in Algeria.

Jean-Marie Bressand was not the only true resistance fighter in France, though he was certainly one of the luckiest. However, by the time of the liberation in the summer of 1944, the number of eleventh-hour resistance fighters surged. When Bressand returned to Besançon at the end of August 1944, as captain in the Free French Forces, he witnessed the grotesque spectacle of French women being shaved, whipped, and paraded naked through the streets for having slept with Germans. "Some of the women were actually informers for the Resistance. The guys who punished them were creeps, collaborationists, and black marketers trying to clear their names. I wanted to tell them that we had not been fighting for four years for this mockery of justice, but I didn't say anything. I really regret not speaking out, but I had a team to move, we had a war to fight, and I wanted to see my parents."

For most of 1944, France was ripped apart by a low-scale civil war between underground resistance fighters and the French militia, propped up by the Germans. When the war was over, de Gaulle was named France's provisional leader, and after he took power in 1945, he began carefully cultivating the myth that all of France had supported the Resistance—morally, if not in their actions. The resistance myth was a healing balm that raised French morale and consolidated de Gaulle's own power. It wasn't until after de Gaulle's death in 1970 that French historians began questioning the myth. Books and documentaries during that period revealed that many of the evil acts attributed to the occupying Germans were actually the doing of the French administration. And that's the question France is still struggling with to this day.

When he came to power, de Gaulle proclaimed that the collaborationist Vichy regime was "not France," yet from at least one perspective, Vichy definitely was France. Some of the institutions Pétain created, like France's telecommunication department and the national police, endure to this day. France's national rail service, which shipped Jews to Germany, is still operating.

Yet, France really was in a state of servitude to Germany; the country was forced to pay Germany a war tribute of four hundred million francs daily. The truth is somewhere in between these two positions. France was not united in resistance to the extent that de Gaulle wanted the populace to believe, but popular support for Pétain's government did dwindle as the war progressed and the French understood that Vichy was keener on executing communists and resisters than it was on taking revenge on Germany.

The events of World War II were so powerful that it is tempting to try to redefine the past in function of the outcome and divide France into heroes and villains. Did France collaborate or resist? Or was it a country of *attentistes* (literally, "waiters")? The debate continues, both inside and outside France. But in reality, none of these labels describe what was really going on. Most people did a bit of everything. Tragic as it was, World War I had been a great unifying experience for the French. But World War II was forty million private wars. Forty million people in France spent four years saying one thing and doing another.

We had many friends in France who had lived through the war either as children, teenagers, or even as adults. None of them had any knowledge of what was actually going on. The radio was all government propaganda and newspapers had been whittled down to mere leaflets. Most Frenchmen never read the conditions of the armistice and they trusted Pétain, who was a war hero, after all. Food was scarce in the cities. Nobody had enough coal to heat more than a single room in any house. One and a half million men were prisoners of war in Germany and their families lived in abject poverty. By 1944, the economy had shrunk by a staggering 80 percent. It was a time of hardship.

The best illustration of the French population's mood during the war can be found in a series of short stories called *Passe-Muraille*, published in 1943 by author Marcel Aymé (1901–63), whose magic realism has inspired much of the literature of Latin America. The first story depicts the highs and lows of a Frenchman who discovers he can walk through walls (literally *passer la muraille*). It's an apt image for the overall frustration the French must have felt being prisoners in their own country. In another story, people are dealing with new restrictions that reduce their rations to fifteen days of living per month. The rest of their time is spent in limbo. The last short story, "En Attendant" (*Waiting*), is a series of fourteen monologues of people waiting in the bread line during the "War of 1939–72"—a joke that shows how nobody in France had a clue of when, or if, the war would ever end. In one of the monologues, a woman talks about the hardship of having only two pairs of shoes for her three children. Some monologues are quite long, but the shortest one, eight words in all, simply reads:

"And I, said the Jew, I'm a Jew."

There was obviously a lot more to say about being a Jew, but Aymé would not have been allowed to write about it. His brevity alone speaks volumes.

There is no doubt anymore that France persecuted Jews on its own. After Pétain came to power in July 1940, racial segregation began almost overnight, but most of the background thinking for this had been done in anti-Jewish circles over the previous fifty years. The new government did not need much help from the Germans to strip Jews of all their rights. As early as August 1940, the Vichy government defined Jewish status, barring Jews from public offices and all state jobs, even teaching. The government went on to produce 168 anti-Jewish laws and regulations. The fact that many French collaborated with the Germans was bad enough, but the truth is that many took advantage of the situation to deprive Jews of their civil rights, their property, and their lives.

No story illustrates this better than that of Jean-Jacques Fraenkel, a sixty-eight-year-old Holocaust survivor whom Jean-Benoît met through his hiking club, and who would become a good friend of ours while we lived in France. Curiously, he was introduced to Jean-Benoît by other members of the hiking club as a "fellow Canadian." Though he keeps a house in Paris, Jean-Jacques immigrated to Canada in 1992, bought a house in Victoria, British Columbia, and acquired Canadian citizenship. Jean-Jacques proclaimed Canadians to be the nicest people in the world. He said he admired them for being moderate and open-minded, although he himself is intense, opinionated, and extremely French. It always seemed a little ironic to us that during long meals with Jean-Jacques at our apartment in Paris our discussions revolved around a common theme: how much he hated the French. But of course, his story explains that.

Jean-Jacques's two parents were gassed in Auschwitz and his life was nearly destroyed by the war. He was eight at the onset of the war. His father, Roger, was the most famous dental surgeon in France at the time, but shortly after the Vichy government came to power, Roger lost his title as officer, then his right to teach, then his driver's license, and was told he could not leave the city. Then the Law for the Exclusion of Jews from the Economy instructed officials to confiscate Jewish businesses. Jews' bank accounts were frozen and they could not work. Eventually, any gentile who wanted the shop of a Jew could ask city hall for a paper that gave them the right to call it their own. The government began establishing quotas for Jewish students, and Jewish lawyers, and Jewish doctors. And they all had to wear the yellow star.

Roger professed his trust that the French government would protect Jews right up until his arrest on December 12, 1941. The police ordered him to pack his luggage with two days of food and underwear, but he refused, saying that he would settle the matter at the station and be back in ten minutes. He never came back—it turned out he was one of the 743 leaders of the Jewish community arrested in the first roundup of Jews in Paris. He boarded a train to Auschwitz three months later and was gassed on May 20, 1942, his wedding anniversary.

Jean-Jacques's mother Jeanine never saw her husband again. Blaming the Germans, she assumed a false identity, joined the Resistance, and moved with Jean-Jacques and his sister Josette to Nice, still a safe haven for Jews in southern France. After a year in hiding, Jeanine had her children smuggled back to Paris, where they could be hidden in safe homes and sent to Catholic schools. Several weeks after Jean-Jacques returned to Paris in November 1943, his mother was arrested and sent to the infamous deportation station of Drancy, in Paris. Five days later she was gassed at Auschwitz, on the second anniversary of her husband's arrest.

After the war, Jean-Jacques believed, like many French Jews, that the Germans alone were responsible for persecuting Jews. Unlike most French Jews, he changed his mind rather abruptly when he discovered a suitcase in his grandparents house, miraculously saved from the ruin of his family. The suitcase, containing papers and documents gathered by his mother between 1940 and 1943, showed how the French government had methodically despoiled the Fraenkels and all Jews, making them defenseless against the threat of deportation—and extermination, as it turned out. Jean-Jacques wrote his story in a book titled *Abus de Confiance* (*Breach of Trust*). "My sister and I survived the war because of the Resistance, because of the dedication of those who hid us, because of Catholic schools," he explained, "but the whole time we were being chased not only by the Germans, but by our own government."

The French will long bear the stigma of these policies. But does their wartime behavior classify them as an anti-Semitic people? It's like asking whether they were fundamentally resisters or collaborators with the Nazis. Nothing about wartime France is that black and white.

In all, seventy-six thousand of the three hundred thousand Jews in France died in Nazi death camps—a low estimate, which doesn't account for those who died in French camps as hostages or resistance fighters. Outside of Germany, this is the highest number of Jews from any Western European country killed. However, the proportion of French Jews saved in France is also the highest of Western Europe. Three quarters of France's Jews survived; the survival rates in Belgium and Holland were below 25 percent. Despite the anti-Semitic policies of the Vichy government and the collaboration of the French administration in persecuting Jews, it's clear a great number of people did not do what the State asked. As Jean-Jacques Fraenkel says himself, the massacre would have been much greater without the secret support of thousands of French people, the Resistance, and the lower Catholic clergy.

Yet there is no doubt that French anti-Semitism was official in character. It came in the form of directives from the State, and many civil servants applied the regulations blindly, sealing the fate of thousands of Jews. The first large-scale roundup of Jews in summer of 1942 was carried out by no fewer than six thousand French police. French Jews were treated the worst of all in French Algeria, where German soldiers never even set foot.

Clearly, it was possible for occupied countries to resist Germany's policies. In Denmark, King Christian X simply refused to accept Germany's racist laws. When it became clear that the Germans would deport Jews anyway, the Danes organized the escape of the last seven thousand Jews across the Oresund Channel to Sweden. It is tempting to attribute France's behavior to the fact that it was Catholic, but Italy—which was not only Catholic but fascist—refused to deport Jews, and only eight thousand Italian Jews died in the camps. The French government did what it was told—and more. The French Bar never protested the treatment of Jewish lawyers, like the Belgian Bar did. When French banks were asked to turn over names and account balances of Jewish clients, they froze and confiscated sixty-eight thousand Jewish accounts.

Jews in France became a general source of unearned income during the war, and the State showed citizens the way: there was a violent legal battle between Vichy and the Germans over who would get the monopoly on the confiscation of Jewish goods. The Germans settled for 10 percent. The rest went into the French treasury or was distributed to individuals. Many French citizens just helped themselves to the spoils. People took all the Jewish possessions they could get their hands on—from furniture and sewing machines to children's books.

French anti-Semitism did, however, have one strange idiosyncrasy that distinguished it from the German attitude: the French differentiated between two types of Jews. In all their laws, French authorities always gave a preference to Jews who had been in France long enough to be integrated (two to five generations), who had fought in World War I, who had distinguished military service, or who had rendered exceptional civil services to France. Still that didn't help Roger Fraenkel, who had been given the *légion d'honneur* for his work in dentistry. According to French senator Robert Badinter, himself a Jew and the author of *Un Antisémitisme Ordinaire*, some French Jewish lawyers, just as xenophobic as the gentiles, tried to exclude themselves from early anti-Semitic laws in France. They argued that recent Jewish immigrants posed more of a threat than they did. This distinction disappeared in 1942 when the Germans ordered all Jews to wear the yellow star.

More than fifty years after the war, is it fair to accuse the French of still being fundamentally anti-Semitic? In 2001, during the second Intifada in Israel, the number of hate crimes in France doubled, from 150 to about three hundred per year. Israeli Prime Minister Ariel Sharon declared that the French were the most anti-Semitic people in the world. Dozens of articles we read in the American, British, and Canadian media echoed him, concluding that anti-Jewish sentiment was still the norm in modern France.

Basically, it depends on how you look at it. On one hand, a member of Pétain's government, François Mitterrand, went on to become the president of France from 1981 to 1995. Mitterrand was not an anti-Semite, but his *Pétainiste* past was well known in *élite* circles. Prime Minister Lionel Jospin (1997–2002) was also the son of a known Protestant collaborator. Author Louis-Ferdinand Céline—so rabidly anti-Semitic and pro-Nazi that he fled to Germany in 1944—is still admired in all classes of French society, and his works are taught in high schools. (Although, we should add that he was enough of an author to keep most of his opinions on the matter outside of his literary works.)

While there's no denying that kind of anti-Semitic thread in French culture, there are other factors that should be considered before labeling the French. Historically, France was a model of integration for the Jewish community, having granted civil rights to Jews in 1794, a good century before any other European country. Since 1936, France has had four Jewish prime ministers. In his book *The French*, author Theodore Zeldin goes as far as saying that the French Jewish community is the most integrated in the world. It is also false to accuse the French of refusing to face their past. While we lived in France, not a week went by without the release of a major new report, book, or film on the behavior of the French during the war.

Terrible as the events of that war were, France as we know it today was forged by them. Most of France's modern structures were created to avoid a repetition of history.

As head of the provisional government from 1944–46, Charles de Gaulle's first job was bringing France's war criminals to justice. Nearly half a million people in France were tried for collaboration and received sentences ranging from death (3,700 executions) to loss of all civic rights (150,000). One hundred and eight members of the government were tried and sentenced along with many others among local politicians. High-ranking civil servants, officers of the army, and even bishops were punished. It was not complete—many escaped any judgment or were wrongly acquitted. But de Gaulle closed the door on the period with his famous declaration that "Vichy was not France."

One fact is rarely mentioned in books on modern France: for better or for worse, France was the only German-occupied country that was allowed to clear up the mess of the war on its own, much the way it had been the only German-occupied country allowed to run things itself. In 1944, while the Americans were still fighting with the French against the occupying

Germans, Charles de Gaulle rejected the AMGOT (Allied Military Government of Occupied Territories). This scheme for post-war reconstruction would have given Americans control over French currency, transport, the appointment of civil servants, and the war tribunals. The AMGOT was imposed on Belgium, Holland, and Germany, but de Gaulle rejected it, fearing that the Americans would use their presence in France to impose their values and customs and turn France into a client state. Whatever the reason, during the liberation process, General Charles de Gaulle, head of the Free French Forces and of the Resistance, quickly established his legitimacy as the head of France's provisional government and got down to business.

De Gaulle set out after the war to renew France socially, politically, and economically. He said he wanted to restore France's honor, independence, and rank among great nations. With that in mind, he and the new generation of leaders he brought with him began by raising the principle of assimilation to the level of a unifying ideal of the French Republic. French citizens would no longer be said to have a religion, a skin color, or even an ethnic origin. Everyone with French citizenship would be French, period; they would be assimilated in the melting pot of the Republic. The government would keep no record or files on French citizens' religion and ethnicity and would not ask for this information in the national census. France reinstated the policy that all children born in France were French, no matter what their ethnic origin. The French State did make serious mistakes in applying the principle of assimilation, namely in Algeria. And the assimilation ideal certainly hasn't eliminated racism, yet it remains one of the strongest, most widely shared values of modern France.

De Gaulle made significant changes in France's social programs and nationalized many industries, but France had to go through another severe political crisis, the War of Algeria, before its institutions would be changed for good, and for the better.

chapter 8

Algeria: The Unacknowledged War

Four months after our arrival, a friend of ours, Éric Marsault, invited us to his parents' for Easter weekend. The family almost adopted us, and their house in the village of Fresnes, in the Loire Valley, became something of a second home to us. Éric's father, Jean-Marie, was a *bon vivant*, a gourmand, and avid accordion player who used to have his own band. But he had been a soldier once. Tucked among the various stuffed fish decorating the walls of Jean-Marie's den was a photo of him and his captain, and a frame with several war medals, a newspaper clipping, and a crest of the *1ère DBFM–Première Division Blindée des Fusiliers Marins* (First Armored Marines Division).

Like most men of his age, Jean-Marie had fought in the War of Algeria in 1956–57—he actually returned a sergeant—and like most, he doesn't talk much about it. Yet as the memorabilia in his office attests, Sergeant Jean-Marie Marsault hasn't forgotten the war. He still mourns his commanding field officer and three of his best friends who died in a skirmish in 1957.

Outside of France, very little is known about the war in Algeria (1954–62). It was certainly one of the most traumatic events in recent French memory, at least as traumatic as World War II. It is no exaggeration to call it the Vietnam of the French—in many ways, this is even an understatement.

The conflicts resemble each other in striking ways. Both were colonial, or neo-colonial, wars. In both cases, two powerful countries were defeated by an enemy considerably inferior in means—the French sent 1.3 million troops to fight against about 330,000 Algerian guerrillas, and lost. And at home the populations of both countries were split over the war, with huge segments opposed to their country's military campaigns abroad to begin with.

That's where the similarities end, though. Imagine if, at the time of the Vietnam War, there had been one million American settlers who had lived in Vietnam for four generations. Imagine if Vietnam had not been "foreign territory," but a part of the United States, a fifty-first state—and if North Vietnamese terrorists had killed twenty-five hundred American civilians in the United States. And just imagine the scenario of the U.S. Army becoming so displeased with its own government's conduct in Vietnam that it attempted to overthrow the American government by staging a coup in Washington. This is exactly what happened to France during the war in Algeria.

Few books and even fewer films tell the story of this war. The French government did not even call it a war until that term was accepted in a vote on June 10, 1999, thirty-seven years after the 1962 cease-fire. Until then, it had been known officially as an *opération de maintien de l'ordre* (a law-and-order operation) to contain Muslim nationalists in French territory. But a war it was. At the height of the operation, in 1959, five hundred thousand French troops were stationed in Algeria. During the conflict, twenty-five thousand French soldiers were killed, and probably ten times more Algerians.

Four decades later, the War of Algeria remains an open wound in France's national psyche. For the French, the physical hardship of World War II may have been greater, but the psychological consequences of Algeria were at least as terrible, partly because, unlike World War II, the war in Algeria was not a "noble" one by any stretch of the imagination. France's attempts to "pacify" Algeria were shockingly out of step with the times; in the rest of Africa the decolonization movement was in full swing. Unlike World War II, the War of Algeria offers no psychological refuge in a "Resistance," whether real or mythical. The millions of men who fought as conscripts or voluntary soldiers in Algeria were either obeying orders or willfully fighting for the cause of a French Algeria. Some of the French who opposed retaining French Algeria protested, but that was all.

The French never speak as openly about Algeria as they do about World War II. But while we were in France, two events brought some unpleasant memories to the surface.

The first was the 1999 trial of Maurice Papon, a former high-ranking civil servant in the Vichy government and former Budget Minister from 1978–81, who was accused of having signed the deportation orders of Jews during World War II. Papon was also head of the Paris police in October 1961 when a disputed number of Algerians were beaten and drowned in the Seine following severe rioting. The French government has always placed the official death count at six, but in his book *La Bataille de Paris: 17 Octobre 1961*, author Jean-Luc Einaudi claimed that as many as three hundred had actually died. Papon interrupted his own trial to sue Einaudi for defamation—and lost, ruining his own reputation and doing inestimable damage to the reputation of the police. (In the end, Papon was found guilty of complicity for a crime against humanity, and sentenced to ten years of jail. In September 2002, a court of appeals released him on grounds that he was too sick to stay in jail. But President Chirac—the first president to acknowledge France's responsibility in the Holocaust in 1995—asked to overturn the appeal.)

But the revelations of the Papon trial were just a footnote compared to the earthquake that shook France when the memoirs of retired general Paul Aussaresses came out in 2001. In *Special Services, Algeria 1955–57*, Aussaresses confesses that he used torture to get information and spread fear among the enemy during the war in Algeria. Although French communists had denounced the use of torture during the war, it was the first time a high-placed French military officer admitted that torture was used regularly and a lot of people knew about it. Aussaresses, who looked the part with his bony face and patched eye, even stated in an interview that he would do it all over again if he had to. The French president stripped

Aussaresses of his *légion d'honneur* medal, and the press published a flurry of articles with testimony and confessions of other military personnel during the period. Aussaresses's book was a reminder that few of those involved in this conflict came out of it with clean hands.

The story of French Algeria started in the 1830s, when France arrived in the North African country with the official pretext of cracking down on piracy in the Mediterranean. Like other countries at the time, France wanted to extend its influence and boost its prestige by acquiring foreign territory. France also wanted to get a hand on Algeria's rich agricultural shores and resume colonial expansion, which had stopped when France forfeited New France to the British in 1763.

However, France would not only settle in its new colony: it would make Algeria part of France.

By 1954, Algeria was the home of one million "Europeans"—referred to this way because half of them were of either Spanish, Italian, or Maltese origin. Writer Albert Camus, whose mother was Spanish, is the most famous of these settlers, who later came to call themselves *Pieds-Noirs* (Black Feet), a reference to workers in the coal bunkers of Mediterranean ferries. *Pieds-Noirs* were the French born in Algeria, as opposed to immigrants from France and native Muslims, and they developed a distinct identity. For one, 80 percent of Europeans in Algeria lived in cities, making them twice as urban as the rest of the French.

The main push for settlement took place between 1848 and 1890 and was carried out pretty much in the fashion of the times—basically, the same way Europeans had settled the western United States, Canada, and Australia. The French seized the best land, bulldozed the Muslims into the worst corners of the country, and installed themselves in some seven hundred towns specially created for the settlers. However, contrary to what happened elsewhere, demographics worked against North African settlers. Between 1830 and 1954, the Muslim population in Algeria tripled from three to nine million. Settlers feared being overrun.

In 1848, the French government declared Algeria part of France—the way Hawaii and Alaska are part of the United States. From then on,

Algeria would not be administered by a single colonial ministry; each French ministry would be responsible for its own affairs in Algeria. The settlers elected their own representatives to the National Assembly and the laws of the Republic were applied there. In 1870, the thirty thousand Jews living in Algeria obtained the same civil and political rights they were granted everywhere else in the Republic. And in 1889, the children of European immigrants in Algeria were granted French citizenship, as was customary in France.

However, the French status was never extended to the Muslim population, whose faith was regarded as incompatible with French customs. The *indigènes musulmans* (Muslim natives) in Algeria had no civil rights; they were mere subjects of the Republic. Over the years, only several thousand Muslims managed to acquire French citizenship. They did so by proving they lived according to French mores, or by performing "exceptional service" to the Republic, in the army or as civilians.

The French government and some high civil servants did see that disaster was looming and periodically tried to improve the lot of Muslims by giving them more political and civil rights and improving services. But the government had to contend with resistance from the European settlers, who lobbied successfully to remove the most pro-native administrators. The settlers' interest was clear: they needed impoverished Muslims to work as cheap labor in their businesses and on their farms. If the government in Paris had managed to break the settlers' resistance to reforms early enough, there might never had been a war in Algeria. But the Muslims never got anything better than the right to manage their local affairs. Muslims in Tunisia and Morocco had retained some capacity of self-government within the French protectorate system, and there had never been as many European settlers in those countries as there were in Algeria. The Muslims' situation in Algeria just kept deteriorating. By 1940, only 8 percent of native Muslims had a formal education of any sort. Settlers' land plots were on average eight times bigger than the Muslims'.

The situation proved to be fertile ground for the rising independence movement, which slowly gained momentum. Until the mid-1930s, Algerian Muslims had asked for the obvious—equal civil rights—but after decades of refusal and arrest, the native Muslim population became more stridently nationalist. Things did not improve under the control of the racist Vichy government. Before the Liberation, de Gaulle's plan was to grant Algerian Muslims citizenship and civil rights after war, but after five years of crippling war, the government in Paris was too weak to break the settlers' lobby. In 1947, when the French government finally granted equal political rights to the Muslim natives, it was too little too late.

Some date the beginning of the Algerian war to May 8, 1945, the day Germany capitulated. On that day, a crowd of ten thousand demonstrators gathered in the Algerian town of Sétif to demand the liberation of Messali Hadj, a nationalist leader who had been arrested two weeks earlier. When one of the demonstrators waved an Algerian flag, French *gendarmes* tried to pull it down and a riot broke out. Nobody knows who fired first, but dozens of Europeans and Arabs died in the massacre, and the strife spread across the rest of Algeria. Facing a rebellion, the French government sent the army and created local militia units to repress it. In the following two months, fifteen hundred Arabs were supposedly killed—although historians now agree that the figure was probably closer to eight thousand.

Nothing serious happened for the next nine years, but Algerian nationalism had reached the point of no return. In 1954, Algeria was the world's last remaining Arab colony. The most extreme faction of the nationalist movement, the Marxist FLN (*Front de Libération Nationale*) organized its own secret army, though it could only arm about eight hundred men. On October 31, 1954, the FLN launched seventy simultaneous attacks against police stations, sentry posts, and isolated farms—and this is generally recognized as the first day of the War of Algeria.

The eight-year conflict went through many phases. The FLN was most effective as a guerrilla army in the rural areas, where it got support from local populations. Algerian fighters were never a match for the French army, so they concentrated on skirmishes, guerrilla warfare, and terrorism, both in Algeria and in France. In total, 330,000 Algerian fighters were involved at one point or another, and half of them were killed. The biggest push was in the six-month battle of Algiers, in 1957, which was in fact a series of continual skirmishes and terrorist raids that the French army eventually broke. In 1958, the French built electric fences along Algeria's border with Tunisia, cutting the FLN from its main supply route.

In strictly military terms, the FLN's secret army had been defeated. It never managed to hold any ground against the French army. But politically, the FLN won, partly because of their terror campaign, but more importantly because their denunciations of France's behavior gained the sympathy of the United Nations, and the French almost found themselves in diplomatic isolation. The two superpowers of the time, Russia and the United States, both stood for an openly anti-colonialist policy.

The French army's military victories only boosted the FLN's diplomatic success. The conflict was brutal, almost of another age. The French army used all the means of repression conceivable at the time. Both sides used torture and terrorism and massacred women and children. In 1956, the French intelligence services even went as far as to highjack a Tunisian commercial flight in order to capture five FLN leaders on board. It worked, but the FLN had no trouble convincing the international community that the French were the villains.

While they fought the enemy, both sides had to deal with severe infighting in their ranks. The Marxist FLN was conducting a war against the French army, but also against the more moderate segments of the Muslim population who wanted to reach a peaceful agreement with the French and non-Marxist factions who were attempting to negotiate with the French government. At stake in Algeria was the question of who would go on to form the independent government. The FLN won, but their internal terror campaign cost at least ten thousand Muslim lives. After the war, most of the thirty thousand *harkis* (Muslim auxiliary troops in the French army) who remained in Algeria instead of taking refuge in France were hacked to death.

Infighting did not cost as many lives on the French side, but it did bring France to the brink of civil war, not once, but twice. For the most part, these divisions were the result of the French governments' ineptitude. From 1946 until 1958, France changed governments twenty times, removing any possibility of a coherent policy. Each new prime minister stressed his resolve to hang on to French Algeria, then appointed a new set of generals, diplomats, and representatives to deal with the issue. Soon enough, Parliament ousted the government over an unrelated issue, and the cycle continued.

All the while, the Europeans of Algeria became restless and increasingly defiant of the government. On one hand, settlers appreciated the fact that the French army was acting with more resolve than it had during the War of Indochina (1945–54), where they were defeated by Ho Chi Minh's Vietminh. But they could not accept the fact that while the French army was fighting, the French government was trying to negotiate a settlement. However, the majority of the French in Europe did not support the war. Some actively opposed it, especially on the Left, and most French were simply indifferent. The government's dual agenda of trying to win militarily while negotiating a settlement was understandable, but the Europeans in Algeria felt betrayed. The most enlightened among the settlers realized that much of the Muslim revolt was fueled by poor living conditions and high unemployment, but they also blamed the French government for this. The situation required a strong hand in a velvet glove, a formula France's frequently changing governments could not offer. Europeans in Algiers became more and more strident in their protests at the same time Muslim nationalists did.

The French government also lost control of the army. Many officers, who had been in Algeria for a while, began blaming the government for the situation, too. That was new. In spite of France's agitated political history over the previous two hundred years, the French military had traditionally been very deferent to the government—except in the cases of Napoleon in 1799 and de Gaulle in 1940. Many soldiers, veterans of Indochina, did not accept the fact that politicians were busy conferring with the enemy while they were losing men in battle.

In the winter of 1958, rumors of a military coup started circulating. Generals let their view be known: France needed a strong leader to get the country out of the Algerian mess. The name of de Gaulle—who had been retired for twelve years—began to circulate. In April 1958, the government changed once more. Both the French in Paris and the Europeans in

Algiers answered with barricades. A group of protesters took over the government's palace in Algiers and declared the creation of a *comité de salut public* (a committee of public salvation)—an allusion to the revolutionary government of 1792–94, which ran the New Republic and defended it against foreign invasion. The army interposed and appointed General Massu, a moderate faithful to de Gaulle, as head of the committee. Then, on May 13, the commander in chief in Algeria, General Raoul Salan, demanded the return of de Gaulle as France's president.

De Gaulle could not be ignored anymore, and he declared himself ready to assume power if Parliament was willing to give him a mandate. On June 1, Parliament voted him prime minister and granted him state-of-emergency powers for six months, as well as the mandate to draft a new constitution. On June 13, de Gaulle went to Algeria and made the famous speech where he declared: "*Je vous ai compris!*" (I have understood you!) His words calmed both the army and the European population, though he never said exactly what or who he understood. De Gaulle then proceeded to reshuffle the army's command both in Paris and in Algiers, in order to break the defiant spirit that had grown among the generals.

De Gaulle accomplished two things. First, he understood that he could not resolve the Algerian quagmire without solid political institutions at home, so he dedicated his time to changing the Constitution first and working to gain the support he needed to get the change accepted. (What he did is described in detail in the next chapter.) Then he invested several billion francs in the economic development of Algeria, in the petroleum extraction industry in particular, which created dynamism in the local economy and satisfied the local Europeans.

The honeymoon lasted a year, until de Gaulle began floating ideas that made it clear he wanted to seek a compromise with the Algerians rather than crush the rebellion. De Gaulle had always demonstrated an extraordinarily good instinct for understanding what France's best interests were. He knew that, in light of the decolonization movement going on elsewhere, the war in Algeria risked damaging France's prestige and reputation beyond repair and undermining its position as a major power. Algeria could not remain French.

By 1960 he was speaking openly about self-determination and the possibility of a referendum in which the whole French population (including native Muslims) could choose between giving Algeria independence, granting it autonomy within France, and/or keeping a French Algeria with a fully integrated Muslim majority. The French supported the referendum idea, but the *Pieds-Noirs* responded with violence, riots, and barricades. The army was having as much difficulty policing the white settlers as controlling the Algerians.

In 1961, European settlers decided that they would not trust Paris to defend their interests and created the *Organisation de l'Armée Secrète* (OAS). For the next year and a half, the OAS carried out military operations and assassinations, bombed the Algerians, and committed terrorist acts in France. The OAS killed a total of about five thousand people in Algeria and Paris.

On April 21, 1961, four retired generals who favored a French Algeria staged a coup in Algiers and attempted to seize power. Panic overtook Paris. Nobody knew who was involved in the coup and rumors circulated that paratroopers would be sent to attack Paris. The coup went nowhere, though, thanks to the personality of de Gaulle. In a TV appearance, wearing his uniform, de Gaulle appealed to soldiers in Algeria to not support the coup. He concluded in his peremptory style: "*Français, aidez-moi*" (Frenchmen, help me). Rank and file soldiers and most officers remained faithful to the general and the coup attempt failed.

Two of the rebel generals, Raoul Salan and Edmond Jouhaud, escaped, went underground, and joined the OAS, which they ran for a year until they were captured in March 1962. Meanwhile, de Gaulle's government fought to maintain control over the army and the police in Algeria and remove elements sympathetic to the OAS.

Throughout 1961, de Gaulle's government conducted secret talks with the FLN. They finally reached an accord in the spa town of Evian, and a cease-fire was called on March 19, 1962. Two weeks later, 90 percent of the French population in France voted in favor of the accord, which granted total independence to Algeria. However, among the 10 percent of the population who disagreed with granting Algeria independence, the grudges were deep, and would last many years.

Realizing that it was fighting for a lost cause, the OAS changed its strategy and decided to fight a defensive battle in Algeria to protect settlers from the threat of massacre by Muslims, which was real. But the OAS also conducted terror operations in Paris, including two assassination attempts on de Gaulle—this was the backdrop for the famous novel and film *Day of the Jackal.*

The French infighting over the question of Algeria produced deep fault lines in the society that are still visible today. Communists and socialists, with their powerful anti-colonial discourse, were vindicated. From this time on, a sizable segment of the French population became militantly and stridently anti-colonialist and denounced neo-colonialism in any form.

José Bové's antiglobalization campaign follows directly in this tradition of French left-wing politics. The McDonald's dismantling was not his first taste of organized protest. In 1989, Bové and other Larzac farmers went to the French territory of New Caledonia to show support for the independence movement there and help organize a clandestine radio. In 1994, Bové protested the creation of the World Trade Organization in Marrakech. In 1995, he went to French Polynesia to protest nuclear tests, and he managed to get onto Greenpeace's Rainbow Warrior. In the spring of 2002, Bové was in Ramallah among the last four European protesters to make it inside Yasser Arafat's compound with a truckload of food and medical supplies, before the Israeli army closed the perimeter. What his protests have in common is a deep rejection of anything resembling colonialism or neo-colonialism in any form—a direct product of the wounds of Algeria.

But the ideological impact of the events in Algeria is almost anecdotal in comparison with the population movements that ensued. In 1962, 99 percent of the one million European settlers packed their bags and took the boat back to France. The government began offering free rides in May, and by July most of the settlers were gone, leaving behind all their possessions except a few suitcases. They moved back "home," but home was not home anymore: most had no family at all, and had no one to meet them in the ports of Marseilles and Toulon. The settlers were refugees in their own country. The government paid two billion dollars to reinstall them and another twelve billion in indemnities, but some members of this group still harbor strong resentment against the French government and the "Arabs" for ruining their lives.

Meanwhile, the French government maintained its special ties with Algeria, including all cooperation programs. The hundreds of thousands of Algerian nationals who came to work in France as immigrant workers did not even need a visa. Many stayed and had to mingle with former settlers and even former Muslim auxiliaries of the French army who had also been repatriated.

The war also produced powerful resentment among those who had embraced the cause of French-Algeria, whether they were *Pieds-Noirs* or old-stock French from the mainland. The most prominent member of this latter group is Jean-Marie Le Pen, founder of France's extreme right *Front National* party. Born and brought up in Brittany, Le Pen belongs to the class of Frenchmen who seek revenge for France's humiliations. The foreign press often accuses Le Pen of being a Nazi, but nothing could be further from the truth: Le Pen's beef is Algeria and Indochina. The fact that Le Pen captured 19 percent of the vote in the second round of the 2002 presidential elections—his highest score ever—shows how resentment about Algeria is still lingering in France thirty-seven years after the end of the war. (More on Le Pen in the next chapter and chapter 21.)

Tensions between repatriated settlers and new immigrants explains some of the anti-immigration sentiment in present-day France. Yet in spite of these open wounds, tensions have never spilled over the limits of democracy. France certainly has Charles de Gaulle and his new Constitution to thank for that.

PART TWO:

structure

chapter 9

The Penchant for Absolutism

We witnessed a strange billboard campaign during our first winter in Paris. The walls of every subway station were plastered with two huge black-and-white pictures, one of an army officer in his twenties, wearing a pre–World War I uniform, the other of a boy sitting on a chair, dressed in a turn-of-the-century suit. The slogan under the photos was, *Celui qui a dit non* (The one who said no). We were in the dark for three months until the same slogan reappeared, this time with a photo of a mature General Charles de Gaulle in uniform. These photos had been taken just about the time de Gaulle had said no to France's armistice with the Germans and fled to London to lead the Free French. The photos were part of an elaborate advertising campaign for a theater production about de Gaulle's wartime experience called *Celui qui a dit non*.

Every child in France learns de Gaulle's story in elementary school, but that didn't prevent *le tout Paris* of politicians, intellectuals, stars, opinion-makers, and business leaders from filling the seats of the Paris Convention Center to hear it again. After the premiere, op-ed pieces starting flowing out with titles like, "*Nous sommes tous Gaullistes*" (We are all Gaullists), or "*Le crépuscule du Gaullisme*" (The twilight of Gaullism). It's a testimony to the man's influence that more than thirty years after his death in 1970, the French still wonder whether his spirit is alive.

Of course, to find de Gaulle's spirit, all the French have to do is look around them. No man since Napoleon has had as strong an impact on the French mentality and institutions. When foreigners hear "Gaullism" they no doubt think of foreign policy and France's tendency to posture on the international stage—both were definitely elements of de Gaulle's legacy. But to the French, de Gaulle is the man who restored their nation's grandeur after the country was humiliated and almost torn apart by civil war during and after World War II. To a large extent, de Gaulle created modern France by single-handedly imposing a reform of democratic institutions after World War II, and again during the War of Algeria.

De Gaulle's story started when Germany defeated France in the battle of France in June 1940. De Gaulle refused the armistice that a group of conservative generals was pushing the government to sign, and exiled himself to London, where he was recognized as the leader of Free France. During his four years in exile, de Gaulle had plenty of time to reflect on France's problems, and he came up with a plan to renew France's spirits, its political system, and its economy.

When de Gaulle was appointed head of France's provisional government in 1944, France was on the brink of civil war, doubly divided between the Resistance and collaborators, and between communists and conservatives. De Gaulle's cherished dream was to create a new constitution. Democratic though it was, the old constitution gave too much power to Parliament and de Gaulle saw this as the root of France's defeat in the battle of France. France's old constitution made it almost impossible for anyone to exercise power. Few parties ever enjoyed absolute majorities and most had to govern by forming coalitions. Worse, since there was no institution to arbiter disagreements between Parliament and the government, whenever Parliament voted against the government on the smallest issues, coalitions fragmented, and governments had to be recomposed.

De Gaulle's own coalition government, in which he had attempted to reconcile France's conservatives and communists, left him too weak to impose a new constitution. After politicians flatly refused his ideas in the fall of 1945, de Gaulle resigned in January 1946.

Busy with post-war reconstruction, the French seemed unconcerned with political instability—there were twenty different governments in the next twelve years. As France became divided over the decolonization wars in Indochina (1945–54) and Algeria, de Gaulle remained in the background. Then, in 1958, he got his chance to return to power.

It is ironic, of course, that the man the French revere for salvaging democracy actually came to power himself through a legal *coup d'état*. When the French military and government called for his return to power, de Gaulle let it be known that he was ready for the job. In June 1958, Parliament elected him prime minister. The next day, he was granted full powers and asked to prepare a new constitution.

The main goal of de Gaulle's new Constitution was to break the power of Parliament and make it possible for a single leader to exercise power. De Gaulle created a presidential regime where the president would have the power to dissolve Parliament, appoint the prime minister, preside over cabinet meetings, and appoint representatives in each *Département*—down to presidents of universities. Three months after he returned to power, 78 percent of the French population approved the new Constitution in a referendum.

Four days before Christmas in 1958, de Gaulle became president by a limited vote of an electoral college of eighty thousand *notables*, all elected politicians. De Gaulle knew that being elected indirectly by other politicians made the French president prisoner of the political class, so his next project was to give the president legitimacy and free himself from favors owed to the political class by making the president elected by universal suffrage. However, many of the politicians who had accepted de Gaulle's new Constitution had done so with the tacit guarantee that they would retain the privilege of electing the president. They were already uneasy with the new regime because it granted too much power to the president, and de Gaulle knew that they would refuse this change.

The 1961 military coup of Algiers provoked the political crisis de Gaulle had been waiting for, and he acted swiftly, announcing a referendum on whether the French wanted a president elected by universal suffrage. Many politicians accused de Gaulle of mounting a legal *coup d'état*, but he held the referendum anyway and the population said yes. At the next presidential election in 1965, de Gaulle won the office with 60 percent of the popular vote.

De Gaulle's new Constitution, known as the Fifth Republic, did manage to overcome the destructive tendencies that had marred French democracy since the Revolution. In a way, de Gaulle took the fundamental weakness of the French and turned it into strength. The Constitution contained France's extremist reflex while being quintessentially extreme, and therefore suitable to all. De Gaulle created an elected monarch—the president—who would serve a term limited in length, but who could, theoretically, be reelected all his life. He gave this figure a lot of power, even power over the Constitution. That made the president the supreme judge of right and wrong, of good and evil, just like France's ancient kings.

The French, it seems, can't resist making kings. Since de Gaulle, the French president has been the most powerful head of state of any democracy. In Europe, most heads of state are figureheads. The kings of Belgium, Spain, and Great Britain, and the presidents of Italy and Germany, are the symbolic incarnation of the State while the real power belongs to the prime minister or chancellor who controls the government and his own chamber. Among presidents, only the American president has real power with his ability to veto legislation passed by Congress and the Senate. Thus, he can say no to a law voted by Congress, but unlike the French president, he cannot dissolve the assembly and call a new election of congress members.

The French president effectively runs the government. By tradition, he appoints the prime minister from the ranks of the party that won the most votes in the legislative elections. But in fact, there is nothing in the law that even holds him to that. If he followed the letter of the law, he could theoretically appoint anyone as prime minister. Because the president presides over cabinet meetings, he has the last say over all matters of government—from budget to defense to immigration. The president decides whether constitutional changes will be approved through a referendum or by a joint vote of the Senate and the National Assembly. The

French president has the power to suspend the Constitution and order emergency measures (although Parliament must approve if the measures are in force more than twelve days).

Aside from the presidency, two more institutions play an important role in de Gaulle's new Constitution: Parliament and the executive. Parliament is made of two chambers, the National Assembly, which makes the law, and the Senate, which acts as its consultative body. The 577 members of the National Assembly are called *députés*, and each is elected in his or her own riding. The *députés* have the power to make and change laws, but must share a part of this power with the prime minister and his ministers, who have the power to make decrees. For constitutional changes, the *députés* can be called to vote jointly in Congress with the Senate, or the president can bypass them with a referendum.

The executive arm of the government is almost completely separate from the National Assembly. The president appoints a prime minister, who then chooses his ministers. By tradition, the prime minister and ministers come from the majority in the National Assembly, but they cannot be *députés* and must resign from the chamber upon their appointment. De Gaulle did this to break the power of the National Assembly over the government: he wanted the cabinet to be independent from the whims of the National Assembly and even gave cabinet members the power to make decrees and override the National Assembly. The executive commands the apparatus of the State, the ministries, and the civil servants. Moreover, the president also heads cabinet meetings and decides the agenda jointly with the prime minister.

Technically speaking, France's regime is semi-presidential and semi-Parliamentarian. It is true that the president's powers are great and that he grants the executive much of its powers. The president can even dissolve the National Assembly and call for a new legislative election. But the National Assembly can make constitutional changes, and the president's power to dissolve it is limited to once in a twelve month period. Furthermore, presidents traditionally appoint prime ministers from the party with the elected majority in the National Assembly. Respect for that tradition has led French presidents to appoint prime ministers of different political stripes three times: in 1986–88, 1993–95, and 1997–2002, a gesture that has considerably reduced the president's power to act.

Only three built-in checks keep the French president from being a dictator: he must follow the Constitution, he must be elected by universal suffrage, and he must obey the laws of the Republic, although a recent court decision made him unimpeachable. Only a tribunal made of chosen *députés* and senators could force him to be tried in the High Court of Justice, and the only crime they could try him for is High Treason. There are no limits on the number of terms a French president can serve and until recently, those terms were seven years long. In 2000, the French population voted to reduce the president's term to five years.

There is one thing that de Gaulle did not change: France's basic electoral rules. The French have always been strong *légitimistes* (meaning that much of their electoral system is geared toward producing clear majorities). This is a direct result of the political instability of post-revolutionary France, when the legitimacy of democratically elected politicians was constantly under attack by conservative groups like royalists, supporters of Napoleon, and Catholics. To produce strong majorities, France operates with a two-round system where electors have to vote a second time if there is no clear majority in the first vote. De Gaulle understood that the French political system needed to bolster the legitimacy of elected politicians. He modified the Constitution so that in the case of the presidential elections only the two candidates with the highest score would make it to the second round, guaranteeing the eventual winner an absolute majority.

While the French president enjoys extensive powers, he also benefits from a rare degree of legitimacy for a democratic head of state because he is directly elected by the people. American presidents are not elected by the people but by an electoral college. The American presidential election in 2000 showed how a president's legitimacy can come into question when President Bush won a majority of votes at the electoral college, but not among voters. In purely parliamentary systems like those of Canada and Great Britain, prime ministers don't even enjoy that much legitimacy since they are elected by their party or their MPs, who, in turn, were voted by their constituencies, not the people as a whole. In France, the prime minister is a mere appointee and *députés* are elected by their constituency, but the president is elected by the French people as a whole.

Other features of the Constitution were designed to enhance political legitimacy. In legislative elections, only candidates who get more than 12.5 percent *of registered electors* make it to the second round, guaranteeing that all small parties are eliminated. Electors rarely have a choice of more than three candidates on the second round.

There is a similar mechanism for creating strong majorities, even in municipal voting. When we watched the 2001 municipal elections, we were surprised to see how interested the entire political class was in city councils. The interest arises from the fact that because of the French custom of cumulating mandates, some of the candidates running for municipal office were already *députés* or even ministers. Winning or losing a local seat can have serious repercussions for politicians at the national level, to the point of shifting the country's entire political landscape and weakening coalition governments.

What truly fascinated us about the municipal elections, though, was the way votes were counted and seats awarded. In France, the first half of the places automatically goes to the majority slate, and the remaining seats are separated between all slates in proportion to the vote. The practice pumps up majorities—a 60/40 win means 80 percent of the seats goes to the winner. When we pointed out to our friends how unfair this system seemed to the defeated parties, their answer surprised us even more. Until 1981, the majority party got 100 percent of the seats at city council! In that light, the present system looked like definite progress. The real lesson, of course, is how important political legitimacy is in France.

One result of the two-round electoral system is that it allows voters to express their opinions across the whole political spectrum. Typically, voters will express their true, often wild, political feelings in the first round, but make a more reasonable or logical choice among the surviving candidates during the second round. Among the sixteen official candidates for the 2002 presidential elections, there were two extreme-right parties and three Trotskyites (extreme left). Neither of these groups of parties truly adheres to democratic values, but they are tolerated because they are certain to be eliminated in the first round.

But as the 2002 presidential elections showed, sometimes the system backfires. We were having supper with a Frenchwoman in Toronto on April 21, 2002, on the day of the first round of France's presidential elections. This day will be remembered as the first time an extreme-right candidate, Jean-Marie Le Pen, managed to arrive second in the first round and become one of the two finalists in the second round.

Our friend Isabelle blamed herself most of the evening for what she had done. A socialist, she had followed her heart and given her vote to a marginal candidate, Elizabeth Taubira, a black, Guyanese, left-wing candidate who had not a chance of winning the presidency, but who obtained 1.5 percent of the total vote nonetheless. That same day, the three Trotskyite candidates mustered 11 percent of the vote, and another million socialists simply did not bother to vote. The result was that to everyone's surprise, socialist prime minister Lionel Jospin only ended up with 15 percent of the vote. That placed him third, after extreme-right candidate Jean-Marie Le Pen, who received 16.8 percent of the vote, and Jacques Chirac, who got 19.5 percent.

All electoral systems have a weakness. In the United States, the president can be elected by the Electoral College even if he doesn't have the absolute majority of votes. In British-style parliamentary systems, the prime minister is a prisoner of the legislative majority, which he doesn't necessarily control. The prime minister in these systems can also be removed by his own party, a private organization—potentially against the will of voters. This party can then appoint a new prime minister, who was never elected. In the French system, the main danger comes from the potential for electors to express too large a variety of points of view, splintering the vote of the big parties with fringe candidates. This is exactly what produced the upset of the 2002 presidential elections. The left spread its vote across too many parties, which allowed the extreme-right candidate to push the left out of the second round. And the extreme right obtained this political victory with only two hundred thousand additional votes!

Like all European extreme-right politicians, Le Pen's platform was strongly anti-Europe, nationalist, anti-immigrant, and law and order. Naturally, all of France and the entire world decried Le Pen's first-round victory. Jacques Chirac, who had come first, called the French to rally behind him and on May 1, one million people gathered in Paris to protest the extreme right.

The aftermath was interesting. Le Pen was completely isolated and hardly made any progress. On the second round, he garnered 19 percent of the vote, which was barely the sum of the total extreme-right vote in the first round. Then, at the legislative elections a month after, Le Pen did not even win 12 percent of the vote. This score proved that most of the presidential vote he had gathered was based on his personality, not on the actual appeal of the National Front. Evidently, few people in France wanted the extreme right to be running the National Assembly. In the second round of the legislative elections, National Front candidates ran in only 31 of the 577 seats of the National Assembly and did not win a single seat. (More on Le Pen and the extreme right in chapter 21.)

It turns out de Gaulle is not the only one in France who says no.

chapter 10

The State: One for All, and All for One

Outside of North America, private American foundations that are in any way related to foreign affairs, like the one that funded us, evoke memories of post-war CIA activities. Not a week went by when we did not have to explain what the foundation was and why they had sent Jean-Benoît to France. The questions were coming mainly from friends, not French authorities, but we still felt we had to be clear to avoid raising suspicion. We told people—truthfully—that the Institute of Current World Affairs was founded a good thirty years before the CIA started the practice of using foundations to cover for their spies, and Jean's notes are public.

Oddly, the most difficult thing to explain to the French was simply what a private foundation was, since they hardly exist in France. One discussion of the issue, with the girlfriend of a friend, led us in a totally unexpected direction. This woman was sure there was a catch, and she was sure she would figure it out.

"You let private interests decide what's good for people?" she asked.
"Yes."
"And the State encourages it?"
"Yes, by allowing tax deductions for charitable donations."
"So then, why do you have a State?"

The conversation was in French, so the woman actually said, *État*, not "State." The meaning of the word *État* in France is so singular that it's better to avoid translating it. In the Anglo-American value system, the State is like a backup. It exists to guarantee individual liberties and to ensure that individuals can reach their full potential. But the French *État* does a lot more than that. It defines culture and language, runs the economy, dispenses welfare and charity, redistributes wealth, levels differences, and defines and defends the common good. It's the skeleton of French society.

The term *État* doesn't refer to a jurisdiction, like an American state does. Neither does it refer to the French government, which changes regularly. The State is a permanent active force; it runs the country. The United States has fifty-one governments and one army, whose purpose is to defend the State. France has one army, one government, and one *État* that amounts to a vast army of civilians whose sole purpose is to create France and keep it working. France is a project. The French never speak of these soldiers of the State as civil servants, but as *fonctionnaires*, people with functions, or as *agents de l'État*, agents of the State.

And the difference isn't just practical. The French State is also the core of French identity. As Adam Gopnik writes in *Paris to the Moon*, the *État* is to the French what the Constitution is to Americans: a binding principle, a totem, and a religion.

The road to democracy in France was a long one that took frequent detours through political instability, but France didn't dissolve into a banana republic or a military dictatorship. The reason? The *État* was always there: a stabilizing and unifying force that counteracted the country's divisive tendencies. This entity was present long before the French Revolution, got a jump-start after 1789, and still gives France its unity and cohesion.

It took us a while to figure out the fundamental distinguishing feature of the French State: it is not passive. The State actually created France out of an extremely divided cultural patchwork—unlike the United States or Germany, where the patches delegated some of their authority to a central government. Long ago, the French State decided that the language spoken in Paris would be the language of the territory, then it forced everyone else to speak it. The State also set standards of beauty and taste and created a French identity.

Needless to say, the French generally believe in the State. They might disagree with its actions from time to time, but they still believe the State should be strong—because it has guaranteed stability for so long. The French look to the State for answers to everything. When a company lays off employees, the workers' first reaction is to organize protest. When they want to start an association, they automatically look to the State for a subsidy. But the *État* has not always *been* good. It deliberately persecuted both Jews and Protestants at different points in its history, and it will undoubtedly commit evil acts again—like all States. But the French are willing to overlook almost anything it's done because of one splendid thing it accomplished: creating France.

It's a political reflex absolutely alien to North Americans.

We passed many schools on our regular walks through Paris, but we never quite got used to seeing the initials RF engraved above their front doors, short for *République Française*. The French prefer to use the word "Republic" rather than "State" because *l'État Français* was the official name of the Vichy regime. But *État* and *République* are really just two names for the same thing. *République* here doesn't have the same meaning as the five Republics, in plural, referring to the five constitutions France has lived under and their corresponding political regimes. (See Appendix 1 on the succession of political regimes.) *République* here carries a meaning closer to its Latin origin—*respublica* meaning the "public thing." The *République Française* refers to the territory of France, to the assets of the State, to the conduct of public affairs, to political life, to law making, and to the gigantic apparatus of six million *fonctionnaires*.

When we looked at the history they teach inside the RF schools, we had a great surprise. French children learn about the contributions many former absolutists rulers made to the State, including François I (1515–47), Henri IV (1589–1610), Louis XIV (1643–1715), and Napoleon (1799–1815)—three kings and an emperor who were not democrats by any stretch of the imagination. The four of them have retained their status among the great men of French history because each incarnates an aspect of the *République*. François I was a patron of the arts. Henri IV was a Protestant who renounced his faith to take the crown, setting the example for the assimilation of all differences into one French whole. Louis XIV was not only a protector of the arts and a builder of the State, he used the arts to impose his vision of the State. And Napoleon built the modern State.

Historians still debate exactly how the *État* came into place. The State-building process was so long and so complex that a summary would be the length of this book. Yet historians do agree on some of the main features of the process. First is the fact that over the centuries the State bulldozed every obstacle that thwarted its goal of becoming the sole source of legitimate power in the unity known as France. France looked much like the Balkans through most of its history. A thousand years ago it was a galaxy of quasi-independent fiefs organized around a weak center, Paris, without a common political, cultural, or linguistic identity. What linked it was an assortment of local chieftains—counts, dukes, marquis, and princes—all vying for power. In 987, these petty lords chose the count of Paris, Hugues Capet, to be king, mainly because he was the weakest among them. None of the lords ever acknowledged Capet's authority over their own affairs.

Meanwhile, the dukes of Normandy became so powerful that one of them, William (the Conqueror) took over England in 1066 and imposed a form of centralization that had up until then been unknown even in France. At the time, "France" merely referred to the region around Paris, the Kingdom of the Franks. The region is still called *Île-de-France*, a vestige of those times. Up until the end of the eighteenth century, half of the population of what is now France didn't speak a word of French. They were Breton, Occitan, Catalan, Basque, Alsatian, Flemish, and Provençal.

Some date the beginning of the *État* to Louis VI, *le Gros* (the Fat, 1108–37), who established his authority in the Paris region by breaking the power of all the petty lords and vassals. That still didn't make much of a kingdom. When Louis the Fat married his son Louis VII to Eleanor of Aquitaine, she brought a dowry one-third of the size of present-day France, making her fifty to one hundred times weightier than her husband. After Louis VII divorced her, she married a Norman duke, Henri Plantagenêt, who became king of England a couple of weeks later. Then most of "France" went back to England—it reverted to France over the next century.

Jean-Benoît's family name, Nadeau, is a vestige of this state-building process at the beginning of the second millennium. A few weeks after he had joined his hiking club, he had a talk with his friend Gustave, who originates from the southwest of France and is familiar with a few of the southern dialects. When Gustave heard the name Nadeau, he told Jean-Benoît it meant "Christmas" in Occitan. This language, also known as the *langue d'oc* (the tongue of oc), was so named because people living south of the Loire used to say *oc* for yes, while in the north, they said *oïl*. Occitan was the language of a brilliant civilization that produced the troubadours, whose vast body of poetry about courtly love was a central influence in Western literature. Eleanor of Aquitaine, whose real name was Aliénor, was well versed in Occitan. Jean-Benoît's ancestor, born in the obscure village of Genouillac, near Limoges, probably spoke Occitan when he migrated to Canada in 1667.

When we were in Larzac, we used this bit of trivia about Jean-Benoît's name as a conversation starter. The area had once been part of Occitan, and many people still understood the language, including two of José Bové's companions. One of them, Jean-Pierre Soulié, even told us about a Toulouse folk band of Jean-Benoît's namesake, spelled "Nadau."

Few reporters in Paris, or from abroad, noted that the slogan the French farmers painted on the McDonald's they destroyed said: *"McDo Defora, Gardarem Roquefort!"* (Out with McDonald's, Save Roquefort!). The peasants may have been protesting against the homogenization of world cultures, but the language of their slogan, Occitan, was chosen to send a message to Paris, which had been homogenizing France's different cultures for nearly one thousand years.

The French have spent most of their history trying to acquire territory and insert a French identity into it, and it has not been an easy task. The reign of the Capetians (the descendants of Hugues Capet) lasted fourteen generations without interruption, allowing them to gradually gain influence through alliances, marriages, and war. Early in the thirteenth century, King Philippe II Auguste (1180–1223) launched what was perhaps the first radical attempt to centralize France. Then there was a first stab at assimilation via religious persecution. In 1216, the pope preached a crusade against the Cathars, a sect of proto-Protestants—three hundred years before Luther—who lived in southern France. A horrible massacre of Cathars ensued. It was a grab for territory disguised as a crusade.

It was not until the end of the Hundred Years' War (1337–1453) that the French began to develop a national sentiment. And by the end of the seventeenth century, the boundaries of France were pretty much what they are today.

During that period, the *État* remained an informal affair. For a long time, the kingdom had been the private domain of the king. Kings had networks of spies, but very little means of collecting taxes or administering justice in their name. They led an essentially nomadic life, wandering from castle to castle with their court of three hundred or four hundred knights, courtiers, and servants. During this period, the State started to be considered a thing separate from the king. By 1662, the king had between four thousand and six thousand civilians on his payroll, not counting the couple thousand functions *owned* by semi-noble or noble families. By today's standards, that wasn't much for a country of twenty to twenty-five million people, but at the time it was regarded as massive. These civil servants worked mostly to increase the king's power and reduce the power held by the aristocrats.

Until the French Revolution in 1789, the king still shared his authority with local parliaments in eleven of the thirty-six divisions of the territory, which included the *pays* of Brittany, Burgundy, Languedoc, and the Navarre. The French *État* was not a pure creation of the Revolution. The State was functioning long before that. However, the Revolution did leave a power vacuum that the State filled. The names of two influential groups of revolutionaries would become almost synonymous with two fundamental features of the French State: the *Républicains* and the *Jacobins*.

The *Républicains* wanted democracy and the end of all monarchs. They were inspired by the philosophers of the Enlightenment, who believed in the perfectibility of mankind. In practical terms, they thought that men were not born citizens, but became them; men needed to be molded to get that way. Their thinking called for a strong State that would create citizens.

The *Jacobins* were an extremist faction of the *Républicains*. Officially, they were the Society of the Friends of the Constitution, and they met in a hospice near the Saint-Jacques Gate in Paris—hence the term *Jacobin*. The *Jacobins* wanted a very powerful central government. *Républicanisme* and *Jacobinisme* profoundly influenced how the French would come to think of their State and its actions. The French still refer to extreme centralizers, or opponents of decentralization, as *Jacobins*.

We always kept an eye on newsstands in France, and early in our stay noticed a type of publication we'd never seen before: books and magazines specifically about careers in the French administration. These publications included information like how many government jobs were available that year, the kind of examinations candidates were required to take for each position, and the wages they could expect. Many of our friends, we found out, consulted these publications hoping to either get jobs in the public service, or get promotions. These fascinating publications spoke volumes about the spirit of the French civil service and its status in French society.

Six million civil servants work in the French administration. That's one French citizen in ten, or a quarter of the entire work force. The biggest Ministry is Education, with one million employees—more than twice the size of the French military. France has the highest ratio of civil servants of all countries in the Organization for Economic Cooperation and Development (OECD), and not because it's the most "socialist" among them (Sweden and Norway are much more socialist than France and have half as many civil servants in proportion).

In the political instability of the 170 years following the Revolution, the French State became more important and more centralized. One of the greatest achievements of Napoleon Bonaparte (1799–1815) was to put order into the burgeoning army of civil servants (in fact, he organized two armies at once). Napoleon was a general. Generals are supposed to win wars, but their chief quality is often forgotten: they are usually talented administrators of vast bureaucracies. Armies are huge bureaucracies, after all. Napoleon won two prizes in a single battle. While he created a mass army to wage wars, he also created an army of civil servants with ranks and uniform rules for pay, promotion, and evaluation. The goal of the second army was, and remains, the creation of France itself.

Although "army" is not too strong a term for France's civil service, "machine" would also be accurate. France's six million civil servants are divided into about eighteen hundred *corps*, according to their qualifications. Like an army, they are remunerated according to their rank and are subject to uniform rules for salaries, benefits, and promotion. The 1999 edition of the *Guide des Concours de la Fonction Publique* lists one hundred people in the *corps* of architects, sixty-seven in the *corps* of second-class research directors, 28,799 in that of tax collectors, 94,043 in the *corps* of police constables, and so on.

Civil servants belong to three categories: A, B, and C. The Cs are the rank-and-file. Like their army equivalents, they rarely have university degrees, and they work jobs like civilian aid to the army's health service, embassy clerk, or school lab assistant. The Bs are technicians, the equivalent of *sous-officiers* (non-commissioned officers). They are tax controllers, social workers, teachers, or civil aviation technician-controllers. The Bs, who may have a university diploma, apply the regulations made by the As. And the As are the officers. Most have post-graduate degrees. They are engineers, professors, inspectors, architects, or city planners. They think up regulations and tell others how to enforce them. Then there is the A+, the top-ranking civil servants, the equivalent of staff officers or executives.

In March 2002, we had supper with a couple of friends, Luc and Armel Dario, at one of their favorite restaurants, Bofinger, specializing in the southwest cooking of Luc's *pays* of origin. Julie had met Luc in Tunisia during a language course in Arabic. He was an engineer, a captain in the French air force in charge of maintenance, but he had not been doing much repair over the last two years because the army paid him full leave to study Arabic civilization.

Luc was not yet cramming for exams that night, but his wife Armel was pale from her own intense studying. Armel was a contract worker for the

Hôpitaux de Paris (Paris Hospitals), and she was trying to get full civil-servant status. To do so, she had to take a series of exams along with 2,200 other people who were competing for 140 positions. The top two hundred from that batch then went on to take an oral exam. Armel was not too pleased about her oral, because she had been asked a trick question, but she did make the cut, we later learned.

Our conversation with the Darios confirmed the two things we had learned from reading the civil-service magazines: the selection process for France's civil servants is severe, and they still have to meet high levels of training after they are hired. Any person who wants to be a civil servant for any job must go through a *concours* (a competitive examination) that can require up to two years of studying and preparation. In order to become an advisor for probation for criminals at the justice department (a B+ job), candidates are screened through a four-hour written test of their general culture. (A question might be, "Media and democracy: discuss.") If they make it through the screening, they have to do a two-hour test that requires them to produce a memorandum. (A question might be, "Outline the reasons for the law of February 6, 1992.") If candidates pass that, they go on to the oral exam, where they are tested on their general culture and their aptitude for the position.

Armel, for instance, had to study the basics of *le droit hospitalier* (a body of French law that applies to the running of hospitals). All her professional life, every time she goes through another examination to get a promotion, she will have to study *le droit hospitalier* again.

Success rates for civil service exams are low. Of the 3,566 candidates for the position of probation advisor in 1999, 160, or 4 percent, got the job. That's the rule, not the exception. Success rates for all jobs vary from 1 to 12 percent. In four cases out of five, people who make the cut then have to go through training in a special school that can last up to two years—even if they already have a related diploma.

In his hiking club, Jean-Benoît also befriended Isabelle, a forty-year-old single mother—a nurse who had raised her seventeen-year-old daughter alone. Jean-Benoît was very much interested in finding out how

Isabelle had managed this, given that salaries in France are not remarkably high. When they were better acquainted, she told him that she had had a lot of help from the hospital that hired her. The hospital had actually housed her and her daughter for free for ten years before she could afford to move to her own place. This sounded quite extraordinary to Jean-Benoît, but he learned from speaking to other people that this was a fairly common perk in France.

For those who make it into the civil service, the perks can be impressive, starting with job security for life. Many employees are lodged at the State's expense, especially police and teachers who have to work in remote corners of the French territory. Those housing perks compensate the low wages—junior nurses earn one thousand dollars per month. But as we found, those salaries are generally for single people without children. Salaries are often modified depending on an employee's family situation—or whether they benefit from free housing.

Because French civil servants have job security for life, one might expect them to sit on their laurels after going through the difficult screening process to get hired. But again, like an army, the French civil service has a built-in incentive to force people to strive: the grading system.

We learned about the grading system from a friend who works as a professor of English at a junior college. She wanted to move out of Paris, so she had to get a new teaching assignment. It seemed like an amazingly complicated process, but the thing that really preoccupied her was her grade, a mark out of twenty that her superiors gave her for her assiduity, competence, and ability to relate to others—highly subjective matters. Like in the army, bad marks won't prevent a *fonctionnaire* from rising in pay and grade, but bad marks will make this promotion slower. Civil servants who are *bien noté* (well marked) get better bonuses and more exciting assignments. They move through the ranks faster and are often encouraged to apply for senior positions that are only accessible by *concours*. So Cs can become Bs or As by going through the same competitive exam process they went through to get into the civil service in the first place. But to do that they have to be *bien noté*.

When we returned to North America in May 2001, one of the first headlines that caught our attention was of the controversy in a suburb north of Toronto over a school-board administrator who had spent $698 on food during a ten-day business trip. This amounted to a bit more than $20 per meal on average, and did not sound like much to us. But of course, we had been in France for two and a half years. We had forgotten that North Americans were so preoccupied with how much civil servants cost. The French hardly ever talk about how taxpayers' money is spent.

The French expect a high level of training and competence from their civil servants, and they do complain about the overall cost of the State. But as we read and compared the Anglo-American and French press, we noticed one big difference: French politicians don't try to get elected with huge promises to cut taxes. The French accept that the State costs money. Actually, when the French are dissatisfied with service, they don't demand their money back. They demand that the State do *more*.

That reaction is all the more surprising given how much they already pay in taxes. According to the 1997 figures from the Organization for Economic Cooperation and Development (OECD), taxes account for 45 percent of France's Gross Interior Product, compared to 29 percent in the U.S., and 37 percent in Germany. Even rent is taxed in France (at around 5 percent). On the other hand, the differences aren't as great as they seem, partly because the French get a lot for their money. If you take what Americans pay in taxes and add the costs of private pension funds and charitable donations, it rounds out to about what the French pay in taxes (on a per-capita basis). Overall prosperity, life expectancy, and standard of living in the two countries are similar. The main difference is that the United States leaves it up to individuals to take care of themselves, while the French State has an absolute monopoly on everything that falls under the heading of "the common good."

It took us a while to grasp the depth of that monopoly. For instance, the French give little to charity. The typical Anglo-American commentator will say the French are greedy, or, more generously, just have no money left over to give to charity because they pay so much in taxes. They are missing the point. Tax money in France does the work that private charities and foundations do in Anglo-American societies. The French wouldn't have it any other way. The idea of leaving the work of caretaking to private interests is completely foreign to them, not to mention suspicious.

During our stay in France, we were lucky to return to North America once in June 2000, for the seventy-fifth anniversary of the Institute of Current World Affairs (the foundation that was funding us). After spending a year and a half trying to understand how the French think, we were amazed at the contrasts we now saw. For one, our American and Canadian friends suddenly sounded awfully dismissive about their respective states. The words "State," "civil servant," or "government" were usually coupled with adjectives like "incompetent," "useless," or "costly." After living in France for a year, we wondered whether that attitude wasn't a self-fulfilling prophecy—maybe the fact that Americans constantly denigrated their governments explained the low quality of service they ended up getting.

Of course, before we returned to France we understood the glitch in our thinking. It's normal for Americans and Canadians to dismiss their governments. Their political systems rely on community life and initiative. Federal governments are only supposed to do what the states or provinces, cities or towns, communities or neighborhoods or school boards can't, at least in principle, whereas the French see the State as responsible for the population's well being. If the State doesn't perform, nothing works. Given this fact, it's not hard to imagine why the French pour so much energy into making their system work and keeping it centralized.

The high expectations from the State are certainly one reason the quality of public service in France is so great. On the whole, the French get what they pay for. While we were in France, a U.N. study ranked their health system first in the world. The U.S. system ranked thirty-seventh, even though the United States spends 50 percent more on health care than France in proportion to their GDP. But this doesn't mean that France's public service is not costly, oversized, or bureaucratic. (There is more on public service in chapter 19.)

One big difference is the sense of purpose. The French State was created to "make France"—to build it and to hold it together. In practice, this means ensuring prosperity and social cohesion by applying the law. Control is a very big part of what the French administration does. A friend of ours, a French doctor now living in Montreal, Quebec, is surprised by the absence of controls in the Quebec health system. One of the main jobs of civil servants in France is to make sure other civil servants are meeting standards. Typically, the government sets very high standards in health and in the workplace, and hires lots of people to make sure they are met.

The French also tend to look at civil servants as people who have a duty to the State. Even though civil servants enjoy benefits that set them apart from the rest of the population, there is a lot of public sympathy for them. That doesn't translate into an unequivocal respect for authority, but civil servants who act in the interests of the State are generally well considered. This value occasionally shows up in the vocabulary the French choose to describe the work of civil servants. When a policeman beats, injures, or kills a demonstrator, convicted criminal, or passerby, he's pejoratively referred to as a *flic* (cop). But when policeman are killed in action, they are called *fonctionnaires de police* (civil servants in the police department) to stress the fact that they were doing their duty on behalf of the State. One of the publications we bought, titled *Profession: Fonctionnaire*, stressed the fact that being a *fonctionnaire* was a "calling."

That of course doesn't mean that all French civil servants are competent and that all French people love them. When a squadron of anti-riot *fonctionnaires de police* charges a mass of protesting hospital employees, neither have nice things to say about each other. When a tax inspector orders a teacher to refund the single-parent family allowance he collected illegally, the teacher will certainly not speak respectfully about the French Treasury. But complain as they may, no one in France has that reflex of always thinking the private sector would do a better job. The French will complain about how oppressive the State is, but very few question the role of the State as a whole.

The whole system works because of centralization. All roads in France lead to Paris, literally and figuratively. Decision-making in France takes the same route: everything goes through Paris. All important decisions are made there, and those that can't are made in Paris's name, because that's where the government is.

Most French cannot imagine life any other way. In 1999, when Kansas decided that schools would teach both creationism and Darwinism, our French friends thought Americans had gone crazy. They didn't understand that what happens in Kansas doesn't necessarily happen everywhere else in the United States, because education in the United States is a state responsibility, not a federal one. "You mean that each state does what it wants?" our friends asked incredulously. When we told them that a resident of Massachusetts moving to Louisiana, or any state, had to change tax systems, education systems, health systems, and even legal systems, they were skeptical. The Americans are modern people, they reasoned. How could they live in such a medieval country?

The reason everything in France is centralized is pretty simple: the French State is one and indivisible. There is simply no such thing as competing jurisdictions in France. That doesn't mean there are no rivalries between regions. But the country remains one big machine managed from the center. In order to make the State work, French leaders created institutions that bear absolutely no resemblance to what we're familiar with in North America—institutions to manage education, language, the economy, law, and even organized protest. (See chapters 12 to 19.) What they have in common is uniformity across the French territory. The State sees to this.

Centralization works because the French embrace three principles: assimilation, the general interest, and equality.

In March 1999, we had lived in our new apartment for a mere two weeks when a woman knocked at our door. It was the national census, which takes place in France every ten years. We told her not to bother with us, since we were mere visitors, but she told us that as residents of France, even temporary ones, we were required to fill it out.

Censuses reveal a lot of things about what matters to a society. France's national census asked us questions about our revenue and occupation. Other questions were actually comical, like whether we had hot or cold water, if we had our own toilet, whether it was in the stairway or inside the

apartment, and if we had a bath or a shower. These questions were a vestige from life in France sixty years ago, when basic sanitation was still a
problem.

The census also omitted a few questions we thought were vital. It
asked us to indicate our nationality, but there were no questions about our
religious affiliation, ethnic origin, or what language we spoke at home.
France's anti-Semitic policies during World War II put an end to that type
of questioning. But the logic of assimilation has the same effect. Once
you're French, you're nothing else. This attitude means the State doesn't
give—or really permit—anyone to have any other identity. Of course, that
means that there is no such thing as affirmative action in France. France
refuses to identify its minorities. It didn't officially start recognizing the
existence of other cultures living inside its borders until the mid-1970s.
But there's an advantage to that. The policy of assimilation virtually elim-
inates the chances of any kind of official segregation. (Immigration issues
are discussed in chapter 21.)

Assimilation is a very positive concept in France. Assimilation means
being integrated into the whole politically, culturally, socially, linguisti-
cally, and economically. No one in France really associates it with a loss of
cultural heritage, ethnic identity, or mother tongue. The policy was
adopted as a complement to centralization and citizenship. Right after the
Revolution of 1789, the French granted citizenship to Protestants and Jews
on the basis that these groups had assimilated French culture and mores.
When France refused to grant citizenship to Muslims in Algeria, it was
because they did not regard them as assimilable.

Assimilation played a fundamental role in France's state-building
process. At first it was a method of breaking ties to local cultures. Its objective now is to break immigrants' ties to foreign cultures. After conducting
a policy for four or five centuries that stripped local cultures of all their distinctive attributes like language, strong community life, and political
autonomy, the French State has pretty much succeeded in convincing the
French that communities with self-rule of any kind will lead to anarchy. In
strictly *Républicain* circles, this stance translates into virulent hostility to
local languages, sects of all sorts, and even private charitable organizations.

The catchy phrase they use for getting rid of these things is *éradication des particularismes* (the eradication of local differences).

The French administration is also overtly anti-sectarian. The French are not opposed to the existence of religious sects, per se. But they do regard any attempt to build a community life around religion with suspicion, as those ties may rival ties to the French State. Foreigners often mistake this as rabid intolerance, but they are overlooking the national obsession the French have with assimilation. The Chinese are, of course, having exactly the same problem with the Falun Gong faith. There's a considerable dose of intolerance in the Chinese attitude, but the root of the issue is also centralization. They don't want potential threats to the authority of the State. It's a story the French know very well, judging by their record of persecuting Protestants three centuries ago. (But French sectarians, being no less *jusqu'au-boutistes* than the others, could not help trying to debase what little State there was back then.) Now that France is a democracy, attacks on sects are subtler, or at least follow the rule of the law.

In the summer of 2001, the French Parliament passed a law that allowed the government to attack religious leaders who were alleged to have committed abuses against their followers. The abuses could include extortion or violence, both physical and moral. Whether this power will be used in a good or a bad way remains to be seen, but its ultimate justification comes from the belief that it is the State's duty to protect individuals against abuse, even if people consent to it.

After the doctrine of assimilation, the second principle that oils the machine of centralization is the concept of *intérêt général* (common good), an idea borrowed from philosopher Jean-Jacques Rousseau (1712–78). The French may argue as to what the *intérêt général* actually is in particular situations, but they don't debate the principle. To understand this intangible concept, we imagined it at one end of a scale with *les intérêts particuliers* (private, special, or local interests) at the other. Private interests are legitimate when they don't contradict the common good, but if they do, the common good wins. In day-to-day life, it is the government and the *fonctionnaires* that decide what the common good is and make sure it prevails over private interests. *"Je suis le gardien de l'intérêt général"* (I'm the guardian of the general interest), said our friend Gustave, when he tried to summarize his career since graduating from *ÉNA*.

The concept of the common good exists because the French value the good of all above the individual good. Naturally, it can be used to justify abuses of all sorts. The *intérêt général* can cancel out civil liberties, so it can lead to the best or the worst. Indeed, it has created a strong ethic of public service, as expressed by our friend Gustave, but it also was used to justify the systematic persecution of Jews during World War II.

During our stay, there was a mini-controversy over whether Parliament should revoke a law that forbade women to work night shifts in industry. We were astonished that such a law still existed. The thinking behind it was obvious: women generally take care of the children in the day so they shouldn't have to work at night. The *intérêt général* was evidently held to be more important than women's individual liberty to decide for themselves. Social programs in France proceed from the same logic: they are generous in spirit and carefully designed, but have a one-size-fits-all philosophy that can make them strangely oppressive. A friend of ours, who was pregnant, was required by the State to attend fifteen mandatory visits to her gynecologist. If she didn't, she would be cut from the family allowance program.

Along with assimilation and *l'intérêt général,* equality is the third pillar of the Republic. Equality has two meanings in France. The first is a belief in equal opportunity, like one finds in any democracy. The French agree that citizens must have equality of opportunity and be equal in law. But there's a twist. The French also believe the law must also be equal to all, meaning identical. The idea that the law could vary, say, from one *Département* to another horrifies them. Since there is one Republic, there can only be one law, and it can only be applied in one way.

Therein lies the wisdom of the French people and their State. The French State built France out of very distinctive parts—sometimes in a brutal manner. But it has perfectly assumed its own logic. In the eyes of the State, the French have only one identity. Citizens may be born Occitan or Breton, Corsican or Tunisian, but when they *become* French, they are

French only. They will get equal treatment wherever they go, and the State sees to that—in the name of the *intérêt général*.

Like the Musketeers said, it's all for one and one for all.

chapter 11

Dogs, Towns, and Local Government

Anyone who has strolled through the streets of Paris knows about the countless souvenirs dogs deposit on the sidewalks there. In all, two hundred thousand Parisian canines leave ten tons of excrement behind them every day. In an average year, six hundred people break a limb slipping on dog droppings or trying to remove the mess from the soles of their shoes. The city of Paris does what it can to avoid these accidents. It spends seventy million francs (nine million dollars) per year on a brigade of sixty green *motocrottes* (motorcycles that streak through the streets sucking up dog droppings with vacuum cleaners). But the effort to rid the streets of dog excrement is futile, thanks to Parisian dog owners' enduring lack of civility.

French authorities have been trying to get dog owners to change their behavior for years. They tried a three-thousand-franc fine for leaving dog dirt behind, to no avail. Jean-Benoît met Patrick Trémège, the then-deputy mayor in charge of environment who was working on adding an incentive to the program in the form of free portable bins.

"Do you know how many fines the police handed out last year?" Trémège asked.

Jean-Benoît speculated, "Five hundred, maybe?"

"Four."

One reason for the general *laissez-faire* over dog dirt, Trémège explained, is that the city of Paris doesn't have its own police force to enforce the dog-dirt policy. The only police in Paris are *Police Nationale*, or the equivalent of the FBI in uniform. These officers obviously don't consider it a priority to hand out fines to undisciplined dog owners. They actually consider it somewhat beneath their dignity.

Trémège was looking for a way around this problem. He said he was trying to beef up the numbers and powers of Paris security guards who patrol markets and parks and who are allowed to fine dog owners. The problem, he said, is that their power is limited. "They aren't police. They don't even have the right to ask for ID. Only the police can do that."

So Jean-Benoît asked the obvious question, "Why doesn't Paris just create its own city police force?"

The answer really got to the heart of the matter: "The government won't allow it. The *Police Nationale* is the police in Paris. The city of Paris can't even make its own bylaws for security, traffic, or sanitation."

The modern French State has always crushed local power, but it seemed odd that this reasoning should even extend to Paris, France's center of power. It turns out that the State is more interested in keeping tabs on Paris than any other city in the country. Authorities are extra-defensive because so many State powers and ministries are concentrated in Paris. They are terrified by the idea that protesters of any kind might get their hands on power and strike at the nerve center of the State. The best way to avoid this kind of situation is to keep a monopoly on police forces. So the French State makes it almost impossible for mayors to control their own paramilitary force—the police.

At least three times a week, we walked south from our apartment to the Champs Elysées all the way to the Seine river. Our habitual route took us through the courts of the Louvre Palace. Now a museum, it was originally built as a castle before becoming the center of government in France. Our favorite feature at the Louvre was not the *Mona Lisa*, nor the innumerable sculptures displayed in its innumerable rooms, but the enormous moat on the east side. The moat was a key feature of the Louvre's old defense system, but against what enemy? Not the English, but Parisian mobs. For that matter, the former castle of the Bastille, three kilometers east, was built so police could hit the mob from behind before it attacked the Louvre.

Distrust of local power is not a recent trend in France. Paris mobs have been a force to reckon with throughout most of France's history. Among the most famous Paris riots was the tax revolt of 1358, when the chief magistrate of the city, Étienne Marcel, led an attack on the Louvre (then the royal palace) and killed a couple of royal councilors right in front of the king. Two centuries later, during the wars of religion, the Catholic League of Paris started a riot in order to bully Henri III out of Paris because of concessions he had made to Protestants. In 1648, a new tax sparked an aristocratic revolt and young Louis XIV, then five, barely escaped the riots. Twenty years later, Louis moved his court to Versailles, twenty kilometers from Paris, to avoid having to confront Paris mobs. In 1789, his great-great-great-grandson, Louis XVI, learned the hard way that even Versailles was not far enough to escape angry mobs of Parisians; the mobs captured him and reinstalled him at the Louvre. Three years later they were fed up with royalty altogether and sent Louis to the guillotine. But that didn't end the riots. In 1871, after the disastrous Franco-Prussian war, Parisians challenged the government of Versailles in another bloody uprising and created their own autonomous government. Following in the steps of the other post-revolutionary regimes, the Third Republic allowed Paris no independent political powers. Instead, a *préfet* was appointed to administer the city.

In future decades, President Jacques Chirac will likely be remembered as the first mayor of Paris, from 1977–95. Although Paris is France's biggest city, the mayor of Paris is, by many standards, the weakest in France. Although the city administration has forty thousand people on its payroll and a six-billion-dollar budget, the mayor has no power over police or transport. Over the last decades, the central government has made small concessions in these departments, like giving the city authority over street cleaning in 1986. But otherwise, France pretty much strangles Paris. The city doesn't even control its own public transportation. In a country where all roads lead to the capital, this is more than a symbolic issue. It's a headlock.

Liberty should probably not be the first word in France's famous motto, *Liberté Égalité Fraternité*. Since local powers are seen as a threat to France's unity, the French government systematically strips local communities of their political liberties. Cities are not even allowed to have their own bank accounts. Until 1982, they didn't even have input into city planing, let alone control over it. At the moment, only towns with less than ten thousand inhabitants are entitled to have their own police, because they are considered less of a threat.

During our stay in France, we met at least half a dozen mayors who explained the various aspects of local administration to us. The most generous was our friend Jean-Marie Marsault, the former sergeant of the First Armored Marine Division, who fought in Algeria. Before retiring, Jean-Marie worked as an insurance salesman. He had had a busy life raising a family of four and acting as mayor of his town, Fresnes (population eight hundred), in the Loire Valley from 1977–89. His biggest accomplishment, by far, was the transformation of a swamp near the village center that used to belong to the local *châtelaine* (castle owner) into a park with a pond.

Jean-Marie spent several hours explaining the ins and outs of local administration to us, showing us papers and copies of budgets. But it was only after reading our notes that we realized one of the most telling aspects of local political life was the language he used, in particular the way he designated his citizens. When French mayors talk about their constituency, they never use the word "citizens." No one talks about "the citizens of Lyon" or "the citizens of Toulouse." Mayors speak of their *administrés* (literally, their "administereds"). The French can only be citizens of one thing: the one and indivisible Republic, and that entity "administers" them at the local level through mayors.

At the time of the Revolution, the doctrine of the *République* was that "nothing should come between the citizen and the State." As we have explained in previous chapters, the French State actually created France by assimilating very diverse populations and giving them a single nationality. To do that, the State eradicated local power, eliminated local languages, and deprived local populations of any sense of community. During the nineteenth century, strict laws prevented local communities from creating associations or even charities. And until about 1885, the job of mayor was almost honorary. The function gradually became more and more important throughout the twentieth century, but local power is still extremely limited in France, and so is the possibility of developing a local identity.

Such a conception of government flies in the face of the political reflexes of North Americans, or anyone who lives in a federation. Whenever a federal system is at work, each Canadian province, American state, German land, or Belgian community is sovereign, making its own laws and managing its own affairs without answering to anyone but its constituents. If New France had remained a part of France, it would have had no power whatsoever to make laws. There would never have been a Parliament in Quebec. Paris would wire decrees and send a representative, called a *préfet*, to enforce them. It sounds colonial, and it is. In a way, all of France is a colony of Paris—even Paris.

Local administration is organized in three levels: the *commune*, the *Département*, and the *Région*. Through our conversations with Jean-Marie, other mayors, and some friends in the administration, we managed to get a clear idea of what each of these levels did.

The *commune* refers to any municipality: a village, town, or city. Paris is a commune, and so is Fresnes. Many *communes* are ancient parishes. They became *communes* during the French Revolution to break the influence of the clergy. One of the most striking features of France's political landscape is the high number of *communes*: 36,851, with an average of 1,650 inhabitants each. France has more *communes* than Spain, Germany, the United Kingdom, and Italy *combined*. The biggest is Paris, with two million inhabitants, followed by Lyon and Marseilles, with about a million each. Toulouse, Dijon, Bordeaux, and Strasbourg make up the third tier, with between one-quarter and half a million inhabitants. Only fifty-two French *communes* have more than one hundred thousand inhabitants. So France is basically a country of small towns.

All these *communes* belong to one of the 99 *Départements*, the basic unit in the French administration. *Départements* were created in the wake of the French Revolution: the remotest corner of each *Département* could be no less than two days by horse from the *chef-lieu* (*Département* capital). The idea was to draw artificial boundaries that would break down and get rid of the local identities that were already there. (Europeans used the same strategy when they were colonizing Africa, except that the French also did it to themselves first.) All ancient duchies, principalities, and *pays* like Aquitaine, Provence, Normandy, and Périgord were cut up or merged into new units with deliberately meaningless names. Brittany was divided up into Finistère, Côte d'Armor, Ile-et-Vilaine, and Morbihan—the region of Brittany only came back to official existence in 1982. In order to mix the cards even more, Brittany's main city, Nantes, was removed from the *Départements* of former Brittany and placed in another *Département*: Loire Atlantique. Half of the *Départements* were given names of mountain ranges or rivers, and all historical reference were erased in most of them. *Préfets* were appointed to run the *Départements*, and their basic mandate was to make everyone respect the letter and spirit of the law of the *République*.

In 1982, the French government realized it had gone too far in break-ing up the natural cultural divisions in France, so it grouped the *Départements* into twenty-six *Régions*. The *Régions* are under the tutelage of a regional prefect who oversees the decisions of the regional council and its president. All of these officials—the mayor, the departmental and regional presidents, and their councils—still answer to the *préfet*, who is in charge of all the administration in the *Département*. (More on this in chapter 22.)

Even though the *Département* is the basic administrative unit of the French Republic, it's no accident that France has held onto so many small *communes*. *Communes* are a very cheap way of running the territory. The position of mayor remained mostly honorific until the end of the nine-teenth century, and the mayor is still practically a volunteer. Most com-munes are tiny and have very small tax bases, so the mayor is often paid only a symbolic amount, which, of course, is one of the reasons mayors tend to join the tradition of the *cumul des mandats*, and stock up on several elected offices at once.

Mayors are basically elected civil servants who do local chores for the government for free. They execute the decisions of the council and per-form mandatory administrative tasks for the government. They organize elections and transmit election results to the government, manage the *état civil* (birth, marriage, and death registries), distribute social programs, organize day care, run school buildings, and even maintain a city plot for *les manouches* (gypsies). Mayors are also in charge of public safety. During the 1999 solar eclipse, they had to distribute protective glasses. They manage the list of men of conscription age in times of war and peace.

Yet wide as the *communes'* responsibilities are, their power is limited. The *commune* builds and maintains elementary school buildings and houses teachers, but the teacher is on the payroll of the State, and the curriculum comes from the Ministry of Education. It's roughly the same division of labor for churches: the *commune* takes care of the building, the Ministry of Culture is responsible for what's inside—stained glass, sculptures, and other artifacts—and the parish buys furniture and provides community services. *Communes* build and repair municipal roads, but don't have any say in national transport policy.

All *communes* are equal, except when it comes to the police. Only towns of less than ten thousand inhabitants can have their own police. The reason is simple. Small towns can't afford very serious police forces. As Jean-Marie Marsault puts it, a *commune* with eight hundred inhabitants (which ranks in the first tier of France's 36,851 *communes*) can barely afford to have a *garde champêtre* (rural warden) on the payroll. And sure enough, this special privilege of small-town mayors has never amounted to much. Together the *Police Nationale* and the *gendarmerie* make up a police force of 250,000, or twenty times more than the twelve thousand municipal police in France. Only one-third of the municipal police have guns.

During a round-table discussion on decentralization organized by the Canadian embassy in Paris, we met Jean-François Copé, thirty-six, the young mayor of Meaux, a town of forty-nine thousand, thirty miles east of Paris. Meaux is one of Paris's infamous troubled *banlieues* (suburbs). Almost half of the population lives in low-income housing projects known as *les cités*, which were built in the 1960s and '70s, but have now turned into decrepit immigrant ghettos. The laws of the *République* are held in high contempt in the *cités*, where riots and car bombings are common. Copé wanted to do something about violence in his city. He could see the short-comings of the *Police Nationale* in this matter; they typically intervene after a crime happens, send in the riot squads, make a few arrests, patrol for a while, and then move on. What Copé wanted to do was create a more visible, permanent police force that would intervene in the shady zone of petty crime, juvenile delinquency, disturbing the peace, fighting, and bad behavior, because he knew that the violence in the *cités* started with small crime.

Copé had a great idea but faced a formidable obstacle: the rule outlawing municipal police forces for *communes* of more than ten thousand inhabitants. Copé appealed directly to the *préfet* and used his many connections to convince him to allow a municipal police force in Meaux. And he won. For less money than Paris spends on its brigade of *motocrottes* (the street-cleaning motorcycles of Paris), Copé hired a police director, built a force of eighty-eight officers, and housed them in four police stations. Meaux's municipal police ranks among the five biggest in France, although the city doesn't even rank in the first one hundred in terms of population. Copé increases patrolling in areas the minute he hears about trouble, and Meaux's police have successfully cracked down on several local networks of thugs and drug dealers.

But the powers of Meaux's municipal police are still strangely limited. They are only auxiliary police to the real force, *la Police Nationale*. They can carry guns and ask for ID, but they can only arrest people who are caught in the act. They cannot question, detain, investigate, or deal directly with the court or the public prosecutor. That's all part of the State's monopoly. Copé finds this stranglehold frustrating. His police are really only the equivalent of university campus police in North America.

But there is another moral to Copé's story. In order to be effective, all mayors must make sure they maintain a good relationship with their *préfet*, who is the appointee of the president, the prime minister, and the cabinet. The *préfecture* is in fact a miniature French government in each *Département*. The *préfet* is the head of each ministry on his territory; he runs the police and commands the army when it has to intervene on his territory. The only authorities who aren't under the *préfet's* control are the Public Prosecutor and the Ministers of Finance and Education. Mayors and local authorities have been steadily gaining more powers since 1982, but the *préfet* still supervises them to make sure mayors perform their administrative duties and respect the letter and the spirit of the laws of the *République*. Until 1982, all city council decisions had to be countersigned by the *préfet*, who personally assured they were in accord with the laws of the *République*. That has changed, but the *préfet* still remains pretty much a quasi-colonial governor in France's *Départements*.

Préfets are a creation of the French Revolution, although the idea of appointing officials to administer on behalf of the centralized authority goes back much further. From 1568 on, the French crown had a network of thirty-six *intendants* throughout the country whose job was to collect taxes, though their functions varied throughout the ages and according to region. In the quiet areas around Paris, the *intendants* performed economic and demographic studies; in the frontiers, they were in charge of lodging the armies; in the rebellious region of Brittany, they acted as local diplomats and spies. By the end of the eighteenth century, *intendants* had fallen into disrepute. The Revolution pulled them out of retirement and gave them a new name: *préfets*. Their mandate was defined as "transmitting the law and orders of the government up to the ultimate branch of the social order with the speed of the *electric fluid*."

Naturally, there is regular friction between *préfets* and mayors. And although *préfets* have all the power, mayors have techniques for thwarting their authority. In the summer of 2000, the French government set out to conduct a national referendum on the question of whether to reduce the presidential term from seven to five years. Two hundred mayors, who were disgruntled for one reason or another, took advantage of the opportunity to become a thorn in their *prefet's* side. Some who didn't agree were against the referendum itself, others just wanted to attract their *préfet's* attention; some were vying for the president's ear or trying to make the news over some other issue. So they decided to exercise a classic protest technique and refused to organize the referendum vote in their *communes*. *Préfets* are stuck when this happens: they have to answer personally to the cabinet and the president about what happens in their *Département*. To resolve the problem, some *préfets* negotiated with their mayors, others simply organized the vote themselves, overriding the mayor's authority for the sake of the *intérêt général*.

A *préfet* can remove a mayor from office, but this rarely happens—there have only been fourteen cases since 1977. Most mayors willingly surrender to the tutelage of the *préfet*. The reason is simple: mayors can use the *préfet's* authority to keep in voters' favors. The *préfet's* powers are so broad that mayors often get them to do their dirty work by simply letting the *préfet* override their authority. If costly repairs need to be done on a church, school, or bridge right around the time of municipal elections, the mayor hands the job over to the *préfet*, who invokes the *intérêt général* and executes the work without causing any political damage to local elected officials.

In the summer of 2000, our friend Gustave invited us to a restaurant not far from the Louvre. That evening he announced that he was being transferred within the next two weeks to the Caribbean *Département* of Guadeloupe, where he had been appointed by the Ministry of Health to run a hospital. We were glad for him, since he felt his career had been side-tracked in Paris for political reasons. But we were sad at the same time to see our friend live a good eight hours by airplane from Paris—excellent though they are, French trains don't go there.

Gustave called us at least twice a month from then on, inviting us each time, and we went to see him in November, just after the hurricane season. Because Gustave worked in close coordination with the *prefecture*, this was a unique opportunity to see how the tutelage of the State over local affairs works in the high levels of a departmental administration.

Guadeloupe is an archipelago in the pearl string of islands in the Caribbean. From the mid-seventeenth century on it was a slave colony, producing rum and sugar for France. After slavery was abolished once and for all in 1848, Guadeloupe remained a French colony with a proletariat of former slaves who still produced sugar and rum. In 1945, Guadeloupe went from being a colony to being a French overseas *Département*, and former slaves became French citizens.

Guadeloupe was a great place to examine the workings of a *Département*. The relative poverty of the islands, and their dependence on

Paris for salaries, subsidies, and welfare, threw a crude light on how the French State treats local communities. In Guadeloupe, we really saw the nuts and bolts of the *République*.

On the whole, Guadeloupeans are better off than most of their neighbors, and the islands make up a little tropical paradise. The standard of living is relatively high. Infrastructure like roads and public buildings are in impeccable shape. Malaria has been completely eradicated. When a destructive hurricane flattens buildings, the *préfet* sees to it that the infrastructure is repaired promptly—it's part of the *préfet's* job to look after the *intérêt général*, after all.

But not all is perfect under the sun. Guadeloupe's prosperity is totally artificial. Subsidies, grants, social transfers, and civil-servant salaries account for 80 percent of the island's income. All civil servants receive a 40 percent indemnity in addition to their salary to compensate for the high cost of living, whether they are native or from continental France. Most of the money that comes in from *la métropole* (continental France) is spent on imported goods and goes back to Europe. Guadeloupe still hasn't succeeded in transforming a plantation economy into something else. Agriculture and tourism are the only industries, and the local economy is just too small to provide a base for developing any manufacturing. Unemployment hovers at around 28 percent. Entire neighborhoods in Guadeloupe's capital, Pointe-à-Pitre, are shantytowns. There is an average of a strike per day, and they are generally violent. In short, the legacy of a slave colony has never been shed.

Bananas are Guadeloupe's only significant domestic industry. Forty thousand Guadeloupeans—a quarter of the workforce—depend on the oblong fruit for their livelihood, as workers in plantations, offices, and processing plants. But banana wars with the U.S. government are making even this industry less viable. When the United States has challenged the measures the French government takes to protect Guadeloupe's banana production, the World Trade Organization has systematically ruled against France. But because of the high standard of living in Guadeloupe and the small size of the plantations, Guadeloupe can't compete against the Banana Republics of the Americas and Africa, whose production is controlled by Chiquita, Del Monte, and Dole.

We visited several plantations and met one banana producer, Sylvestre Mardivirin, in his office. He ran a twenty-eight-hectar plantation with two associates, but since he was an accountant by trade, he worked in one of the nondescript office buildings in the new section of Pointe-à-Pitre. Mardivirin, who is mulatto with some Indian parentage, had been in charge of overviewing trade talks. He complained bitterly that French Foreign Affairs did not defend them strongly enough in international trade talks. Naturally, we responded like North Americans.

"Instead of harping on the government for not doing its job, why don't banana planters send their own representatives to trade talks?" we asked.

His response: "We can't. Only the government can go to trade talks."

In France, foreign trade is the prerogative of the State. There is only one State so there's only one voice. Unlike Canadian provinces, which send their own representatives to negotiate trade rules and regulations in trade disputes with the United States, French *Départements* are powerless to represent themselves.

The way power is shared, or not shared, in the French system explains many of the problems in Guadeloupe, but also many of the good things about the Republic. After all, the State maintains a very high quality of infrastructures and services that Guadeloupeans could not afford if they had to pay for them on their own. However, Guadeloupeans cannot take their economic problems into their own hands. The entire structure of the system forces them to adopt a wait-and-see attitude that clearly fuels social unrest on the islands.

After our meeting with Mardivirin, we decided to discus the banana issue with our friend Gustave when he returned from his hospital. Our take on the situation was, again, typically North American.

"Why doesn't France give more power to local governments?" we asked him. "Clearly this is what Guadeloupe needs. Give local government more authority and autonomy, and they'll find solutions."

He looked at us with puzzlement. "What do you mean by local government?"

"Well, municipal governments, *Départements*, Regions," we said.

"That's not government," he replied. "That's local *administration*. There's only one government in France."

French Regions may be the size of some American states, small Canadian provinces, or German lands, but they have no political sovereignty whatsoever. Varied as they are, geographically, economically, and even culturally, regions cannot make their own laws or "take" responsibility for running their own affairs. *Communes*, *Départements*, and Regions have basically the same function. They administer the same things at different levels: safety, culture, transport, schools, social programs, welfare, and planning. *Communes* take care of the school buildings for grades one to five; *Départements* take care of grades six to nine; and Regions handle *lycées* (grades ten to twelve). But none of them have authority on standards of education any more than they set their own standards for social welfare. They handle the buildings—period.

It's all a matter of their power to tax—or lack of it. *Communes*, *Départements*, and Regions all get by on revenues from the same three taxes: real estate, rent, and business. The regional council decides what cut the Region, *Département*, and *commune* each get, and then each level decides how much it wants to take. But none of them can create new taxes to get more money. And there is nothing to suggest that France is moving in this direction. On the contrary: the *Département* used to have its own tax, *la vignette* (annual license tag for cars) until September 2000, when the French Finance Minister cancelled it without consultation or explanation. The lost revenues will be made up with other transfers, but the decision shows how reticent the French State is to grant autonomy to any level of local government.

The picture is harsh, but in a way, it doesn't make sense to think of the French government as "repressing" local government. Centralization is more fundamental than that. The French wanted it this way, after all. Not so long ago, France was as divided and divisive as the Balkans. To make it work, France leveled local differences and centralized power. Cultural groups *demanded* political, cultural, and economic assimilation. Assimilation brought peace and order, but erased political liberty at the local level.

In 1945, the Guadeloupeans demanded, and were allowed, to be fully assimilated into France. Other former colonies, like New Caledonia and French Polynesia in the Pacific, have retained a degree of autonomy, but the Guadeloupians, like the populations of Martinique and French Guiana, insisted on becoming a part of France like other *Départements*. It would be false to pretend that integration took place without a hitch, or that it even succeeded completely. Guadeloupe has a violent separatist movement, and it has taken all the might of the Republic to suppress it. But Guadeloupe is much better off than most of its neighbors and its people know it. The situation of Dominica, an island that became independent from Britain in 1978, is bleak and practically hopeless in comparison. Guadeloupe chose to become part of France, but unfortunately, France can't seem to find a middle ground between total assimilation and recognizing local differences.

Given how much the French value history, we were expecting to see many monuments commemorating Guadeloupe's past, and museums documenting its history, particularly the dramatic story of abolishing slavery on the island. Slavery was abolished in 1794, reinstituted in 1802, and abolished again in 1848 after a long and violent struggle. It seemed to us a perfect illustration of the Republican ideals of *liberté*, *égalité*, and *fraternité* at work.

But France's policy of assimilation went very far in Guadeloupe, and until the 1980s, textbooks completely omitted this heroic period. The *République* doesn't value local heroes—it's one of the casualties of assimilation. Like French kids everywhere, Guadeloupean children are taught that French history starts with "Our ancestors, the Gauls..." There is only one small statue in Guadeloupe commemorating Ignace, a black officer who lost his life leading the last battle against Napoleon's army—a local hero! The memorial wasn't raised until 1998.

The only thing the French government adapts to local conditions is its techniques for assimilation. The French government created mandatory, non-religious, national education in the 1880s to undermine the influence of the church in rural areas. This was an especially important step in Brittany, where the church was the main defender of the local culture and the Breton language. A sizable segment of French popular literature until the mid-1960s is written about the clash between clergy and teachers, whose job it was to teach French and transmit the values of the Republic. But the government took the opposite approach in Alsace, a territory that had been annexed by Germany in 1870, returned to France in 1914, reannexed in 1940, and restituted again in 1944. Germany had made intense efforts to get Alsatians to speak German while it was annexed. To counteract German influence, the French government allowed Alsatian schools to remain religious, reasoning that this would keep the Alsatians happy and break their loyalty to Germany. Some local customs in France are preserved, but only when it's in the interest of the *République*.

Guadeloupe also allowed us to see in stark detail how France's administrative system mixes populations and breaks local ties. France's well-known, blue-clad, anti-riot police are never posted in their region, let alone town of origin. If they come from the south, they are posted somewhere else. The idea is that they will be more willing to use force against people they don't know. The same logic is applied to prefectoral officers. There is an unwritten rule that *préfets* are never appointed in their own *Département* of origin, to prevent them from establishing local power bases. That custom is one of the reasons Guadeloupe is not run by locals. Félix Éboué, the first black governor of Guadeloupe in 1936, was a native of French Guiana.

There are advantages and disadvantages to this custom. Because the *préfet* has no local ties and is appointed for only three years, he is the natural arbitrator in local conflicts, like strikes or solving quarrels between mayors. *Préfets* don't owe anything to anyone, so they are hard to buy. However, having outsiders as leaders can backfire, and Guadeloupe is a good case in point. Regardless of their training, *préfets* from continental France aren't very likely to know how to deal with local realities as elementary as hurricanes or conch-wielding separatists.

The process of assimilation and the leveling of cultural differences was never fully completed in France, partly because the government recognized that total assimilation was unnecessary, and partly because it recognized at one point that mass media and television were doing the job for them. Regional languages still exist, though many, like Occitan and Catalan, are barely spoken. In Alsace, German is the mother tongue of many French citizens. Residents of Alsace and Lorraine refer to France as "the Interior." Some three hundred thousand Bretons still speak Breton. And there are other marked cultural differences from one region to another. The favorite sport of the southwest region of France is rugby, not soccer.

Some cultural differences have arguably flourished *because* of centralization. Cuisine is one case where this is almost indisputable. Over centuries of assimilation efforts from the central government, cuisine was one of the few outlets local cultures had to express themselves.

North Americans have an ingrained resistance to the idea of political centralization. Yet when we returned to Canada after three years in France we saw that centralization has its merits. Whatever their origin or class, the French enjoy the same social services wherever they go in France, even as far as Reunion and Guadeloupe. They speak the same language everywhere, use the same legal system, get the same education, listen to the same radio and TV, receive the same health services, and get the same holidays. In that sense, the French enjoy a level of equality and uniformity that cannot exist in federations, even the richest ones like the United States, Germany, Canada, or Switzerland.

Community life is never as strong as it is in North America, but when we moved home to Toronto we got a very different impression of what community life was really about here. In the United States, like in most other federations, community life is the pillar of the entire social edifice. Everyone is expected to contribute and cooperate to make society work, whether it's funding Christmas food drives, recycling garbage, or volunteering to take students on school outings. North American communities have very little means of enforcing policies like these, so they appeal to people's morals, through advertisements and even during private conversations. Society self-regulates in ways that are really pretty subtle. One of the first things our neighbors joked about was how people would notice the excessive number of wine bottles in our recycling box (of course, the very same neighbors already had noticed themselves). If we didn't remove the snow from the sidewalk in front out of our house, neighbors would let us know we've erred, even if all they did was glare.

In France, most of these responsibilities are shouldered by the State. It is easy to think the French are uncivil and inconsiderate, especially when they refuse to observe basic courtesies like scooping up after their dogs. But people pay high taxes and expect the State to do its job. And the State does do its job. The French don't have very rich community lives. But they do draw a limit on moralizing individual behavior. We found that there was a certain *liberté* to that.

chapter 12

Strong Language

We were surprised when some of our old-stock French friends and acquaintances told us their parents or grandparents had never spoken French. A couple of weeks after our arrival, we were invited to dinner at the home of Bénédicte Rozeron, a thirty-five-year-old systems architect for an insurance company, who was introduced to us by a French friend in Montreal. Over the course of the supper, she mentioned she was from the *pays* Basque and we spent much of the evening on the topic.

There are approximately eight hundred thousand Basques living on each side of the Franco-Spanish border along the Atlantic coast. Nobody knows where the Basques originally came from or exactly how they ended up inhabiting this area. The roots of the *Euskara* (Basque language, in the Basque language) go back at least four thousand years, before Latin was spoken and possibly to the Neolithic age, which would make it one of the oldest languages still spoken today. Although Bénédicte likes playing *pala*, a traditional Basque game similar to squash, she counts herself among France's assimilated Basques, much to her regret. Her grandmother spoke the Basque language and her mother understood it, but Bénédicte can't make out a word of it. She doesn't know why her grandmother didn't transmit the language.

As the evening progressed, we saw for ourselves why Bénédicte never learned Euskara. We asked her why she didn't get her daughter to learn the

Basque language and she replied:

"I wouldn't want my child to lose her French. It's too important. She couldn't function."

Throughout our stay, we met many other old-stock French of Catalan, Provençal, Alsatian, or Breton origins who had exactly the same attitude about their regional language or dialect. Everyone regrets the loss of regional languages but defends the need to speak good French—as if French was fighting a zero sum game against other local languages.

Whenever we returned to North America from France, people often asked us why the French were so obsessed with protecting their language. Although something told us it was really North Americans who were obsessed with the question, there's no denying how vocal and explicit the French are about protecting their language. Language is a national complex in France. Anglo-Americans consider language a tool, but the French regard it as an accomplishment, even a work of art. They love and cherish their language in ways that are almost incomprehensible to English speakers. It's their national monument.

The obsession goes much deeper than grammar and sentence structure. Language was one of the main tools France employed over the centuries to solidify a common identity—thereby reinforcing France's territorial, political, and administrative unity. Efforts to impose a common language go back as far as the time of Charlemagne (742–814 A.D.), French emperor of the Holy Roman Empire, who tried to make the whole empire speak Latin. Later French kings used aggressive, even violent methods to impose the French language—and apparently, they never quite won.

Modern French is a derivative of *Francien*, the language spoken in the Paris region at the beginning of the second millennium. By the fourteenth century, Francien was already widespread throughout the kingdom, especially in the cities, because Paris was already an important center of trade. Students flocked to its universities and artists entertained the court.

The process of penetration during that period was very akin to the spread of English today: no one forced French on anyone. The language became important because of the sheer weight of Paris in the French kingdom, and of the French kingdom in Europe. France's population in the fourteenth century equaled those of England, Germany, Italy, and Spain combined. France's neighbors recognized the French language long before it became the official language of France. Most treaties in Europe were written in French. The language had no real standards, and French borrowed and absorbed words from other languages much like Shakespeare's English.

Six centuries later, Jean-Benoît is a North American native and French speaker. The French spoken in Quebec is as different from Parisian French as American English is from British English, but the numbers and the ratios of the two groups are very different: Americans outnumber the British five to one, whereas the French outnumber Quebeckers ten to one. As a consequence, Americans impose their own standards on the English language, whereas Quebeckers have to conform to the French norm. Jean-Benoît learned to read and write in French using mostly French dictionaries and reference books, with French examples and French definitions. For instance, if you open a French dictionary of *noms propres* (people's and place's names), the entry for the town of Besançon is followed with the number 45000. This is not the population, but the postal code. And naturally, only the biggest cities of Quebec are listed in the same dictionary—without their postal code.

The reference point of the French language has always been, and will remain, Paris, and Paris still dictates the standard today. This has to do with demography as well as the history of the language after the Renaissance.

The first language ruling of the modern French State took place in 1539. At the time, the French crown was still busy vying for power with members of the aristocracy and the Catholic Church. Looking for ways to chip away at the Church's influence, King François I (1515–47) passed the ordinance of Villers-Cotterêts, which stated that French would be the language of France's tribunals—not Latin, the language of the Church. The same ordinance made French mandatory in all administrative documents, although that rule wasn't widely applied until the French Revolution.

The French poet François de Malherbe (1555–1628) had a decisive influence on the French language because he managed to impose the idea of a "norm." Malherbe convinced a group of followers that France's class of "honest" men—meaning people of "value" like aristocrats, clerics, and artists—should employ language that was clear, precise, uncorrupted, and followed rules of *bon usage* (correct use). In 1634, Cardinal Richelieu (1585–1642) gave his protection to some of Malherbe's followers. The next year, Richelieu created the *Académie Française*, whose founding goal was to give "undebatable rules to our language, to make it pure, eloquent, and capable of addressing the arts and sciences."

The *Académie* published its first dictionary by 1694. Its work consisted mostly of pruning the language of synonyms and rigidly defining each term so that no two terms had the same meaning. But even before the publication of a French dictionary, *bon usage* was rapidly eliminating French words. François Rabelais (1483–1555) used forty thousand words in the Gargantua and Pantagruel cycles. A century later, a playwright like Jean Racine (1639–99) wrote the entire body of his tragedies using about three thousand words. The French are always surprised to hear that there are from five to ten times *more* accepted words in the English language than in French (they will typically talk about how much "richer" the French language is than English and assume by deduction that French has more words). In French, the boundaries between what is acceptable and what is not are clearly defined and enforced by the *Académie* and the government. In English, there is no body that rules out words.

Starting in the seventeenth century, two French languages actually developed side by side: the language of the court and literature, and the common language, of which we know practically nothing now. French grammarians and language purists became very influential during this period. But they never really succeeded in imposing their standards on the general population. People just refused purism, even people of relatively high standing, like the playwright Molière (1622–73), an intimate of King Louis XIV, who mocked the precious language of the court in his work.

The French Revolution fueled the efforts of the language purists. A 1790 survey of spoken languages showed that half of the French population did not speak or understand French. This was clearly a problem for a regime that proposed making the people sovereign. Henri Grégoire (1750–1831), a priest and Républicain cleric of the extreme Left, who openly decried regional dialects and the influence of foreign languages, demanded that French be taught to the whole nation.

A couple of generations passed before the Abbé Grégoire's demands were met. But French continued to make great progress in the countryside during this period thanks to two seemingly unrelated factors: a road system centered on Paris, and mandatory military service. Because of the road system, most tradesmen had to pass through Paris, and they had to be able to speak and understand the language. Like all branches of the State, the military spoke French. Millions of men in France's mass armies were forced to speak and understand it. After the Revolution, the Villers-Cotterêts ordinance, which made French the legal language for all written documents, was finally applied. The new State also required educated civil servants who could speak French. More and more people entered the school system in the 1830s. Spelling became state business, and the French government started to rule on what was acceptable and what was not.

The *Académie* and the promoters of *bon usage* never succeeded in forcing the French to speak the pure literary form of the language that was their model. The State vilified regional languages and dialects, but artistic schools like the romantics and the naturalists extolled them as "natural" languages. Accelerating economic and social changes also called for a constant redefinition of the norm. New technologies and new ideas called for new words. The process of erasing regional languages was slow. At the end of the nineteenth century, the only people who spoke French in many *communes* were the mayor, the notary, the priest, and the teacher. By 1910, 90 percent of the French understood French, but 50 percent of the population still understood a dialect.

While the idea of language norms is very strong in France, the French have always nurtured a counterculture of dialects that subvert these norms. In the nineteenth century, French criminals developed a language called *Argot* so they could communicate without being understood. Honoré de Balzac and Victor Hugo were militant defenders of *Argot*— popular characters in their novels spoke in dialects and used colloquialisms rather than the language of *bon usage*. Many *Argot* terms crept into standard French and are still used, like *mec* (man), *bidule* (thingamajig), or *fric* (money).

Slang exists in all cultures, but the French are famous for building theirs into systems. One interesting case was *Loucherbem*, a slang developed by butchers in Paris markets in the nineteenth century. In *Loucherbem*, the first letter of a word is taken off, replaced with the letter "l," tacked on the end, and followed by *em, oche*, or *oque*. *Loucherbem* is the *Loucherbem* word for *boucher* (butcher). Some terms from the slang are still used, like *loufoque*, from *fou* (crazy).

The liveliest form of *Argot* now used is *Verlan*, which is common in the French Arabic ghettos of the suburbs. *Verlan* just reverses the syllables of a word—the term *Verlan* is itself a reversal of the term *l'envers* (reverse). Many *Verlan* words are commonly used, even in the media and publicity. The second generation of Arab immigrants call themselves *les Beurs*, a Frenchification of the Arabic term for "Arab." In *Verlan*, Beur is reversed and becomes *Rebeu*. Another common *Verlan* term is *ripou*, which means cop, but is actually *Verlan* for *pourri* (rotten).

Despite the proliferation of *Argot*, language purists have not given up: the idea of a norm remains strong in France. In 1997, after the Socialist Party won the legislative elections, a group of high-profile female ministers demanded they be called *madame LA ministre*—a very bold break in tradition. Unlike English and German, there is no neutral gender in French, and titles were customarily masculine. Traditionally, *la ministre* is the minister's wife. And *la mairesse* is the wife of the mayor, *le maire*. A female mayor has always been *madame le maire*.

The battle over these titles was a showdown between France's purists and non-purists. The purists argued that a masculine title refers to the institution. Being summoned by *madame le juge* means you're being summoned by justice (the institution). A summons by *madame la juge* means you're being invited (by the person). Naturally, the *Académie Française* bought this argument and opposed changing the gender of titles. The government appointed a committee to decide, but most people just adopted the change anyway, including the press. Even relatively conservative publications now speak of female ministers or judges as *madame la ministre* and *madame la juge*.

This is the kind of language quarrel you get in the *République*: common usage always wins, but the purists never give in without a fight.

Anglo-American commentators accuse the French of being insular and xenophobic whenever the French government attempts to outlaw the use of English terms in France. Yet when one considers the effort the French government has put into getting rid of its own regional languages, there's nothing remarkable about the fact that it regulates English. Language purism is part of the fabric of France. The old idea of *bon usage* remains very strong, and linguistic innovations of any type are carefully considered before being accepted. Normal French people speak in a way that is far more refined and formal than anything one would hear in North America—either in English or French. The French have fewer words to choose from, but they use more of the ones they have. The hierarchy between oral and written standards is opposite of that of English. Typically, good English writing tends to conform to the spoken word. But the French try to adjust the way they speak to reflect the way they write—or should write.

We found the French remarkably welcoming when it came to housing us, feeding us, helping us out, and becoming our friends, but intolerant when it came to language. As French-speaking foreigners with "exotic" Quebec accents, we got to observe their fastidiousness close up. Sometimes they mocked our Quebec accents. Sometimes they made double-edged compliments—telling us our accents were *mignon* (cute). Sometimes they even tried to imitate us. In television interviews for a special on Quebec singer Céline Dion, her family members were even subtitled (French Canadian TV never subtitles Parisians, even when they are incomprehensible).

Even so, it wouldn't be fair to categorize this behavior as arrogant. We eventually understood that, in France, correcting a person in mid-sentence in not considered impolite, as it is in the Anglo-American world. Jean-Benoît was often corrected for not making the liaison between words. In Quebec French, the silent consonant at the end of words is not always pronounced before a word that starts with a vowel. The French are absolutely manic about liaisons, which can be very elaborate. *Vous essayez d'étirer un élastique trop épais* (you try to stretch too tight an elastic) becomes *Vous z'essayez d'étirer un n'élastique trop p'épais.* Making every available liaison is a mark of good education in France. Quebeckers can take or leave the liaison, but generally consider it precious sounding.

Julie found herself in an interesting situation. She speaks Quebec French with an English accent, yet the French tended to hear only her Quebec accent. Quebeckers had very little contact with the French for nearly two centuries, from 1763 to about 1940, so the languages, understandably, are quite different. Because Quebec is in direct contact with a predominantly English continent, Anglicisms crept into Quebec French in a different way. Julie discovered this firsthand when she tried to buy a bottle of iced tea at our local bakery on Avenue St-Ouen. Iced tea has been around for a long time in Quebec, long enough for them to just translate it into *thé glacé*. But when Julie asked the French baker for a *thé glacé*, the woman almost dropped her baguettes.

"You mean an *eese tee*," she said, twisting the English words "iced tea" into something that sounded like certified French.

Julie was in the odd situation of having a Parisian instruct her on how to mispronounce words in her own language. Eventually she got used to that (and she got into the habit of explaining that English was her first language). The French have an irrepressible habit of correcting language use, and they do so indiscriminately. France has dictated the standard of *bon usage* for so long that nobody really questions it. The standard French dictionaries used in Quebec, for instance, are French. Examples for word use refer exclusively to French reality, as seen from Paris. So it's no surprise that Parisian French consider their language to be the standard.

In France there is also a sort of residual belief in the intrinsic genius or superiority of the French language. These days, that prejudice is clearly being fueled by France's rivalry with Anglo-American culture. Many people we met in France, even highly educated ones, spoke to us matter-of-factly about how the French language was infinitely "richer" than English, with a "wider vocabulary." English has approximately five times more words than French, so the argument about richness is definitely open to debate. But the French believe their own story (partly because they do *use* their language more richly).

Again, the roots of the belief go back centuries. One of the creators of the doctrine of *bon usage*, Dominique Bouhours (1628–1702), a grammarian, wrote that the French language "may be the only one that follows exactly the natural order and that expresses thoughts as they rise to the mind." The idea that the French language was innately superior had triumphed by the eighteenth century, when author Antoine de Rivarol (1753–1801) wrote his *Discours sur l'Universalité de la Langue Française*. He claimed, "Of all languages, the French language is the only one that has an element of probity attached to its genius. Defined, social, and reasonable, it is not only the language of the French, but the language of humanity."

By the nineteenth century, most who learned French disagreed with this kind of chauvinism, but the idea of its superiority still has sway in modern France. What's clearly not debatable is that the French love and value their language and use it with great care. Many people in France simply mistake good language use for an intrinsic quality of the language itself.

You might say the French lack perspective. But all cultures are self-centered. Now that English is the dominant global language (replacing French), it is common to hear or read nonsense like Rivarol's about the genius of the English language.

Interestingly, the British abandoned the idea of creating a French-style English academy after a heated debate over the issue in the eighteenth century. But even if the British had created an academy, their successful colonial policy meant that they would have lost control of it early. Only 10 percent of those who speak English as their mother tongue now live in Britain. English, of course, has its purists too, but there has never been a single authority to enforce good language use. Because so many people speak English in so many different ways, "getting the message through" is the spirit that dominates the use of English today. Contrary to what many French believe, English is not a simple language. As a French *académicien* once put it, English is a language that is relatively easy to speak poorly. The real difference is that, unlike the French, English speakers tolerate poor use of their language.

The French have a complex relationship with English. In pre-revolutionary France, there was actually a wave of Anglomania. During the French Revolution many political terms were picked up from English, including *gouvernement* and *révolution*—a term that applied only to astronomy prior to the English Revolution of 1688. Yet in the same period there was also a shift against foreign influences in the French language. All European cultures were going through about the same process at the time. The British and the Germans were modifying spellings of foreign words to make them look native. In France, the Abbé Grégoire preached against the use of foreign words and dialects, which was ironic since, by chanting the merits of the Revolution, he was using an Anglicism.

The idea of protecting the language against Anglicisms actually started in Quebec. In a population of seven million now, six million can be considered native speakers of French. This is a very small French pool in a sea of three hundred million English speakers—no other linguistic group has a similar situation except, maybe, Baltic-language speakers with respect to Russian, or Hebrew speakers with respect to Arabic. Starting in the 1960s, Quebec leaders became conscious of the necessity of protecting the French language, and they implemented various policies, including a policy of official bilingualism in Canada. The Quebec government also created a set of language laws that carefully circumscribed the use of the English language on signs, enrollment in English schools, and in public communications. The French followed the trend ten or fifteen years later.

Until the 1970s, the French were very *laissez-faire* with respect to the English language. Oddly, one of the first high-profile initiatives to protect French came from IBM France in 1954. At the time, IBM was trying to popularize the use of computer mainframes. Most cultures adopted a version of the English term in their own language—like *computador* in Spanish or *computer* in German. In French, the first two syllables of the word computer resemble the worst insults imaginable—*con* and *pute* (meaning cunt and whore). So IBM France created its own trademark term, *ordinateur*, which the French government officially adopted ten years later.

The idea of language control oozed in the French political class in the 1970s, mostly as a result of foreign influence from Quebec and French-speaking countries in Africa. In 1975, the National Assembly passed a law making it mandatory to use French in publicity, though the measure didn't prove very effective in the long-term. In 1992, the Constitution was modified to state that "the language of the Republic is French." In 1994, a new law modified the publicity law of 1975 and added fines of up to four thousand dollars for companies that didn't use French. More importantly, the new law forbade publicly traded companies and individuals in the service of the State from using any language but French in their communications.

Language rules have always been controversial in France. In the 1990s, the government wanted to forbid the use of English terms outright. The *Conseil Constitutionel* (Constitutional Court) ruled against such a prohibition, no doubt taking into consideration the realities of daily life in France, where English words abound. Quebeckers, who are very purist about Anglicisms at the official level, constantly reproach the French for using English terms. In reality, each culture just uses different Anglicisms. As one common joke puts it: Quebeckers *parquent* the car in the *stationnement* (parking) while the French *stationnent* in the *parking*.

Legal measures will not stop the French from using English terms. At best, they will slow the process down. One need only walk down a street in Paris or any provincial French city to notice the proliferation of English words and expressions. As Quebeckers, we were surprised to see that French people use English expressions to project a kind of *cachet* or sophistication, much like English speakers use French expressions to project sophistication when they are talking about cuisine, fashion, or even international affairs. The French go to do their *shopping* with their *caddie*. After work, they do their *walking*. Stylish young French businessmen and women speckle their vocabulary with English business terms. The influence of English is evident everywhere American culture is imported. The Belgian fast-food chain Quick sells *les chicken wings*. McDonald's meal deals are called *Best of* meals.

The borrowing of English terms is the source of ceaseless arguments between France's language purists (who reject them) and linguists (who actually welcome them). Linguists argue that French borrows from all languages, so why should there be a stigma attached to *le scanner* or *le shopping*, but none on *le spaghetti* or *Beur*? Half of the basic vocabulary in English comes originally from old French, not including the more recent adoption of cooking and military vocabulary. At the moment, English dominates the vocabulary of new technology, but that does not pose a threat to the existence of the French language. As the history of the French language shows, ordinary use and fashion eventually prevail over purism, but purists never go down without a fight. (There's more about anti-Americanization in chapter 20.)

Given the French penchant for controlling vocabulary and language usage, it should not come as a surprise that they refuse to hand their culture over to "market forces." Culture in France has always been closely associated with the country's national and international ambitions. François I (1515–47) made French mandatory in dispensing justice, but also created the *Collège de France,* the Royal Library, and a policy of public works, and hired writers as diplomats and high civil servants in his court. Art, for him, was not simply a matter of decoration, but a means of affirming French power. At the same time that he created the French Academy, Cardinal Richelieu founded an institute for the promotion and development of science and the arts, of which the French Academy is only one part. Louis XIV oversaw and encouraged an impressive quantity of artistic production, mostly in architecture, with the single goal of affirming his own *grandeur.* He also subsidized men of science, even outside of France, the most famous being the German mathematician Gottfried Wilhelm Leibniz (1646–1716), who invented calculus.

In the second half of the twentieth century, while France was aggressively affirming its place in international institutions, the State created scores of organizations to promote the international presence of the French language. In 1962, President Charles de Gaulle (1944–46, 1958–69) set out to increase France's *grandeur* by giving André Malraux (1901-69) the mandate to create a Ministry of Culture. Malraux had a lofty objective: he proclaimed France's mission "to propose to humanity the means and the method of an intellectual and spiritual action." In 1981, socialist president François Mitterrand appointed a prodigal Minister of Culture, Jack Lang, who embarked on a vast program of subsidies to all (some now say, any) avant-garde artists in France. Artists, like intellectuals, are very influential in left-wing circles in France. Mitterrand needed to unify the Left to stay in power, and he reasoned that keeping artists happy was a good means to this. It didn't hurt. Mitterrand won two consecutive seven-year mandates. (The best source on the issue is *Le Gouvernement de la Culture* by Maryvone de Saint Pulgent.)

Now, radio and cinema are the main transmission belts of popular culture and language. So the French government conducts an open campaign to defend these industries against the incursion of English. The French government does everything in its power to promote the French film industry, to the envy of many of France's neighbors. The French film industry is notoriously well funded. The proceeds from an 11 percent tax on movie tickets go directly toward funding national film production. The government pays French producers advances on box office earnings so they don't have to wait for profits before making their next movie. Hollywood considers these perks unfair, yet French cinema is one of the few national film industries that has survived the onslaught of American cinema.

Americans are quick to accuse the French of subsidizing movies they don't watch themselves. In bad years, less than 30 percent of French moviegoers watch French films; 2001 was a vintage year with 50 percent. But compared to other countries' performances, this isn't bad. In 2000, Britain produced 115 films, Italy 87, and Germany 61, while France churned out 163. Most of the measures France uses to encourage cinema started in the 1960s and even the fifties. French cinema was in complete disarray at the time and government funding spawned an entire generation of influential filmmakers. As a matter of cultural choice, the French put much more energy into cinema than television. They produce six hundred hours of original television material per year—half of Britain's thirteen hundred hours, and one-third of Germany's two thousand hours. French TV chains are big investors in cinema. They play a lot of films, and since French TV doesn't show many commercials, watching films on TV is actually pleasant.

Measures in the field of music are much more recent. In the early 1990s, the music on French radio stations was mostly American. One of

France's senators, Michel Pelchat, decided to do something about it—a logical reflex because French senators can introduce bills unlike their Canadian peers. Pelchat looked across the Atlantic and saw Canada's radio regulation system, which specifies how much air time each radio station must reserve for national production. Most English Canadian radio stations must devote 40 to 60 percent of the their airtime to Canadian artists. And most French Canadian radio stations must play a similar percentage of French language music, or music in a language other than English.

Pelchat launched a campaign to get similar regulations applied to French radio. Many French opposed the idea, arguing that they should be allowed to listen to whatever they wanted. That was no coincidence—French music was regarded as corny. But Pelchat's camp won by arguing that the only way to protect French culture was to guarantee radio time for French artists. Interestingly, this measure had the support of many French executives at big labels like Warner and Sony, who sought a bigger outlet for their own domestic production. The regulations actually apply to language, not nationality, so one interesting result has been a boost to a new generation of Quebec musicians who were largely unknown in France until then. Many Quebec artists have become celebrities in France as a result. Following the new regulations, French rap also took off. French rappers are quickly entering the musical mainstream, but they are still very influential in defining France's new counterculture. The stars are mostly Beurs fluent in *Verlan*.

While we lived there, not a week went by in France without talk of *l'exception culturelle* (the cultural exception). Since its creation, at the beginning of the 1990s, *l'exception culturelle* has become the rallying cry of all of those who oppose the idea that culture should be left to markets alone. The idea first surfaced during the 1993 round of discussions before the signature of the GATT, where issues of intellectual property and subsidies to arts and cultures were on the table for the first time. At the time, the U.S. film industry was calling for the elimination of French film subsidies. French filmmakers and intellectuals rallied together and put forward the concept of *l'exception culturelle*. They argued that the arts could not be treated like mere commodities to be traded freely, since they were the vehicle of culture. France wanted protective measures for the arts to be permitted and even encouraged international trade agreements in the name of fostering national identities. Canada also supports the idea, although Canadians tend to be less confrontational than the French in promoting it. The French managed to win over other European countries, then other GATT member countries, with the idea of *l'exception culturelle*. The World Trade Organization now accepts the notion that culture has to be protected and subsidized.

In the meantime, the term *exception culturelle* has become a catch phrase the French use to justify any form of resistance to Americanization. French trade negotiators and government officials have become defensive about the protectionist overtones the term has internationally, so they have started to use the expression "cultural diversity" instead. It is, of course, ironic that a nation so bent on leveling cultural differences now preaches the virtues of distinctiveness and diversity. On the other hand, France's language and cultural policies have always been determined by the interest of the State. In a way, the French language *is* the State.

chapter 13

Élite Education

At fourteen years of age, Benjamin Chabert asked his father if he could go study in a U.S. high school for a year. It was a novel idea for a French teenager, but not that surprising given his background. Benjamin's father, Jacques, a friend of ours, has a degree in English literature and translates travel literature for a living. Jacques approved of the idea and found a high school in California that agreed to admit Benjamin and a family to billet him. There was only one condition: Jacques suspected his son's academic performance would suffer from spending a year abroad, so he made Benjamin promise he would put in extra hours at school when he returned to France.

Benjamin got back safe and sound and with his French education intact. Two things surprised him about life in America. Academically, his American peers were way behind. Benjamin knew more about English grammar than they did. That's not surprising given the drill-type education French children receive and the number of hours they spend at school— up to forty per week. On the other hand, Benjamin said, American teenagers were much more "socially mature" than his French peers. Most of the high school students he met had part-time jobs and earned their own pocket money. They came and went as they pleased between home and school, setting their own schedules and taking responsibility for their lives.

Most expected to be driving at age sixteen and to own their own car soon after.

What Benjamin said matched closely with what we had observed. In the two years that we stayed in France, we never met a child under eighteen who had a part-time job—not in a gas bar, a restaurant, or even a variety store. To be precise, the only child we saw working was the sixteen-year-old son of the "Arab"—as the French call mom-and-pop grocers, generally run by North Africans—on the first floor of our apartment building. And the child was not really "working" as much as filling in when his father had to be somewhere else.

The banal facts of teen life in America seem strange to the French. Regulations in France make it difficult to hire anyone on a temporary basis, in particular children younger than sixteen, so French teenagers don't tend to hold part-time jobs while they're at school. They don't uniformly drive, either, partly because cars aren't a necessity in most French cities, but also because they don't need them to drive to their part-time jobs. Compared to Americans, French parents shelter their children; they try to preserve them as long as possible from outside influences and the necessity of work. It's not because French parents are unnaturally protective. They just know that their children have to study hard to succeed. Diplomas are everything in French society; they follow the French everywhere they go, all their lives.

So French parents do everything they can to maximize their children's performance. We met middle-class parents who still gave allowances to their twenty-two or twenty-three-year-old children. We met students in their twenties who had never had a job. They weren't all from the upper or even middle classes. One, a twenty-five-year-old, told us he had never earned a *centime* in his life. He had a master's degree in law and was the son of a barber. The reason he never worked, he said, was that it looked bad: only the truly poor work while studying. Good results are so important in the French system that in the summer many parents buy their kids *cahiers de vacances* (holiday exercise books) to prime them for the next school year. *La rentrée* (back to school) is a very serious affair in France. The papers are filled with advice about how to get little ones off to the best start possible.

One column even advised parents to get their children's feet checked for warts so they wouldn't be distracted by the problem during the school year.

In 2001, a study from the Organization for Economic and Cooperative Development compared randomly chosen elementary and secondary students from thirty-two countries. French students placed in the top quarter for math skills but were average for understanding written texts. These mediocre results in this category should not be surprising. Raising the overall level of education is not the only objective of the French education system. The system is designed so people will find their place in society. As part of this, it singles out the *élite* students who will go on to run the country and manage large companies. Students who are underperforming at age twelve or fifteen are often channeled into a trade. Others just find their own place in France's pecking order.

The French education system is specially designed to serve the interests of an extremely centralized country. It's founded on a curious mix of egalitarianism and elitism. A good basic education is available to all, but those who don't make it to the top are stuck on the same rung of the ladder for the rest of their lives.

Elementary and secondary education are very similar to what you find in most advanced societies. The big differences are at the beginning and the end of the process. At the beginning of the twentieth century, France had a high percentage of women in the workforce: 30 percent in 1901, 48 percent in 2001. France was one of the first countries to establish a state-run system of day care, known as *la crèche*, and kindergarten schools, known as *la maternelle*. Kindergarten is mandatory at age five but optional at age three, and 88 percent of French children are placed at *la maternelle* at this early age. So French children learn to adapt to social norms very early in life. They are generally *propres* (toilet trained) by age two, a year earlier than American kids. Children attend primary school from ages five to eleven. After that they go to *collège* (secondary school) for four years. Then, between age sixteen and eighteen, they go to *le lycée* (three years between high school and university). Many *lycées* serve the purpose of technical colleges these days, but their original function was to give students exposure to higher learning and the classics. In the general *lycées*, the curriculum is heavily oriented towards philosophy and math.

Establishing a public education system in France was one of the great accomplishments of the State. In 1833, the Minister of Education, François Guizot (1787–1874) passed a law making school mandatory. By 1870, a mere forty years later, there were six and a half million students in France and 110,000 *instituteurs* (teachers). The population recognized early that a good primary education was the ticket to social promotion. Even then, written exams were mandatory for almost any kind of job in the ever-growing civil service. Until the 1970s, pupils had to pass an exam to get their primary education certificate, which was required to enter a *collège* or *lycée*. Usually only the best students (chosen by the teacher) were allowed to take the exam, and only 10 percent of students passed it. Students who didn't earn the certificate either quit school or went to technical schools known as *primaire supérieur*. The proportion of primary-school graduates increased progressively until the mid-1970s when the government decided that university should be accessible to all. The *lycée* went from being a prestigious school to an institution for mass education. In 1985, the Minister of Education, Jean-Pierre Chevènement, launched an ambitious program to ensure that 80 percent of *lycée* students would graduate.

All pre-university education in France has three common features: national standards, uniformity of education, and authoritative teachers. National standards are enforced by the exams students must pass to earn *le Bac*, short for *Baccalauréat* (the end-of-*lycée* diploma). Napoleon created the *Bac* in 1808 to ensure that people entering university and training schools would meet a uniform standard. He didn't predict that schooling would spread the way it did. In 1889, five thousand students passed their *Bac*. By 1936, that number had jumped to fifteen thousand. That figure doubled by 1948, and again by 1963. In 1973, 150,000 students passed their *Bac*, and since the mid-1980s, that number has been around half a million per year. Traditionally there were three categories of *Baccalauréat* exams: science, letters, and commerce. In the 1960s, the government added categories for technology and economics, and because of the 1985 reforms, there are now nearly twenty types of *Bacs*.

The *Bac* is not just the certificate students get after twelve years of primary and secondary education. It is also the equivalent of an admissions test for the university. The French rarely refer to their university diplomas by their real name. They say they have a *Bac* plus the number of years attended. *Bac* + 3 means they have done three years of university. Education requirements for jobs use the same terminology, with postings calling for *Bac* + 2, +3, + 4, +5, etc.

Fifty years ago one could get a good job with a *Bac*. That's no longer true, but the *Bac* remains the universal reference point in the post-secondary education system. The *Bac* exams in June are always covered by the media, starting with talk shows that invite guests to discuss and comment on the questions for the philosophy exam. Students spend months studying for the exams, which are graded by committees of teachers (who never mark their own students, according to the same logic by which *préfets* are given postings away from home). Typically, students must go through six or seven exams for all mandatory disciplines and a couple optional ones, and the experience can be traumatic. In the Paris area, the exams are centralized so students often have to travel to other, unfamiliar cities. The German exam may be in Bagnolet, east of Paris, and the math exam in Neuilly, a western suburb. Results are then posted publicly.

France has some 950,000 teachers, a number that is not particularly high compared to the United States, which has four million teachers, and it is only a slightly higher than normal ratio among advanced democracies. But in France, those 950,000 teachers and professors belong to one single system called the French Ministry of Education.

The main objective of the Ministry is to dispense education uniformly throughout the French territory. There is no concept of local needs or particularities. Teachers are theoretically interchangeable from one region to another. They belong to twenty-five different *académies* (school boards) that manage the allocation of resources for a territory corresponding roughly to administrative Regions. *Académies* decide where teachers go, but teachers who want to move from one territory to another must apply to a national committee. That committee weighs all candidates through a complicated point system that takes into account years of experience, marital status, and whether or not a teacher has a family. The schools are run by *proviseurs* (school directors) who have no control over which teachers are placed in their school. A cohort of some eighteen hundred full-time inspectors makes sure everything works.

As with everything in the French administration, uniformity is one of the underlying principles of national education. The French believe fervently in the virtues of uniformity in education, because it fosters cultural uniformity across the territory. When we explained how the American and Canadian education systems work, our French friends could not fathom why a country would delegate authority over education to lower jurisdictions. But uniformity in education is a bit of a myth. There actually are huge discrepancies in quality and resources between France's regions. Some *académies* lack schools or even teachers. Poor towns and violent suburbs generally get stuck with teachers who have little experience and are ready to leave as soon as they can. And cities typically attract better teachers than rural areas do. About 20 percent of the twelve million pre-university students attend private schools, but four private schools out of five are actually subsidized by the State and follow the national syllabus, which is controlled closely by the State. That means that only 5 percent of students go to purely private schools.

The existence of the private system has always been a very controversial issue in France. State education is militantly *laïque* (non-religious, and, frankly, anti-religious) to the point of banning all traces of religion like crucifixes, prayers, and religious education. This has been the official policy since the early 1880s when Minister of Education Jules Ferry (1832–93) nationalized the school system. At the time, schools were managed by local communities and the clergy, neither of which exhibited much enthusiasm for the Republic. The clergy agreed to step out of education when the government gave students one day off a week for religious education (it was Thursday then, it is now Wednesday). As a concession, the government allowed private schools—often religious or community-oriented schools—to operate.

The third outstanding feature of French education is the authority of teachers. The French don't regard childhood as an age of innocence, but see it as an age of ignorance. Children must be set straight and corrected. French parents are, on the whole, quite authoritarian about child rearing, and they teach their children to respect rules from a young age. Parents' work isn't lost when kids go to school because the same authority is granted to teachers. French children generally exhibit good manners and speaking ability at a very young age.

At the invitation of a friend, Jean-Benoît visited a high school and was astonished to see students standing up to greet their teacher when she entered the classroom. Students dutifully followed as the teacher led them from class to class in rows. One student raised his hand to ask for permission to blow his nose. When Jean-Benoît remarked on this respect for authority, teachers sighed and told him: *Ce n'est plus ce que c'était* (Things aren't what they used to be). It seems to be a standard refrain in France these days.

For all their love of rules, the French aren't strong on pedagogy. Teachers get their certification by passing an exam and teaching experience is not a requirement of the training process. But of course the point of school in France is not to develop personalities. Teachers see their objective as the transmission of knowledge. Education is theoretical and formal. Pupils are expected to take a lot of notes and ask few questions. The only schools where students call their teachers by their first names are experimental ones. It is considered good practice to be as demanding as possible. Evaluation processes are strict and marking is almost tyrannical: typically, all exercises are marked on a scale of 20, and a 14 out of 20 is regarded as a good grade. For bad students, zero isn't bad enough: French teachers even give out a *zéro pointé* (a pointed zero).

How can the French stand this? The short answer is: they want it. The French tolerate authoritarian teaching because they are an authoritarian society. They want a uniform education because they want uniformity. But French parents also hope some day to hear the magic words from a teacher, "Your child has the right stuff for *l'École National d'Administration*." The

ÉNA is the most prestigious of the five hundred or so *grandes écoles* that train France's *élite*.

French parents don't want to send their children to university. We couldn't believe this until we understood just what the *grandes écoles* were. French parents do everything they can to make sure their child *won't* go to university, but will go to a *grande école*, even the least prestigious of them. The only university that still garners some sympathy among the *élite* is *La Sorbonne*.

Like law, medical, or graduate schools in the U.S., the *grandes écoles* are very selective. Candidates have to go through a severe written and oral examination process. French universities, meanwhile, don't even look at candidates' marks. Any student with a *Bac* can enter a university, no questions asked. The catch is that not everyone who enters a university finishes. Students are weeded out by year-end exams. Entering a university takes little effort and money, but the outcome is uncertain. Anyone with a *Bac* can begin studying medicine, but 90 percent don't make it through the second-year exam.

Since 1985, university attendance has nearly doubled to 1.3 million students, and resources are strained. In comparison, only about 150,000 students enter the parallel *grandes écoles* system. The admissions policy for French universities was put in place before the government launched its campaign to get more students through the *Bac*. French universities have been put under enormous pressure because of the tide of potential students this policy created.

On the whole, French universities contributed very little to the advancement of society over the last five centuries. In the eighteenth century, the universities were producing armies of theologians and jurists, many of who had simply bought their diploma. During the eighteenth century, the French government realized that this situation would lead to ruin in France, so it started creating the *grandes écoles*. France was the biggest country of Western Europe at the time in both territory and population. To deal with the budding industrial revolution, France needed more *encadrement* (managerial staff) in public administration. The solution was to train *cadres* (managers). In 1747, the king created a school of civil engineering called *Ponts et Chaussées* (Bridges and Roads). In 1783, a mining school was created.

At the time of the Revolution, France's twenty-two universities remained hotbeds of feudalism, clericalism, and intellectual conservatism. In the 1790s, the government simply shut them down. But existing *grandes écoles*, royal though they were, remained open, a tribute to the quality of the education they provided. In fact, the revolutionaries created even more *grandes écoles*: the school of Public Works in 1793, as well as the *École Polytechnique*, which would expand the pool of military officers beyond the aristocracy. From that point on, gray matter replaced blue blood as a condition for being an officer. And in 1794, the *École Normale Supérieure* was created to train *élite* professors in letters, philosophy, and science. This *école* system continued to expand and diversify throughout the nineteenth century as chambers of commerce and industrialists created their own business and engineering schools.

In 1896, the French government reopened the universities, but the faculties (medicine, law, theology, and philosophy) kept their autonomy and conservatism remained the norm. After WWII the government saw that France would go nowhere with such bad universities. Universities needed more autonomy, a higher standing, and a higher intellectual stature. The student revolts of May 1968 have gone down in history as a story of students protesting against the establishment and President de Gaulle's semi-authoritarian government. This may be so, but they actually started out as student protests against the universities themselves, which were overcrowded, decrepit, and controlled by conservative faculties.

Six months after the student revolts of '68, the government launched a set of university reforms. Universities were granted administrative and pedagogical autonomy, meaning that they could manage their budgets and create the programs they wanted. French universities had actually never enjoyed these basic powers until then, and the changes were so drastic it took universities years to act on them. French universities didn't create their own engineering faculties until the 1980s. When they announced the introduction of 172 new programs in the summer of 2000, the public and press were taken aback. No one ever thought universities could have initiative.

French universities are still not fully autonomous, and progress is slow. University rectors are still appointed by the President of the Republic. There are very few provisions in French law for philanthropic foundations, so universities rely exclusively on subsidies and grants. There is no such thing as an alma mater. Only the *grandes écoles* have alumni associations that solicit donations. Libraries in French universities are notoriously bad; they close early, and students often don't have access to the books they need because the best collections are reserved for professors. Students pretty much have to consider their professors as their libraries. Lectures, which are authoritative, are meant to suffice; questions are not encouraged. Faculties remain very conservative and discourage students from pursuing unconventional paths of study. A student who earns the equivalent of an honors degree in political science can conceivably pursue a masters and a Ph.D. in history, but if they do that they will forfeit any hope of being regarded seriously in their field, or of being hired. Forget about fancy combinations like political science and public health or economics and social work.

Universities also do very little research and have few links with industry, although those connections have steadily increased since 1968. Most researchers in France either work at a *grande école* or the *Centre National de la Recherche Scientifique* (National Center for Scientific Research), which employs thousands of researchers in dozens of offices throughout the country. In France, researchers are paid to research in a research center, and professors are paid to profess. A friend of ours, a Canadian pediatrician, did her second fellowship in neonatal surgery at a French university. She decided to return to Canada when she found out that the French system would not allow her to do research *and* clinical work at the same time.

No matter how hard we looked, we never saw a sign in French universities of the cross-fertilization and hybridization that is common in American universities. French universities are getting better, but general opinion about them probably won't change for decades, and with good reason. Still, French universities do not produce morons. The system guarantees a high degree of excellence because it is designed to separate good students from bad ones and dispel the latter. By the time they reach the masters or doctorate level, university graduates have survived a *parcours du combattant* (obstacle course), and it shows. But of course, that doesn't make a dent in the dreams of French parents who want their children to attain the glory of attending a *grande écoles*.

Professor Thierry Leterre belongs to the group of friends we made outside of the hiking club. We met him at a round table on the topic of new technologies that was organized by the Canadian embassy. Leterre was starting the European business program of the *Institut d'Études Politiques* (Institute of Political Science, known as *Science Po*) in Paris. He was both typical and atypical of the *Science Po* group. Born in a working-class family, he got into the prestigious *École Normale Supérieure* at the age of nineteen, where he trained to be a professor and was paid to study political philosophy. When we left France, he was about to become a fully tenured professor and the vice-dean of the faculty of political sciences at a Paris university, this at the age of thirty-seven. Thierry and his wife, Marie-Line, who had graduated from two very good business schools, gave us by far the best insights on the workings of university-level studies in France.

There are now roughly five hundred *grandes écoles* that train students as engineers, chemists, professors, business administrators, judges, historians, agronomists, biologists, mathematicians, architects, artists, designers, fashion artists, cinematographers, musicians, journalists, and more. Only law and medicine are not taught at the *grandes écoles*.

The key word in the concept is *grande*. The explicit function of the *grandes écoles* is to create France's *élite* class. That is why no university degree can match the luster of a diploma from *Poly*, *l'École des Hautes Études Commerciales*, or *Normale Sup*. A diploma from these schools brings honor to graduates and their families and guarantees an influential management job either in the private or public sector. For France's real stars, a diploma from *Poly* or *Normale Sup* is not enough. The supreme prize is a diploma from *École Nationale d'Administration* (National School for Public Administration), the famed ÉNA. (The prestige and influence of ÉNA are the reasons we devoted the whole next chapter to the topic.)

By American standards, all the *grandes écoles* are rather *petites*. The biggest, *Science Po* of Paris, which trains public administrators and managers, has four thousand students, making it the size of a very small American university. The business schools are the largest, but the most prestigious among them, *l'École des Hautes Études Commerciales* (HEC) admits only four hundred students per year. The average *grande école* has around one hundred students. Some, especially business schools, are private and very costly by French standards, charging up to ten thousand dollars per year for tuition. Others are public and even pay their students to study—at ÉNA they pay up to two thousand dollars per month. Getting into one of the *grandes écoles* can be like having a super-fellowship with all the perks. Our friend Thierry Leterre, who entered *École Normale Supérieure* at nineteen, was paid one thousand dollars per month to study and was entitled to full social benefits as a civil servant from the day he started. The majority of all 230 engineering schools are under the administrative supervision of the Ministry of Education, but the ministries of Industry, Agriculture, and Defense, to name only a few, also have their own engineering schools. The famous *École Polytechnique*, for instance, is part of the Ministry of Defense. ÉNA is under the direct supervision of the prime minister's office. Business schools belong to chambers of commerce, but most have a diploma recognized by the Ministry of Education.

It is the *grandes écoles*, not the universities, which have ensured the standards of excellence of post-secondary education in France. Whatever the universities did wrong, the *grandes écoles* have done right: they have excellent libraries, strong links with academics of the highest standing, and a highly collegial relationship between students and professors that favors discussion. Most *grandes écoles* require applicants to know a second language. German was required for admission to Mining School starting in 1783 because, at the time, Germany set the standards in mining. The central school of engineers, founded in 1830, required students to know English because the industrial model of the time was Britain. Most of the best schools still test candidates for foreign language proficiency and require that students do field training or even a school term abroad.

Grandes écoles have produced the best minds of the nation in research, industry, and politics. Henri Becquerel (1852–1908), who won the Nobel Prize for physics with Pierre and Marie Curie in 1903, was a graduate of *Ponts et Chaussées*. The president of Nissan-Renault, Carlos Ghosn, is a graduate of Mining School. Jean-Marie Messier, former president of Vivendi-Universal, was from *Polytechnique*. So was André Citroën, who created the eponymous brand of automobiles popular in Europe. Three presidents of the Republic were also *Polytechniciens*—Sadi Carnot, Albert Lebrun, and Valéry Giscard d'Estaing. Louis Pasteur studied at *Normale Sup*, which has also produced ten Nobel Prize winners. Graduates from the Central School of Engineering include Gustave Eiffel and André Michelin, two names that need no introduction.

One thing all *écoles* have in common is the *concours* (a competitive examination for a limited number of places). Only one in ten candidates gets admitted to the best schools. The *concours* can last up to a week in total. (The next chapter gives more details on what these *concours* entail.)

Only the most brilliant minds can pass these *concours* without first attending one or two years of *classes préparatoires* (cramming classes) that prepare students for the very competitive entry exams. Students who attend *la prépa* must assimilate high doses of math, philosophy, history, or science— whatever subjects their school of choice requires. The *prépa* includes up to eight hours of classes per week, per subject. Most students take three or four courses simultaneously. Students are not trained in the scientific model of experimentation and proof: they're trained to be quick, precise, and to get it right. They have to learn to work efficiently and reason well.

Attending a *classe préparatoire* is a risk. It takes two, or sometime three years, can cost up to ten thousand dollars per year for private classes, and there is no diploma at the end. If students do not manage to get into a *grande école*, they have wasted two or three years of their lives. Fortunately, there are a lot of not-so-*grandes écoles* that accept not-so-great candidates, and students do not tend to pin their hopes on one school alone. The typical ÉNA candidate, for example, also prepares for the *concours* at Foreign Affairs, or at the *école* for hospital directors. ÉNA's entry examination has the reputation of being one of the hardest in France.

The French are quick to claim that their *concours* system is a pure meritocracy. They argue that it levels the playing field between different socioeconomic groups by rewarding talent and intelligence. But the reality is not that simple. There is no *concours* for getting into the quasi-mandatory *classes préparatoires*. These schools select students on the basis of their past marks, but also according to which *lycée* they attended or how they performed in their previous studies. Whether private or public, *prépa* schools are very selective about the students they admit because their reputation depends on the number of students they later place at the best *grandes écoles*. Placement statistics for these schools are well known. The *classes préparatoires* of some *lycées* in Paris, Versailles, and Lyon place 90 percent of their students. Parents are said to move to certain neighborhoods of Paris just to give their offspring a better chance of being admitted to the right schools. Kids who grew up in bad neighborhoods (the poor ones) are often weeded out at this stage. So there are limits to the system's claim to egalitarianism.

On the whole, the great benefactors of the system are Parisians and people living in the Paris area: that's where the best *grandes écoles* are, and where the biggest pool of students live. The famous *école* known as *Science Po* shows how strong Paris's stranglehold on the *grandes écoles* system is. There are six *Instituts d'Études Politiques* (Institute of Political Studies) in France. Only one is known as *Science Po*, the original school in Paris. All six follow about the same curriculum, but the students that make it into ÉNA are generally the ones who studied at the true-blue *Science Po* in Paris. You find the same ranking with *Normale Sup*: there are six in France, but only the Paris school attracts the Nobel Prize professors. The situation for engineering and business is exactly the same.

Why Paris? France is a very centralized country, where the capital is both the seat of the government and the country's intellectual and economic center, so the choice is easy. The best teachers and lecturers want to be where the action is. Parisians' attitude of superiority over people living in the "desert," as they call the rest of France, just amplifies the city's appeal. Who wants to preach and study in the desert? You have to be in Paris if you want to be somebody! If France were a federation of fifty states, and if Paris, like the capital of the United States, had been built on a swamp in the eighteenth century, there would be no Paris clique.

There is a much-repeated French proverb that "Paris is not France." But for the most part, it is.

chapter 14

The Enarchy

When Jean-Benoît first met him on a hike, our friend Gustave was extremely discreet whenever his professional life came up. Jean-Benoît learned from other hikers that Gustave was an an *énarque*, a pun combining the words ÉNA and monarch, which is used for all former students of ÉNA.

North Americans could be misled by the word "administration" in the school's name, *École Nationale d'Administration*. Although some graduates do go on to manage private companies, ÉNA does not produce MBAs. ÉNA's main task is training senior civil servants. ÉNA is certainly one of the most prestigious, but also one of the most secretive, of all French *grandes écoles*, to the point that few French people actually have a clear idea of exactly what ÉNA students do. Everyone knows what it means to study at ÉNA, though. Since the school was created in 1945 by a decree of President Charles de Gaulle, fifty-five hundred people have attended it, and 80 percent of graduates have gone on to occupy top functions in the French administration. Each year, the prime minister reserves top positions in each ministry for ÉNA's 110 graduates; they begin their careers where the best civil servants usually expect to end theirs. No school in France can match ÉNA's influence. About one-half of the ministers in any present cabinet, six of the last nine prime ministers, and two of the last three presidents were *énarques*. By talking to Gustave and interviewing other graduates, we managed to piece some information together.

Shortly after our arrival in France, one of the French TV networks broadcast the best report on the topic to date. The one-hour documentary, titled *Mirror of a Nation*, followed ÉNA students through one school year, beginning with the director's famous welcoming speech: "You are now entering the *élite*."

Local and foreign critics often accuse ÉNA of creating a mandarin class of technocrats that run the country from on high, never coming into contact with the day-to-day realities of the country. That may be true. But it is also a little absurd to criticize ÉNA for being elitist. The school was founded for the very purpose of creating an *élite*. Everyone who applies to ÉNA knows this, and their only wish is to become a member of that *élite*. Those who don't earn a place among the *énarques* will spend the rest of their lives trying to keep up with them.

It is incredibly difficult to get into ÉNA. It is the only school in France that requires candidates to have either two university degrees or one *grande école* degree before applying. Before the entry exams, candidates attend one year of special *classes préparatoires* called *prep-ÉNA*, managed by the *Institut d'Études Politiques de Paris*, the famous *Science Po*. Candidates fight for spots in one of three groups: fifty-five places are reserved for students under twenty-eight; forty-five places are for mature students under forty-seven who have five years of experience as civil servants; and ten places go to candidates under forty who have eight years of experience in politics or the private sector.

The *concours* is divided into two parts: written and oral. Candidates write five tests of five hours each on public law, economy, political thought, second-language proficiency, and the European Union (or social affairs). They are required to discuss issues like the "recent reforms of the qualified majority in the European Commission" or, "the place of the contract in administrative law." Then they have to read sixty pages of documents and produce a ministerial memorandum on an issue like "amendments to the language law of June 1994."

The written tests eliminate six out of seven ÉNA candidates. Those who pass become eligible for the real *concours*, the oral examinations, which will eliminate half the remaining candidates. The first part consists of three half-hour oral exams to test candidates' capacity to speak a second language and their general knowledge of public finance, foreign affairs, social affairs, and the European Union. That's the easy part. The fourth oral examination, dubbed *le Grand O* (Grand Oral), is worth as many points as the first three combined. For forty-five minutes, a five-person jury questions candidates on *anything,* with the explicit goal of destabilizing them. Even worse, *le Grand O* is public.

Jean-Benoît attended one *Grand O* where twelve people watched— mostly friends of the candidates about to be grilled and other about-to-be-grilled candidates. In the front of the room was a table where five judges sat. Between the judges and the crowd was a chair. The Big O began with an usher announcing the candidate's name: Monsieur Antoine Le Bout de Château-Thierry. Antoine (for short) was thirty-three, black-haired, and impeccably dressed. The second he sat down, the clock started: like all candidates, Antoine had forty-five minutes to impress the jury and keep his head above water. During those forty-five minutes, the jury bombarded him with sixty-five questions. Some were easy. The jury asked him why he waited so long to get to *ÉNA,* what services he wanted to work in, and what the last film he saw was. Other questions were clearly meant to desta-bilize him: should minimum wage be indexed to economic growth? How many people are on welfare? What do you think of piggyback transport for trucks on railways? What elements of your personality would help in a for-eign posting and what ones would be detrimental? They were exactly the types of questions any head of a minister's cabinet would have to face on a daily basis.

A couple of weeks later, on the second Thursday of December, Jean-Benoît returned to the *ÉNA,* this time to witness another ritual: the post-ing of the results on the billboards in the entrance at 5 P.M. sharp. He arrived late, but still in time to see the TV crew packing its gear after film-ing the event. During the fifteen minutes that Jean-Benoît stayed, four or five dozen people passed by to see the results. Some were candidates, but most were wives, children, friends, husbands, uncles, and parents of candi-dates. Most were talking on cell phones the whole time, transmitting the result to a candidate or the candidate's family. Like everyone around, Jean-Benoît checked the list for the one he knew—and Antoine Le Bout de Château-Thierry did indeed make the cut.

According to tradition, results are posted on the second Thursday of December at 5 P.M. because the director's welcoming speech is always on the second Friday of December at 9 A.M. Admitted candidates must be present for the welcoming speech the next morning at nine—it's mandatory—no matter how hung over the successful candidates are from celebrating the previous night. This struck us as one of the many insidious traps that Parisians lay to thwart the ambitions of outsiders. Candidates from remote towns like Marseilles, Dijon, Bordeaux, or Toulouse have to either stay overnight in Paris on the night of the results or find a way to get there fast to make it to the director's speech the next morning.

ÉNA's program lasts twenty-seven months, starting with two six-month *stages* (internships) in a Prefecture, an embassy or a French multinational corporation. The validity of ÉNA's training is a subject of continued debate among students and former students. But no one in the school's six-decade history has ever criticized the field training—including the eight graduates Jean-Benoît met for his article.

It's not surprising. The *stage* is a remarkable experience. *Préfets*, ambassadors, and even French CEOs are required to take ÉNA trainees under their wings. They bring them to all executive meetings and give them executive tasks like speech writing, working as liaisons, or carrying out studies. When we were in Guadeloupe, we met an ÉNA trainee at a party at our friend Gustave's home and later crossed paths with the young man at the old citadelle known as Fort Delgrès. He was researching sites in preparation for the visit of the Minister of Culture a couple of weeks later. Otherwise, most of his days were spent at the Prefecture—he even slept there—acting as Apprentice Deputy *Préfet*. His job was to decide whether calls should be directed to the *préfet* in person, his deputies, or some other service.

Students love the practical experience. It's exciting and exceptional by any standard of French education, which is very theoretical, even in most of the *grandes écoles*. Students who attend the *École Normale Supérieure*, France's school for *élite* professors, do not get actual teaching experience in front of a class during their four years of study. They are not even given a course on pedagogy. The only practical experience *Normale Sup* students gain is from giving private lessons, a traditional and lucrative sideline in a *concours*-obsessed society.

ÉNA's field training tradition was actually accidental, the product of circumstances in post-war France. Since roughly 1830, French ministries had been progressively moving toward selecting recruits through examinations, then training them in-house. As a result of the post–World War II purges of 1944–45, France desperately needed to replenish the higher ranks of its civil service. In 1945, ÉNA's first year of operation, the school didn't even have a building, let alone a curriculum. The only thing new students could really do was field training. Soon after, directors realized the wisdom of giving students contact with the real world after so many years in the education system *à bachoter* (cramming for exams). As Gustave told us, knowing the Constitution and the Civil Code won't help you handle a miners' strike.

After the field training come the classes. The courses cover administration of a *préfecture*, control of community affairs, and management of public affairs. In formal courses and through role-playing, students learn about economic analysis and decision-making. They are taught how to handle administrative issues, evaluate a budget, and assess diplomatic efforts. In teams of twelve, they produce a group report on weighty topics such as assessing France's energy policy, the minimum wage reform, or the unification of Germany. Everyone we met said this was by far the hardest exercise they had ever done. Each group has to come to a consensus on the approach and strategy, a process that requires compromise. That is a challenge: teamwork isn't taught in the French education system and first-class students with powerful egos typically have little experience with it. ÉNA students are not usually accustomed to compromise, but the group exercise is good for them, since most ÉNA graduates will spend their whole lives dealing with other brilliant, uncompromising prima donnas like themselves.

196 sixty million frenchmen can't be wrong

Students and graduates debate the program ceaselessly, but it is difficult to assess the validity of ÉNA's program primarily because there is no
such thing as ÉNA anywhere else in the world (and all the more so because
ÉNA students are trained to debate). To get a more objective opinion, we
asked two of the forty foreign students who attend ÉNA what they thought
about the program. They gave us entirely contradictory viewpoints.

Isabelle Roy, a Canadian diplomat who attended the school in
1995–97 as a mature student with professional experience, said: "ÉNA is
not a school of substance. I tell other Canadians who get there, 'don't
make the mistake of studying.' It's all about buzzwords, jargon, and language. If you can master that and use the proper buzzwords, you will do just
fine."

Her peer and friend, Hartmut Kramer of Germany, who now works for
a private consulting firm, was fresh out of a German university when he
entered ÉNA. He came out with the opposite view. "German university
education is very scientific, very theoretical. ÉNA's memorandum system
is fundamental: people are shown a problem and they have to find solutions and recommendations."

Roy and Kramer are among the two thousand foreigners who have
studied at ÉNA since the Franco-German rapprochement between de
Gaulle and Chancellor Konrad Adenauer in 1963. Each year, forty students from thirty countries are admitted to ÉNA and follow exactly the
same courses as the French students, but with a lighter *stage*. Canada and
Germany send the largest contingents, with four students each. On the
whole, foreigners represent 25 percent of each ÉNA class, which is exceptional; the average at other *grandes écoles* is well below 10 percent.

ÉNA wanted foreigners for several reasons. Foreigners bring fresh air
and new ideas. Their presence enhances networking in a changing world
(foreign governments who send students to ÉNA also get to train some of
their own to deal with the future technocrats of France). Adding foreign
students to the mix at ÉNA also reduces the danger of intellectual inbreeding in the French administration. The risk is great because most ÉNA students come from the same milieu and schools and most are Parisians, a
problem the French government has been conscious of since World War II.

ÉNA unfortunately doesn't go as far as it should to encourage diverse thinking. Foreigners do bring in new ideas and perspectives, but French students have virtually no incentive to listen to them. Foreign students are a separate class at ÉNA. They don't go through France's stringent entry-exam process to get in. The government of each country chooses its own representative, and ÉNA just screens out obviously bad choices. More importantly, foreigners can never hope to get into the French system, and the French students know this. No matter how well foreign students perform, the French civil service will never hire them. It is as though great American universities told foreign students they could never be professors in the United States. For French students at ÉNA, foreigners are not the competition.

ÉNA students are graded on everything they do during their twenty-seven months of study. Each course ends with a five-hour exam, during which students must read eighty pages of material on the topic of study and produce a four-page ministerial memorandum. At the end of the twenty-seven months, their grades are added and yield a numerical grade that will, in turn, determine much of what happens in the rest of their professional lives. This is the really peculiar feature of the *grandes écoles*. All countries have institutions that foster an *élite*: the United States has Harvard and MIT; Britain has Cambridge and Oxford. But France places its *élite* graduates in exact order, from top to bottom, according to their final grade. This rank is nothing like getting a Ph.D with honors, with praise of the jury, or with recommendation for publication.

That rank then translates into a pecking order for the pool of jobs the prime minister sets aside for ÉNA graduates each year. The *major* (the number one student) has first pick; the rest, in order of rank and number, take what's left. (A complete list of postings is given in Appendix 2.) It's that simple. Ranking is inherent to the French system. *Polytechnique*, the school of engineers, proceeds exactly the same way. In medicine, all students choose their specialty according to their rank, based on grades in the final examination. Graduates of the school of hospital directors pick locations according to rank. The U.S. Army uses this system for the graduates of West Point, but to our knowledge the only country that applies a rank-ing system to civilians is France. But then, as we saw, the French State is run like an army of civil servants.

ÉNA's strict numerical ranking system strikes foreigners as narrow, but it does have many advantages. It is one way to make sure accepted candi-dates do not just sit on their laurels after writing their *concours*. To receive a good posting at the end of the program, students have to perform. The choice-by-rank system also serves a broader purpose. It helps prevent the kind of thickly woven network of contacts, friends, political sympathizers, and family that governed the appointment of high civil servants in France from the Middle Ages to 1945. Before ÉNA existed, families, associations, and political parties monopolized ministerial services. The system of choice-by-ranking frees the administration from the influence of elected politicians. Ministries have no choice about which *énarque* they hire. The government is forced to cooperate with a corps of *préfets* and a *Conseil d'É-tat* that wasn't put there by friends.

The problem with the ranking system is the conformity and rigidity it perpetuates. The jobs themselves are not officially ranked, but everyone knows what the best ones are, starting from the *Cour des Comptes* (Revenue Court) and moving all the way down to agriculture and fishing—roughly the order of prerogative in official protocol. It's extremely difficult for stu-dents to deviate from the traditional order of choices. Customarily, the first fifteen graduates, known as *la botte* (the bunch), take the fifteen best jobs in the top three corps: those of magistrate at the *Conseil d'État*, the *Cour des Comptes*, and the Ministry of Finance, which will assure them high-profile duties and maximum visibility. If the *major* chooses the *Conseil d'État* (which he or she inevitably will), number two doesn't because it would give him or her an automatic second-place ranking there. Number two becomes number one in the next most prestigious corps.

The choosing ceremony is the most secretive rite of the ÉNA, but our friend Isabelle Roy was allowed to attend it as an observer, even though she was a foreigner. The students agreed to this after some debating. Those who were against letting her in argued that "the ceremony actually does not show people at their best." But Isabelle's friends argued that "she has already seen us go for two years, so what's the difference?" She was allowed in, and indeed, what she saw was not nice.

The ceremony, which takes place in ÉNA's *Grand Amphi* (amphitheater), is actually rehearsed up to eight times until all students are certain of their choices (because every time a candidate changes his or her choice, the selection of remaining jobs is altered). Students are called in the order of their ranking. They sit down beside the director, declare their choice, and sign the employment contract in front of their peers. When they make the right choice, the other graduates clap. If they don't make the next best choice, the other graduates boo them. And if students actually do not choose what has been rehearsed eight times, everyone yells.

This is the fundamental flaw of ÉNA. The school takes the most talented students in the country and gives them rigorous training in public administration, but the graduates then end up choosing a posting almost entirely on the basis of prestige, peer pressure, and a quarter of a grade point. Students can't heed their hearts, or follow a "calling" for a vocation. The pressure to conform is too great. If they don't choose what everyone agrees is the best posting, their peers publicly humiliate them. A top-ranking graduate who is inclined to work in the Ministry of Health probably won't, even if he wants to, because if he did so, his peers would consider him an underachiever. Meanwhile, the Ministry of Health will probably get a student who doesn't want to be there. A graduate with last-minute hesitations is yelled at mercilessly by others still waiting in line.

The other consequence of allocating jobs by rank is that the top jobs tend to go to those with the least professional experience. All ÉNA statistics support this: mature students rarely finish in *la botte*. The highest-ranking students are generally from the under-twenty-eight category. It's not surprising when circumstances are factored in. Younger students have spent their whole lives in school and still master the art of performing well on tests (it's practically all they've ever done). They are also less likely to be distracted by family obligations during their twenty-seven months of study. Mature students, who generally have family obligations and domestic matters distracting them, don't perform as well on formal tests. The

200 sixty million frenchmen can't be wrong

marking system also works against them by awarding more points for academic performance than for field work. Until 2001, field training took up
40 percent of schooling time, but only counted for 20 percent of the final
mark. In 2001, ÉNA raised field training to 30 percent of the overall grade,
which gives more of an advantage to mature candidates.

Thanks to ÉNA, it is common to see cocky twenty-three year-olds with
top jobs at the *Conseil d'État*. The promotion of inexperienced *énarques* is
one of the most controversial aspects of ÉNA, and probably the least studied. Most people agree there are pros and cons to it. A mature civil servant
of thirty-six or forty is better suited to sit as magistrate, ruling over cases of
corruption. Yet a Canadian consultant we met in Paris who frequently dealt
with young *énarques* swore that the French system worked well in the end.
"The system brings in fresh minds and gives them fantastic opportunities at
a young age," he said. "And the graduates get enough rope to hang themselves." In other words, fast-track candidates who succeed rise quickly and
stay in the system for a long time, but those who fail end up in the slow
track. History shows that age hasn't always been a prerequisite for administrative skill. Napoleon reformed French education, law, and the administration between the ages of thirty and forty, and his reforms have endured.

Decrying ÉNA as elitist is missing the point. Because of the way
French society evolved and the way it is structured, France needs an *élite*
just as an army needs officers—leaders who are not the rank and file (and
without its *élite*, France probably would be an army without officers).
People in all democracies accept the idea that army officers have higher
status than other soldiers do. In France, the same distinction is made
among civilians: some civilians are trained with the express goal of turning
them into leaders. The idea would certainly not pass muster in the United
States or Canada, yet it's not anti-democratic or undemocratic *per se*.
France's technocratic *élite* does not attain its status through blood relations
or by bribes. Even if the children of the middle and upper classes do have
an advantage, the *élite* still attains its status through hard work and personal merit, even if that merit is rather narrowly defined and boils down to
the ability to perform well on tests. Still, it's hard to knock the powerful

drive to excel in France's meritocracy. It has been the drive of French excellence for two hundred years.

Critics who accuse ÉNA of perpetuating a clique mentality and encouraging intellectual inbreeding are closer to the mark. ÉNA is a clique. Even though the school was created to break the clique mentality that ruled the selection of top civil servants prior to 1945, it only replaced one clique with another. ÉNA graduates are a caste who attain their status through hard work and merit, but they are a caste nonetheless. And the clique mentality is very real. ÉNA's active alumni association mainly serves the purpose of allowing *énarques* to keep in touch and help promote each other. Naturally, this means that people end up rising through the system for reasons that have nothing to do with personal merit.

Does the *énarque* clique breed incompetence, as many critics claim? Nobody knows and everyone wonders. The *Crédit Lyonnais* case is often used to demonstrate the failure of the *énarque* system. In the 1980s, the publicly owned bank lost tens of billions of dollars in bad business ventures. The bank's president was an *énarque*, as was the prime minister, the Minister of Finances, and even some of the auditors who investigated the case. But there are plenty of success stories: Thierry Desmarest, the president of Elf-Total-Fina, the fourth-largest petrol company in the world, is a graduate of ÉNA. In truth, anecdotal evidence illustrating the pros and the cons of the system can be found by the hundreds. But in all fairness, cliques can work well, too. In spite of all the doom-and-gloom predictions regularly published, France's post-WWII *élite* of civil servants and politicians has not yet taken France into a black hole as in the 1940s when the country collapsed totally in front of adversity.

North Americans are offended by the idea of people being promoted because of their diplomas or school marks alone. But of course, ÉNA was created to put an end to an even worse system of promotion: blood and class. Many top civil servants are still recruited from schools other than ÉNA. Only one-third of France's *préfets* are *énarques*. It is difficult to say how the other two-thirds got their jobs, but networks of friends, family, and associates still help people rise through the French bureaucracy. "Clearly, then, ÉNA's function has been to bring in some clarity in hiring and promotions," says Hartmut Kramer. "It is a way to break the old-boys' clubs."

It is true that a high proportion of France's ministers, prime ministers, and presidents since 1945 have been *énarques*. The clique mentality certainly contributes to this phenomenon. Even more influential is a simple rule in the French administration that allows French civil servants to take a leave of absence to run for a political offices while retaining their status as civil servants the whole time (even after their election to the post). Civil servants do not run much of a risk when they take a shot at a political career. The result: 41 percent of all French *députés* are civil servants on leave, and a quarter of those are *énarques*. It sounds like an unusually high proportion of *énarques*, but of course it's only normal for the top performers to get the top jobs. And 99 percent of *énarques* never become politicians.

The clique mentality is not exclusive to ÉNA either. Graduates of French business and engineering schools behave exactly the same way. Even though they are often the first ones to criticize the *énarques*, they use their alumni associations to co-opt their peers across the country the same way *énarques* do. Hartmut Kramer, who worked at the French branch of Arthur Andersen at the time we met, told us that quarrels between graduates of HEC and ESSEC (two prestigious business schools) are incessant. Graduates vote for their peers' proposals and against those of rival graduates. Contracts inevitably go to former classmates. The same pattern exists in engineering firms. Some *écoles* are known to monopolize the entire management of companies. Petrol company Elf was said to be ÉNA-controlled, while its French competitor Total was *Polytechnique*-controlled. When Elf made a takeover bid for Total, the entire alumni networks of both schools contributed to the public-relations war to win over shareholders and receive government support—Elf won. The same thing happened when the BNP bank made a bid for a double takeover of competitors Paribas and Société Générale.

In the last several years, directors of ÉNA have been wrestling with a trend that started in the mid-1990s and took everyone by surprise. Since then, the number of yearly ÉNA applicants has dropped from a high of about fifteen hundred to less than one thousand. Even more surprisingly, the number of *ÉNA* applicants who came through *Science Po* has dropped by half. *ÉNA* directors have wondered if candidates are being lured away by lucrative offers from large businesses. They have also wondered if the European Union isn't making government jobs less appealing by rendering the national governments less important. They have even asked whether students from outside of Paris might be tired of *Parisianisme* and are boycotting the capital. The other possibility is that the State is simply less important to the French than it used to be.

No one knows exactly what is changing in France, but the sharp drop in applicants to *ÉNA* is one sure sign that something is happening. *ÉNA* is trying to adapt before it is too late. The oral examinations have been modified to allow juries to evaluate candidates' personalities and goals, and field training now counts for more in students' final marks. Many business schools in the *grandes écoles* system face similar shortages and have moved beyond the *classes préparatoires* to recruit candidates from second-year universities. Engineering schools now have to compete with engineering faculties that universities created twenty years ago.

However, it would be a mistake to conclude that France's *élite* is disappearing. It's probably just, once again, taking a new form.

chapter 15

In the Name of the Law

Among the friends we made in Paris, at least a dozen lived on avenues with names commemorating significant people and events from World War II. These include Avenue Charles-de-Gaulle, Liberation, 6 Juin 1944 (D-Day), 18 Juin 1940 (date of de Gaulle's famous radio message to the Resistance), 24 Août 1944 (date Paris was liberated from the occupation), and so on. Or they lived on streets honoring heroes of the Resistance such as Jean Moulin and Colonel Fabien, or liberators like General Leclerc and General de Lattre de Tassigny.

The French do not name streets and avenues with numbers, like in America, partly because their cities are not built on grids, and partly because numbers are neutral while names confer the much sought-after quality of *grandeur*. Yet while the French have plenty of heroes to honor, oddly, the one figure who is strangely omitted from this custom is Napoleon. There are streets in France named after some of Napoleon's famous battles, like Austerlitz and Marengo. But the gigantic, golden dome of the Invalids, where he is buried inside a sarcophagus of six Russian-doll-like tombs, is still known as Les Invalides, not as Napoleon's tomb.

It is strange the French downplay him so much. Granted, Napoleon hardly embodied the values of modern France—he was a despot. But on the other hand, he was the maker of modern France.

Although he was barely French, Napoleon Bonaparte turned out to be one of France's most important state-builders. Napoleon was born in 1769 to a family of lesser nobles on the island of Corsica just a year after the French government purchased it from Genoa. He flirted with Corsican separatism at the onset of the French Revolution, but his sympathies quickly veered toward the centralizing Jacobins. He settled in Paris in 1791, but did not gallicize his name as "Bonaparte" until 1796. Yet, by 1795, at the age of twenty-five, he had become a living legend among French generals. By 1799 he had propelled himself to the position of First Consul. And in 1804 at thirty-five years of age, he crowned himself Emperor of France.

Napoleon was obviously no democrat, but he was a brilliant statesman. After the Revolution, he was able to look at his exhausted country with the eyes of an outsider. He was young, not completely French, and had played only a peripheral role in the Revolution. All these factors helped him realize his ambitions. He took the best of the Old Régime and the best of the Revolution and merged them. First, he made peace with neighboring countries and the Church and gave amnesty to exiled aristocrats. Then he embarked on an ambitious campaign of reforms, the result of which still forms the foundations of modern France. He installed an administrative tribunal and a *préfet* in each of France's *Départements*. He structured the administration like an army, establishing a hierarchy and fixed rules for promotion in the civil service. In education, he created the *lycées* and the *Baccalauréat*. He created the Bank of France and labor tribunals. And finally, he reformed the entire legal system to such an extent that even modern French citizens could be said to be living out his vision. During his exile on the island of St. Helen, Napoleon said: "My true glory is not to have won forty battles; the defeat of Waterloo will erase this. But what can't be erased, what will be remembered forever, is my Civil Code."

Le Code Civil (as the French call their system of private law) is only the most famous of Napoleon's legal and judiciary reforms. He also performed a complete overhaul of French criminal law, established the working rules of tribunals, and created a third, unprecedented body of law: administrative law. This law, invented to deal exclusively with the relations between citizens and the administration, would become central in the lives of the

French for at least the three centuries to come. It would also make it hard for the French to see the importance of separating the judicial from the executive powers of government—or judges from politicians—a problem that remains with them even today.

Most foreigners know the *Code Civil* as the Napoleonic Code, a name that came into use several years after the Code was created. Prior to the Revolution, as Voltaire said famously, a Frenchman traveling across the country changed legal systems more often than horses. The kings of France had made several attempts to create a unified legal system out of the mix of Canon law, local customs, Roman law (in the south), and Germanic law (in the North). The Revolutionaries wanted to rid France of this legal *collage*. In their modernizing spirit, they wanted to invent a unified system that worked on clear, logical principles. They tried four times and failed, but Napoleon made sure the job was completed.

The *Code Civil des Français*, as it was known, was finished in 1804, but it was only one part of a reform of the entire legal system that would create new, modern foundations for law. In the next six years, Napoleon's government produced four new legal codes: a code for commerce, civil procedures, criminal investigation, and a penal code. Most of these were based on previously existing codes, except the Civil Code, which was built from scratch. In legal terms, the word "code" refers to the systematic statement of a body of law that is supposed to include everything. Foreigners often associate the Civil Code with Roman law because both are codes, but Roman law is actually a set of rules and punishments recorded in chronological order as new types of crimes appeared with the evolution of society.

The makers of the Civil Code started from clearly stated universal principles that were divided into broad categories. The Civil Code sets the rules for contracts dealing with issues like family relations, inheritance, and acquisitions. Its creators discarded Old Regime concepts like primogeniture, hereditary, nobility, and class privileges.

The Code established the family as the fundamental unit of society and the father as the head of the family: women became subjects with approximately the same status as children. It stated the limits of property rights, how leases could be worded, the conditions for inheritance, and confirmed the right of all children to a share of their parents' estate (a law which is still in effect today).

The Civil Code is often compared to Common Law because both are systems of private law, however their doctrines are radically opposed. But because law is fundamental to the workings of society, it is rare to find a specialist of one system capable of comprehending the other system outside of Quebec; in Canada, common law prevails except in Quebec, where the legal system follows the French model. Fortunately for us, we did meet a couple of Quebec lawyers who had come to work in Paris: André Beaulieu, who worked as a technology consultant, and his wife, Francesca Trop, who was in charge of legal affairs for a film production company.

As frequent guests in their superb apartment near Parc de Monceau, we had plenty of opportunities to discuss the differences between the Civil Code and Common Law, among other things. It was Francesca who came up with the best analogy to illustrate these differences (passed on to her by a law professor): the difference between the two systems is like the difference between English and French gardens, she said. English gardens are intricate and bushy; French gardens are orderly and geometrical.

Common Law is based on customs, and as such, takes the form of long lists of cases and precedents. Judgments on past cases are what judges consider first. In the absence of precedents, the judge falls back on the law, and in the absence of law, the judge refers to moral principles. Judges would use a Common Law precedent that John Homeowner could not eat his neighbor's carrots to decide whether he could not eat their tomatoes, too. It is up to lawyers to prove or disprove that the tomato case can be judged according to the jurisprudence of the carrot case. The lawyers present their argument and the judge (or jury) decides.

The Civil Code approaches the question from the opposite direction. A Civil Code judge starts from stated principles and works out a verdict on any situation, in theory, by using deductive logic. In the case of a man eating his neighbor's tomatoes, the principle might state that nobody can appropriate what belongs to a neighbor without proper compensation, and that a person must pay damages if use was made without that consent. The issue is whether by eating the tomatoes the man committed that crime, not whether what applies to carrots also applies to tomatoes.

In many ways, the Civil Code created contemporary France as much as the State, language, or education did. It was common for farmers in the nineteenth century to have a copy of the Civil Code at home. A lot of people in France criticize the Civil Code for being "antiquated," but in fact, it is very modern. Its fundamental principles are individual freedom, freedom to enter into contracts, and the inviolability of property. The Revolution, with all its excesses, still managed to generate a system of law that is a model of prudent liberalism and enlightened conservatism. As a framework guiding private law, the Civil Code was universally accepted, and the justice system could administer the law with very little interference from changing political regimes.

The Civil Code's clarity and efficiency are the chief reasons French business thrived during the nineteenth century in spite of political instability. Its universal acceptance and the overall economic stability it ensured explain alone why France did not turn into a second-rank European country in spite of all the upheaval between 1789 and 1962. Most European countries and their former colonies adopted the Civil Code or, later, a variation on it. After the metric system, it is one of France's greatest exports.

A French judge of civil law is expected to arrive at a judgment using logic and the stated principles, with little consideration of precedents and jurisprudence. But this is only the theory. The Civil Code was meant to be a starting point, not a fixed monument of law. It has evolved as society has evolved. For example, the original version included provisions only on damages inflicted by animals, but a century later, it was adapted to include damages caused by automobiles. Some subjects had been entirely omitted in the original version, like real-estate mortgages. Labor unions did not even exist when the Code was written. Napoleon's prejudices about women (heavily influenced by his own marital problems, no doubt) were transformed into extremely sexist laws just at the time in history when women were beginning to be regarded as human beings with equal rights. Facing these new realities, judges had to innovate, and they did so by checking precedents and developing jurisprudence. But the Civil Code did not turn into lists of jurisprudence; legislators periodically reworked it, updating rules, developing new principles, and rewriting entire chapters when necessary.

Despite the rewrites, the Civil Code still turned into a maze of laws and precedents as Byzantine as the Common Law. When we were looking for an apartment in Paris, we discovered that there are three separate laws governing apartment leases in France. Most apartments (including ours) are ruled by the law of July 6, 1989, which specifies both the obligations and privileges of tenants and landlords, like signing a standardized lease, an obligation for landlords, a privilege for tenants. However, we learned that some 8 percent of apartments in France are still covered by the law of 1948, which was created to curb inflation—meaning some tenants in these buildings still pay 1948 rents! Most foreigners are not aware of these complications because they often rent furnished apartments, a third category of dwellings that is excluded from the two other laws. Leases in furnished apartments are still guided by Civil Code rules on leases, which allow verbal contracts!

In all this mess, two elements of the original spirit of the Napoleonic Code prevail: the drive to update principles and define a clear starting point. Unlike Common Law, the Civil Code is not a collage of obscure writs from 1329 and rulings from 1627.

During our first six weeks in France, we stayed in the apartment of a friend who is a lawyer in civil law. Her spouse had just finished serving a sentence for a drug-related crime. It was an oddly matched couple, much like French civil and criminal law.

French criminal law, known as *le Code Pénal*, is just as "modern" as the Civil Code. What makes the Code distinct is not so much its structure as the way it determines guilt or innocence. The French system of criminal law is often characterized as inquisitorial, as opposed to accusatory. In accusatory systems, such as those in the United States, Britain, and Canada, the judge is an arbitrator between the prosecution and the defense—the two parties that lead the trial. The judge's function is to ensure that rules are followed as the prosecution and the defense make their arguments. In an inquisitorial system, such as the French system, the judge does not just arbitrate; he or she actively participates in the search for the truth even to the point of questioning witnesses or the accused.

The difference struck us as we were watching *La Vérité (The Truth)*, a 1960 film about a murder trial featuring Brigitte Bardot in the most dramatic role she ever played. Bardot plays a provincial girl who comes to Paris, adopts the Bohemian lifestyle, and ends up murdering her lover. The events are relayed through flashbacks Bardot recalls while she is on trial for the murder. For two viewers acquainted with the accusatory tradition of law, the trial scenes are nearly incomprehensible. The judge bullies and yells at Bardot as much as the prosecutor does. At first we thought this was just dramatic embellishment (there probably was a bit of that), but actually, the judge was just playing the role the *Code Pénal* assigns to him.

This difference in tradition shed some light on another feature of French criminal law that puzzled us at first: the *juge d'instruction* (investigative magistrate). Public prosecutors usually give the mandate to investigate crimes to the police. But in the case of serious crimes or murders, if the circumstances or the nature of the offense are not clear, or if suspects can't be found, the prosecutor gives powers of investigation to a *juge d'instruction*. This magistrate is an ordinary judge who has been delegated, temporarily or permanently, to investigate a crime. A successful *instruction* establishes the facts and determines whether a crime was committed, and who should be accused. One merit of the system is that victims can appeal directly to a *juge d'instruction* (if say, a case being investigated by the police is closed) to convince a judge to investigate a case for them. *Juges d'instruction* can investigate cases on their own without being formally assigned to them, often against the desire of the police or the public prosecutor. The logic of the system is, after all, the search for truth, not simply justice.

Because they enjoy such extraordinary powers, the *juges d'instruction* are among the most controversial figures in the French judiciary system. When they are investigating a case, they are free to decide whom they want to question and where they want to do their research. They can even take advice or leads from suspects themselves. The *juge d'instruction* can demand that the police bring them witnesses or suspects to testify and force them to testify against their will. Primary suspects can be detained without trials for six months (since 1984, lawyers of suspects can contest their client's detention). At the closing of the investigation, the *juge d'instruction* decides if the case should be referred to the public prosecutor.

In theory, the work of the *juge d'instruction* is confidential and the testimonies brought forward are secret until the trial is over. However, in cases involving politicians, information about judges' investigations often leaks out via unidentified sources (in other words, the judges let it leak). Most of the spectacular corruption scandals of the 1990s never actually reached trial. The news was about the investigations being carried out by a *juge d'instruction*. Judges leak information either for self-promotion or for protection, when the careers of important political figures are at stake. (The particular brand of disrespect for the law that the French exhibit is the topic of the next chapter.)

There is one last feature that closes the circle of France's inquisitorial justice system: the importance placed on confessions. Presumption of innocence is, of course, the core of all modern criminal law. In 1791, the French Constitution clearly stated that crime suspects are considered innocent until proven guilty. In practice, however, the French are far more ambiguous about this principle than Anglo-Americans are, partly because it conflicts with their tradition of considering a confession to be a central element of proof. To obtain confessions, police in France can place suspects in custody without filing charges and without giving them a lawyer for up to twenty-four hours (renewable at the prosecutor's discretion). The drive to obtain confessions leads police to commit all sorts of abuses, including torture in some cases. In 2001, the government tried to limit these abuses by introducing a regulation that would allow suspects to contact a lawyer in the first hour of detention, but police and judges protested it. The regulation has never been applied systematically. Because of their high regard for confession as the proof of guilt, judges are known during trials to commonly harass suspects into confessing crimes—hence the judge pushing Brigitte Bardot around in the film.

Civil law and criminal law make the two basic legal bodies of most countries, but the French created a third one: administrative law. This by-product of the Revolution is certainly the most distinct feature of the French judicial landscape.

Jean-Benoît first heard of the existence of this body of law during a hike along the cliffs of the Seine river, from the mouth of our friend Daniel Roux, who worked at city hall. The topic was very much on Daniel's mind because he was applying to a special ten-month training program at ÉNA. And in order to pass the *concours* securing his admission to the program, he had to plough through the great jurisprudence of administrative law. Daniel did not pass the *concours*, and the great jurisprudence of administrative law quickly left his memory—but not ours.

There is nothing like French administrative law. The French were the first to create an entire parallel system for matters of the State, including specialized judges, administrative tribunals, administrative courts of appeal, and even a specialized supreme court called the *Conseil d'État* (Council of State). Common Law countries like Canada, the United States, and Britain reject the idea that civil servants should enjoy any special privileges: they assume that the same law and the same tribunals should apply to everyone. The French view is exactly the opposite. Because the State carries the responsibility of seeing the general interest prevail, civil servants must enjoy privileges, prerogatives, and authority that are different than those of normal citizens. Administrative law is analogous to martial law, a special body of law for the army that is justified partly by the army's exceptional responsibilities. Administrative law applies to the relationship between France's army of *fonctionnaires* and normal citizens.

The variety of cases that are tried in front of administrative tribunals is staggering. Administrative law covers the whole spectrum of decisions that can be made by any bureaucrat in the gigantic army of civilians managing the French administration. Was a *préfet* in the right when he ordered the expulsion of an immigrant? Did the deputy *préfet* misuse his power in sending someone to the psychiatric ward? Can a violent police arrest be regarded as abusive if the altercation took place during a riot? Did the State have the right to terminate the contract of a supplier? Can the State prevent the sale of a work of art regarded as part of the national heritage? Can people control what information is held on them? Is a regulation on air transport voted by the Cabinet respectful of the residents in the vicinity? Administrative tribunals can decide whether a contract between the government and an individual or a private company is legal, and if not, whether the State will pay reparations. The tribunals can even force the government to repeal regulations.

Administrative law began to be applied in 1799, when the Revolutionary regime mutated into a form of enlightened despotism run by Napoleon. Napoleon created the *Conseil d'État* (Council of State) six weeks after he became First Consul. The Council had two functions: write the bills on the First Consul's (Napoleon's) behalf and advise him on litigation between the administration and private citizens or companies stemming from unfair contracts and regulations. In 1800, Napoleon created a *conseil de préfecture* (prefectoral council) in each *Département* to act as a sort of administrative tribunal, and as a check against the influence of the *préfet*. By 1872, the *Conseil d'État* had reached the status of a full court ruling over matters of the administration and functioning as an appeal court for the administrative tribunals. The same year, the government created *le tribunal des conflits* (jurisdictional court) with the mandate of deciding whether cases fell under the jurisdiction of administrative, criminal, or civil law.

In 1926, the government reduced the number of *conseils de préfectures* from ninety-nine to thirty-five, and in 1953 it gave them full status as courts. In 1987, administrative courts of appeal were added. And in 1990, the government put the entire structure of administrative tribunals and courts of appeal under the direct management of the *Conseil d'État*.

Thanks to these administrative tribunals, France did not become a dictatorship of technocrats. Administrative law is one of the strongest bulwarks the French have against the authoritarian tendencies of the French administration. Administrative tribunals, which often rule against government and the State, continue to be an efficient check to the power of *préfets*.

In 1999, thirty-five administrative tribunals settled 117,000 cases; the courts of appeal settled sixteen thousand cases and the *Conseil d'État* made pronouncements in eleven thousand cases. Statistics do not show the proportion of decisions that favored either the government versus citizens, but the sheer number of cases brought forward by the citizens attests to the faith the French have in this institution. The people working at the *Conseil d'État* are not magistrates, but civil servants judging their peers. Although the State is both judge and judged, administrative law works because the lawmakers who created it were fundamentally liberal and the administration accepts this system of voluntary limitations on its powers, albeit begrudgingly at times.

Contrary to the civil and criminal law systems, which have been codified, France's administrative law is based on precedents, not on stated principles. Magistrates have progressively worked out jurisprudence case by case over the two centuries it has existed. During that time the *Conseil d'État* has come up with original ideas on how to address grievances while preserving the prerogatives of the State and ensuring that civil servants perform their duty to make decisions as a function of the general interest. One such method is never having civil servants declared "guilty" by administrative tribunals. Civil servants are declared to have committed a *faute de service* (act of administrative negligence). Administrative law went as far as creating the notion of *responsabilité sans faute* (responsibility without fault). This keeps the language out of the register of crime, but doesn't lighten the severity of the recrimination.

The term *faute* (fault) is very grave in the French mind-set. "Worse than a crime, it's a blunder!" were the famous words of diplomat Charles de Talleyrand (1754–1838). This thinking is one reason the French are loath to admit being at fault over even the smallest mistakes, even in private. Politicians are even less willing to admit to being at fault.

The system of administrative law had to adapt to the rising complexity of the French administration throughout the twentieth century. After World War I, the government embarked on a campaign of new commercial ventures, including telecommunications, broadcasting, and nationalization of businesses like banking that brought the administration into a domain governed by civil law. As a result, certain government-owned businesses are excluded from administrative law, even though they are run by bureaucrats. But when the government created nonprofit organizations in 1945 to manage Social Security, it decided to include these spheres of activity in administrative law since nonprofit welfare organizations act in the general interest.

New competing bodies also added another layer of complexity. For instance, the *Conseil Constitutionnel*, created in 1958 with the mandate to rule over the constitutionality of the law, also deliberates on disputes between Parliament and the executive branch (which runs the administration). The *Médiateur de la République* (the Mediator of the Republic), created in 1973, has the job of finding ways to resolve conflicts between citizens and the administration outside of the courts. Two other bodies can also challenge the authority of the *Conseil d'État*: the administrative tribunals of the European Union's Court of Justice and the European Human Rights Court (both of which are structured on the French model, interestingly).

Justice, the administration, and politicians form an uneasy triangle in France. We understood this while we watched the strange controversy surrounding the resignation of Finance Minister Dominique Strauss-Kahn in late 1999. A *juge d'instruction* had summoned Strauss-Kahn to question him about a series of false invoices that he had allegedly produced before he entered the government. Two things made the case particularly uncommon. Compared to his peers, DSK (as he was commonly called) had demonstrated a really uncommon respect for the principle of accountability by resigning. Few *députés* and ministers facing the same situation in the past had ever resigned before the trial even began (some didn't even resign after they were found guilty of the charges). In 2001, DSK was released for lack of evidence. But the strangest thing was the almost unanimous indignation of French politicians and the press at the idea that a non-elected judge could "dictate the composition of the cabinet" or "set the political agenda" (i.e., make an elected official resign). We were stunned, coming from a system where the independence of judges and political accountability are considered sacred. But newspaper columnists and a host of other experts in France denounced DSK's resignation as the result of judges having too much freedom of action. They called it the *gouvernement des juges* (the government of the judges). Politicians were "losing their independence" in the face of these *petits* (upstart) *juges*, they said.

The explanation for the press's defiance is fairly straightforward. The French have never fully applied the theory of the separation of powers to their justice system, although, ironically, it was a Frenchman, Charles de Montesquieu (1689–1755), who came up with the idea in the first place. In his 1748 book, *L'Esprit des Lois*, Montesquieu argues that in order to protect citizens, a constitutional government must make a clear separation between the legislative powers (Parliament), the executive powers (the government, cabinet, and the administration), and the justice system. This principle is the foundation of most modern constitutions, though with considerable variations.

Americans were deeply influenced by Montesquieu's ideas and applied them quite literally. In the United States, the president (executive) runs the government but is not part of Congress (legislative). The French never really separated the three powers, partly because a series of despots, kings, emperors, and dictators made a strong imprint on the system, partly because Napoleon placed the administration (the extension of the executive power) at the center of the system. And contemporary French citizens still believe justice should be subordinated to elected representatives, not the other way around. In practice, it means that ministers have insisted that judges keep them up to date on any cases that have political ramifications (like corruption trials) and have even instructed judges on how to rule. The upside of this subordination of justice is that non-elected officials like judges rarely rock society with rulings—the assumption being that the people, through their elected representatives, shape society, not judges.

Charles de Gaulle almost separated France's legislative and executive powers in the Fifth Republic. His Constitution clearly specifies that when *députés* become ministers they must resign their seats. But de Gaulle did not exactly erect the Wall of China between justice and government. He simply stated that justice was a distinct authority, like any other ministry (education, finance, and defense). Prime Minister Lionel Jospin was the first to make serious efforts to separate judiciary power from other government powers. When he came to power in 1997, he instructed his ministers not to interfere with the work of judges. The policy has been respected on the whole, but it will take several generations of governments before this policy becomes an engrained tradition, and before *députés*, ministers, and senators stop complaining that judges have too much power every time a *juge d'instruction* questions a politician. President Jacques Chirac, who was reelected in the spring of 2002, and who now controls the executive, does not share Jospin's scruples on this matter.

Meanwhile, the viewpoint among the French population is changing slowly, as we saw from the reaction to DSK's resignation. Ordinary French citizens seem to instinctively resent the "government of judges," not for distinct political reasons, but because they value politics so highly. In January 1999, the French president was even granted quasi-total judiciary impunity. It's easy to see why the French think this is desirable. Since the president stands as the ultimate magistrate in France, in the sense that he is the one who has the last word in all matters of the administration and the law, he must not be subject to pressures like threats of impeachment for his sexual conduct, for instance. The French also believe their president is justified in lying about certain things. (This follows from their understanding of *grandeur*, which assumes that the president is in power to run things, not to set an example.)

The process by which the president acquired this immunity was questionable, however. Around 1994, a *juge d'instruction* began investigating cases of embezzlement and corruption that allegedly took place at city hall while Jacques Chirac was mayor of Paris from 1977 to 1995. In 1997, Chirac, now president, asked the *Conseil Constitutionnel* whether the president had immunity from these charges. The *Conseil Constitutionnel* at the time was run by Roland Dumas, a former Foreign Affairs Minister of the socialist government. But Dumas was himself named in some other corruption cases. Dumas granted the president immunity—probably in the hopes that he would gain presidential protection for the charges against him in exchange. As the evidence mounted against Dumas, the pressure became so strong that Dumas took a leave in March 1999. He was later found guilty and sentenced to six months in jail (he resigned in February 2000). In January 2003, six months after Jacques Chirac was reelected with a solid majority, he was discharged by the court of appeal.

Old reflexes are hard to suppress. During the proceedings, Dumas made a veiled threat to the judges, saying that they would "hear from him" when the trial was over. In the United States or Canada, he would have been thrown in jail for contempt of court. In a country where politicians are known to interfere continually with justice, Dumas's threat only added some *piquant* (spice) to the trial.

However, Dumas's ruling regarding immunity was maintained. The National Assembly wanted the ruling not to apply on cases that applied before the presidency, but the *Conseil Constitutionnel* ruled that immunity applied on everything during the presidency (save High Treason, which is difficult to imagine a president doing)—but only during his presidency. That means that a former president becomes liable for acts committed outside of his presidency once he's out of power, but also that the president-monarch is immune for the duration of his presidency and only for that. It's a compromise *à la Française*.

Because French judges are subordinate to politicians, they cannot challenge the constitutionality of a law. In the French judiciary tradition, law-making and constitutional issues are the sole domain of elected officials. Judges are expected only to administer the law; neither they nor citizens can challenge a law's constitutionality. Under American or Canadian traditions, it is possible for a judge to rule a law or a judgment as unconstitutional and send it back to the legislature to be revised. An American or Canadian citizen who is dissatisfied with a law can challenge its constitutionality before the court. These cases often rise to the Supreme Court and if the Supreme Court proclaims the law or an article of the law to be unconstitutional, it becomes null. It's then up to the legislature to draft a new version (unless the government chooses to override the Supreme Court, which also happens).

In France, only the National Assembly, the president, the *Conseil Constitutionnel*, and the *Conseil d'État* can question a law, and this capacity is limited for each body except the National Assembly, whose law-making powers have no limits.

Means available to challenge laws in France exist, but they are complicated. After laws have been voted in by the National Assembly, they must be "proclaimed" by the president. The president has fifteen days to proclaim legislation. During this period he can order Parliament to debate and vote the law again or he can refer the law to the *Conseil Constitutionnel*, a body of nine non-elected members appointed in equal numbers by the President of the Republic, the Senate, and the National Assembly. The *Conseil Constitutionnel* is responsible for controlling election results, but it can also rule a law unconstitutional before its proclamation and application. Of the twenty-seven hundred decisions the *Conseil Constitutionnel* has rendered since 1958, four hundred were over the constitutionality of a law.

However, ordinary citizens can't use the *Conseil Constitutionnel* to challenge laws. Before 1974, only the president, the prime minister, the president of the Senate, and the president of the National Assembly had this privilege. Since then, the law has allowed *députés* or senators to do so if they have sixty signatures from their colleagues supporting their motion. In spite of the limitation on who can challenge a law, the system works. When changes to the language law in 1994 included restrictions of the use of foreign terms, the *Conseil Constitutionnel* ruled these provisions out on the basis that nothing should interfere with individual liberty. Needless to say, the kind of monopoly *députés* have on challenging laws is one reason elections are so important in France. *Députés* and senators are not only lawmakers. They have powers North Americans grant only to magistrates.

Ordinary citizens do have a back-door method at their disposal for challenging the constitutionality of laws. In a way, French laws all have a loophole—before a law can be applied, there must be a *décret d'application* (decree of implementation) by the government. Citizens can contest a decree in part or in its entirety by using administrative tribunals, claiming, for instance, that the application of a given law would "wrong" them. This system can put laws in limbo for many years. The law creating the metric system is a famous example. It was passed in 1799, but the decree of implementation was only made in 1840.

It seems like a circuitous way to exercise a democratic right, but the right is there, and the French use it. For all its faults, the French legal system seems to work. It gives the State a significant amount of power, but the French have their ways of checking this power.

chapter 16

Civil Society: Invisible Helping Hands

While we lived in France, the French economy was outperforming all the others in Europe. This had put the French in a state of dazed wonder. They spoke about their business sector as if they had just noticed it for the first time in history. Foreigners have long joked that French capitalism is an oxymoron, but the fact of the matter is that most French think so, too. Unlike in North America, business is not a subject of public fascination in France. The French don't glorify their business leaders or boast about the accomplishments of their business sector very often, either in public or in private.

Yet France's economic success didn't happen overnight. The country has always been known for dominating the wine, cuisine, and fashion industries. The French are also world players in aviation, the automobile industry, chemistry, pharmaceuticals, and water management.

Why doesn't anyone in France ever talk about business? One reason is that the State occupies such a large place in public discourse the French tend to forget there is anything else. Yet there is activity outside the State: the French call it *la société civile*, or civil society, an expression referring to private initiatives like businesses and associations. Civil society is also not openly affirmed. The French tend to consider these areas of life as part of the private sphere, and anything certifiably private in France is pretty much omitted from public discourse. In fact, France is like the alter ego of America, where private enterprise is so valued that few people have a clear appreciation of what the State does, let alone how much the State fosters the private sector.

Even if foreigners, whether travelers or observers, tend to confuse silence with non-existence, France doesn't lack either businesses or associations. People working for private enterprises, including business leaders, just tend to keep a relatively low profile. Business leaders are not public heroes in France. Journalists do not quote their opinions about anything besides business, not even the economy.

French business is also somewhat self-effacing by its very nature. Private businesses in France tend to be small. Of France's 2.4 million private enterprises, 2.25 million have less than ten employees. Not even two thousand have more than five hundred employees. France even has a special term for small- and medium-size businesses, la PME—an abbreviation of petite et moyenne entreprise.

Napoleon accused the British of being a nation of shopkeepers, but as Theodore Zeldin explains in A History of French Passions, France has always been the paradise of small business owners. Most of France's entrepreneurial energy in the nineteenth century, he writes, went into trade rather than industry. The result is that France's industrial sector today remains much less developed than its service sector. The impact of French innovations in trade are felt everywhere—like the development of the grands magasins (department stores), a French idea that inspired Americans in the 1800s. But the trade and service industries are inconspicuous—there is no "made in France" label on what is traded, and that invisibility helps push the economy even farther off the public stage.

Contrary to their reputation, French businesses are primarily entrepreneurial, not bureaucratic, in spirit. Relatively few follow the large corporate model—"corporate" being the Wall Street euphemism for private, financial bureaucracy. This is an old tendency. During the nineteenth century, while France was the kingdom of the cottage industry, small entrepreneurs and artisans were very individualistic and seldom pooled their resources. The French still value small businesses to the point of allowing special legislation to preserve them. A glance at the Fortune 500 listing shows U.S. businesses at the top, followed by some Dutch, British, and Japanese companies. The first French businesses are usually around the fiftieth mark. The same pattern appears in each sector: French business will be second, third, or fourth in their category, but rarely first. In pharmaceuticals, Novartis is third; in tires, Michelin is second. It's as if the French don't want to be number one.

One reason businesses stay small is that the French finance their companies privately rather than publicly; they only recently began turning *en masse* to the stock exchange. About 8 percent of French households hold stocks, compared to 40 percent in the United States and 75 percent in the Netherlands. The public prefers saving money at lower interest rates in more secure investments. French entrepreneurs prefer financing their ventures by borrowing rather than selling a chunk of their business to unknown people. They don't want to end up answering to people they don't know.

The Alps is one of the best-known mountain ranges in the world, but the towering Pyrenees that make the border of Spain and France are equally impressive. We visited them often, to explore caves, hike, or visit friends. The best view of them is in the city of Pau, southeast of Bordeaux—or more specifically, from the old castle of Henri IV, where you get an excellent view of the range's mountains and their typical conical shape. The last time we were there, we were guests of our old friend Marc Naige and stayed with his parents, who initiated us to a few local specialties. Pierre's father had just bought a sheep farm in one of the deep valleys of the area for his older son François. And he did not "officially" pay much, he told us.

We were a bit puzzled. Marc's father explained, "There is a price for the government, and there is the real price that is stated in the *contre-lettre*."

Literally, the *contre-lettre* means counter-letter. It is a private document between parties that states the real price of a transaction, usually higher than the declared one. Parties exchange the difference in private, in cash.

Strict government regulations have the effect of keeping business low-key in France, if not underground. A lot of economic activity in France takes place in secret and remains outside of what is accounted for in statistics. The French even have a name for this parallel economy; it's called *le système D*—D stands for *débrouille* (sort things out on your own). The impact of taxation in encouraging the black market is well-known, yet the government continues to pass regulations that push the French into *le système D*, like the law passed in 1999 limiting the working week to thirty-five hours. The law's intent was to force businesses to hire more workers, but most companies just turned to the *le système D* to find a way around the regulation. Everyone knows what's going on, but no one talks openly about it.

At least once a week, we walked from our home to the *Arc de Triomphe*, a good ninety-minute walk. About halfway there, at Gare Saint-Lazare, we would pass through a gathering of anywhere from fifty to 150 poor and homeless people, depending on the night, who had turned out to get a meal from the famous charity organization, *les Restos du Coeur* (restaurants of the heart). The charity was founded in the 1980s by the famous actor Michel Coluche, who wanted to take surplus food that big grocery chains were throwing out and give it to the poor instead.

Les Restos du Coeur is one of France's biggest successes in non-religious charities. In 2000, the organization's forty thousand volunteers distributed sixty million meals to six hundred thousand people. If such an organization existed in North America, people would be constantly solicited for money or time or food, and the organization would do all it could to be as visible as possible to keep a high profile and encourage donations. The *Restos du Coeur* is quite well-known by French standards. But if we had not known the significance of the small heart attached to the trucks that distributed food next to Saint-Lazare station, we would have walked by for two and a half years without knowing exactly what the gathering was all about.

Associative life is as discreet in France as the business sector. In a way, it's surprising that associations even exist in France. The State has always looked suspiciously at any kind of community life. In 1789, Revolutionaries believed that no intermediary body should exist between the State and the individual:

they forbade communes, universities, professional associations, and the clergy. There was a double purpose behind this: first, it broke the capacity of opponents to organize; and second, it made it complicated to contest the centralization of the regime since no intermediary body was allowed to exist and do anything noteworthy. As a good despot who did not like opposition, Napoleon believed in the same principle and pushed the measure farther: he decreed that all associations of more than twenty persons had to be approved by the *préfet,* who made sure that these approved associations were not subversive in any way. Throughout the nineteenth century, most associations were prohibited.

However, during the nineteenth century the State realized it could not do everything and began to see associations as a way to fill the gap. Progressively, the administration agreed to grant status to political clubs, unions (in 1884), and some charities. After the beginning of the Third Republic in 1871, associations remained theoretically subject to a *préfet's* approval, but the law was not systematically enforced. Associations had to get initial approval to exist and further approval to become legal entities and hold a bank account. It was hardly ideal, but it was progress.

The big breakthrough occurred in July 1901, when socialist president Pierre Waldeck-Rousseau (1846–1904) passed a law that allowed the creation of any kind of association and made registering them a mere formality. The main exception was made for religious orders. Originally, all Waldeck-Rousseau wanted to do was remove religious orders' rights to run schools, but members of the radical left wing of his party used the law to banish most religious orders altogether. They were not allowed to appear again in France until a decade later.

Many people in France are convinced that their country has the most active not-for-profit sector in the world. In spite of the reticence of the State, associations have indeed become an important element of French society. To our surprise, there turned out to be no less than nine hundred thousand associations and charities in France, with about sixty-five thousand new ones created every year. They employ 1.3 million people—about 5 percent of the workforce, compared to 10 percent in the United States—and rely on the voluntary work of another ten million people, for a total budget of forty billion dollars. Nearly half of them deal with health and social services and a quarter are active in education and research. The southwest city of Angoulême, which has forty-five thousand inhabitants, is a typical case. It has a network of two thousand associations, from a *pétanque* (a sort of French bowling) club to a theater club and numerous tourist information centers.

There are three kinds of associations in France: non-registered, registered, and *reconnue d'utilité publique* (state-approved). Nobody knows the number of non-registered associations. There probably are some, but they are no doubt just small, ad hoc entities that can't do much. Because they are not legally recognized, non-registered associations cannot open a bank account, sign a contract, or even sign a lease.

To get official status as "registered," associations have to fill out a form. The Minister of the Interior reserves the right to disallow, or dissolve, associations if they are deemed to be "for the pursuit of an illegal activity, are contrary to accepted standards of good behavior, or if they attack the integrity of the national territory or the republican principles of the government"—which means that associations that promote hatred or subversion can be simply forbidden. But otherwise, registering associations is a formality, and that status gives them the right to hire personnel, open a bank account, and own material and property. They can be structured any way they want and sell membership, goods, and services.

The 1901 law on associations is so liberal that many private companies were able to create associations as a means of getting government subsidies or giving themselves the aura of a public service. The fashion in the 1980s and 1990s was for companies to create nonprofit organizations that offered cleaning, laundering, and day-care services. These organizations collected generous subsidies to hire former welfare recipients as cheap labor. Legitimate private-sector operations that offer the same services have denounced these associations, but they are legitimate private associations, so nothing can be done to stop them.

The French administration also makes use of liberal laws for associations to remove some of its own activities from public scrutiny. In Angoulême, for instance, the city decided to create the Technical Center for Help to Associations to provide services to its network of community associations. The center could have been a municipal service, but city hall decided to create an association instead, mainly because the association structure gives them more flexibility if they ever need to close it. Comically, a lot of public-sector unions call these administration-made associations *les faux nez* (literally "false noses," but it sounds curiously like the English word "phony").

To be *reconnue d'utilité publique* (state-approved), an association must be registered, have existed for three years, and be approved by decree of the *Conseil d'État*. State-approved associations are the only ones that can collect donations or inherit money or property from an estate. To earn this privilege the association allows the government to control how they run their affairs. State-approved associations must have permission from the French administration for any decisions related to borrowing, purchasing, or selling property. The most famous of this type of association is the French Doctors, which is in fact two associations: *Médecins sans Frontières* (Doctors without Borders) and *Médecins du Monde* (Doctors of the World). These two organizations, famous for sending medical teams to conflicts and catastrophes all over the world, have always lived up to their reputation of being the first to arrive and the last to leave. They also share another feature that is very French: they are not neutral like the Red Cross. The French doctors are known for making inflammatory speeches about the conduct of local governments or rebel groups. The oldest of the two, *Médecins sans Frontières*, was created in 1971 by an idealistic doctor, Bernard Kouchner, who became Minister of Health in 1997 and the first UN administrator in Kosovo. These associations run on budgets of seventy-five and fifty million dollars, respectively. *Médecins sans Frontières* also receives an additional two hundred million dollars from foreign sources.

In a way, French associations deserve a lot of credit just for managing to exist—most importantly because the French are not very generous donors. In 2001, they gave two billion dollars to private associations, two-thirds of which came from companies (the rest from individuals). This is not much money for a country of sixty million; it amounts to thirty-three dollars per person per year. Only a quarter of households give at all. A total of 44 percent of associations' budgets come from subsidies—39 percent from their own generated income, 12 percent from membership, and a mere 5 percent from donations, compared to 13 percent in the United States.

Fiscally speaking, the French have no incentive to give. The tax-deduction system is simply too complicated and too restrictive to make donations worthwhile. Donations are only partly deductible, and figuring out whether to apply the 40 percent or the 60 percent rate is not a simple task. In addition, the French are not permitted to deduct more than 1.75 percent, or 6 percent of their total income, depending on which tax category they fall into.

France's social safety net also works against private charity. French social programs are generous, and the French pay a lot of taxes to maintain high-quality public services. They have no choice about being generous taxpayers, but the consequence is that they don't see the rationale of giving generously to private associations, particularly because nearly half of the funding for associations comes from government subsidies in the first place. The philosophy is contrary to that of Anglo-American societies, where, in theory at least, the State is expected to pick up the slack for whatever communities cannot achieve on their own. People in the United States give generously to private charity and community initiatives because they believe it's the right thing to do, but also because tax deductions offer incentives for giving. The French decided long ago that only the State would decide what the common interest was. Associations are there to pick up the slack, and not any way they want to, either.

Associative life in France has several peculiarities. The French State doesn't like letting much happen outside of its control, mostly because the State discourages self-interested charity of the kind that is typical in the American system, keeping foundations weak. Private foundations are the most underdeveloped segment of French community life. As a matter of fact, few French people even know what they are. Various sources put the number of private foundations in the United States somewhere between twelve thousand and thirty thousand; in France, the estimates vary from only five hundred to two thousand. The ratio is anywhere in between one in twenty-four or one in fifteen, but France scores low in either estimate.

France's most famous foundation is the Pasteur Institute, which mainly funds medical research. The biggest is *La Fondation de France,* created in 1969 to collect endowments and inheritances. Its total endowment is estimated to be around 350 million dollars, which is not much (because it is private, there are no exact statistics on the total endowment).

In France, the common good is considered the State's business, so the French government never encouraged the creation of foundations, and it has never made any kind of provision in the law for them. State authorities grant foundations status on a case-by-case basis and keep control over them by appointing delegates to their boards—either civil servants or former elected officials. Strict regulations on fund-raising keep foundations weak. Estates can be left to associations, but only foundations can inherit them if they have permission from the *Conseil d'État.* Companies can create their own limited foundations, but they must apply for authorization from the *préfet,* and they cannot ask for donations or receive endowments.

Joint foundations of the government and private enterprises are more common, the most famous being the *Fondation Nationale de Science Politiques,* which runs the *Science Po* school in Paris. However, as we were told by our friend Thierry Leterre, a professor there then, the school's alumni association does not try to raise a lot of cash through fund-raising campaigns because the government deducts these earning from the school's subsidy.

In addition to his hiking club, Jean-Benoît also joined the *Spéléo-Club de Paris,* a speleological society dedicated to cave exploration. Some twenty-five thousand French people are known to do some cave exploration in France, and with reason. France has thousands of caves; seventy-five thousand of them are classified, and new ones are discovered every year. It harbors the world's deepest cave, *la Mirolda,* which goes 1.1 miles down. The most famous is the Grotto of Chauvet, found in 1994 by a group of French cave explorers in the South of France. This cave, regularly featured in prestigious publications like the *National Geographic,* contains the oldest prehistorical paintings in the world, made an estimated thirty-two thousand years ago.

France's biggest speleological association, *la Fédération Française de Spéléologie* (French Federation of Cave Exploration), has ten thousand members and actually shoulders some of the State's responsibilities.

Because the State has trouble giving up control of civil society, it often ends up co-opting associations to the point that they are turned into adjuncts of the government and become quasi-institutions or mini-bureaucracies. This can go very far, to the point that some associations end up functioning like miniature French governments. Federations in France are not loose, decentralized galaxies of smaller associations that team up under a central umbrella organization: they are official bodies that answer to the State about the activities of a group.

Like many other sports federations in France, the French Federation of Cave Exploration has a say in government policies that affect its activities, even when it comes to police matters. It is financed in part by the Ministry of Youth and Sports, which gives it an annual subsidy of $250,000 (U.S.), about a quarter of the annual budget. More interestingly, the Ministry lends five civil servants to the Federation who act as managers and serve as liaisons with all levels of government. In exchange for this staff, the Federation performs a series of duties. It must provide an elected speleo-logical committee in seventy-eight of France's ninety-nine *Départements* and twenty-one of its twenty-six Regions to debate safety subsidies and exploration campaigns. And, more importantly, it is responsible for rescue missions. French speleologists are the only ones in the world legally responsible for their own rescue efforts. Since the early 1980s, each *préfet* has a technical advisor for speleological rescue. This advisor is consulted for all caving emergencies, which happen often in a country with seventy-five thousand caves available for recreational exploration.

Because it is responsible for safety, the *Fédération* even created its own *grande école*, the *École Française de Spéléologie* (French Speleological School), which trains beginners and advanced speleologists in rope techniques, rigging, anchoring, and rescuing, and in the scientific method and techniques for the incredibly specialized practice of cave diving. In addition to all of this, the school studies proper techniques and material and sets standards for the sport.

The farmers' union, *la FNSEA* (National Federation of Farming Companies and Farmers), is another example of a co-opted federation. It is a gigantic organization, representing six hundred thousand farming families who are members of thirty thousand local farming unions. The *FNSEA* enjoys incredible influence in the Ministry of Agriculture thanks to departmental chambers of commerce for farmers called the *chambres départementales d'agriculture*. These bodies have a direct say in France's agricultural policy, make rules about what activities can be carried out on local lands, manage programs, and even decide who will be eligible for government loans.

The role of federations is especially striking in the case of religion. France is the only European country that enforces a very strict separation between State and religion. Religions are not outlawed in France, but to have any dealings with the State, they need a national federation, which means they have to organize themselves like mirrors of the French State. Since the French Revolution, the government has spent a great deal of energy trying to erase the influence of the Catholic Church in France. A 1905 law separating Church and State stripped churches of their property and put them under the control of *associations culturelles* (local religious organizations outside the church). For all its dealings with the State, the Catholic Church has official representatives that mirror each level of the State structure. The bishopric level corresponds roughly to the *Département*. The highest level is the *Conférence des Évêques de France*. Protestant churches created a federation in 1904 in order to communicate with the government about issues that affect it such as laws, subsidies, and tax credits. The Jewish community has exactly the same structure, called a *consistoire central*, which serves the same function. Most other religious groups, though smaller, have similar structures, with the exception of Muslims.

The Muslim community long resisted the idea of creating a structure with a national representative that would act as a *vis-à-vis* to the State and speak with authority for all believers. This lack of representation is one of the reasons no one has a clear idea how many Muslims and mosques there are in France. Islam, Protestantism, and Judaism are not structured according to a clear hierarchy the way the Catholic Church is. However, French Jews and French Protestants, having been assimilated into French culture over many centuries, have always understood the necessity of structuring themselves and giving themselves representatives who could speak with authority on their behalf. The vast majority of Muslims, however, are not old-stock French. It has taken this community a long time to understand that it has to organize itself in a way that would allow the government to communicate with them. Most of France's great mosques are financed by foreign Muslim regimes, and only 4 percent of the Imams of each mosque are native French. Many of the other 96 percent of France's Muslims are immigrants, or even civil servants of a Muslim state.

In 1992, the Muslim community finally gave itself a council to represent all Muslim associations, but it split in 1995. Finally, in January 2000, the Minister of the Interior, Jean-Pierre Chevènement, convinced France's five main Muslim federations to sign a six-page text outlining how the administration and the Muslim faith in France should relate. The signatories affirmed their adhesion to the principles of the *République*, in particular the separation of State and religion. As a trade-off, their religious organizations are entitled to tax benefits. They agreed that mosques should be used for religious purposes and to support community life only, and foreign activism and matters related to foreign policy are strictly forbidden. The federations recognized that only national and local construction standards would apply for the building of mosques—and the government agreed that building permits could not be refused for other reasons.

The federations also agreed that religious leaders could be remunerated by their own religious association, but not by a foreign government, and that a majority of these ministers should be of French nationality. By all accounts, this agreement was a remarkable achievement. It solves many of the problems Muslims had with the government (and vice versa) and will probably go a long way toward easing relations between the French government and France's Muslim community. (There is more on the issue of integration in chapter 21.)

chapter 17

The Choreography of Protest

We did not have a car while we lived in Paris, but whenever we rented one, we checked the day's protest schedule in the Paris daily *Le Parisien*. The schedule, right next to the weather forecast, shows where roads are blocked on any given day because of protests, strikes, parades, or demonstrations. Like the rain, protests and demonstrations are regular features of daily life in France's capital. The forecasters make their predictions based on the protest permits the police hand out every day. With the exception of the odd wildcat protest, like the spontaneous May 1999 public-transport strike in Paris, the schedules are pretty reliable.

On the day of the May 1999 strike, we luckily hadn't planned to leave town. The wildcat strike had turned France's capital into a parking lot. Jean-Benoît learned about it first thing in the morning when he tried to enter the Guy Môquet Métro Station on his way to an interview. The doors to the station were locked. A note Scotch-taped to the window said the workers had gone on strike to protest "violence inflicted on them by the public." According to radio reports later that day, the strike was declared because a subway inspector had been killed fighting illegal vendors. By the middle of the afternoon, all the buses in Paris and the regional trains transporting commuters in and out of the capital had ceased operations in solidarity with the Métro workers, and Paris was paralyzed.

The real story—which came out the next morning—was somewhat different, though. A subway inspector had indeed died on the job, but the cause was a ruptured aneurysm of the aorta, not a violent passenger. The inspector was chasing an illegal vendor when he died. We expected a public outcry, followed by an apology from the union, but that is not what happened. The union did not call the strike off; it just changed its rationale and claimed that the striking was to protest understaffing and stressful working conditions. Transport employees stayed home for the next day and a half, and Paris remained paralyzed.

Although the strike was actually illegal, the union was never fined or punished for keeping Paris in limbo for so long. Even more surprisingly, Parisians didn't seem to care that the union had erred on day one. During the strike, they displayed the calm of Canadians in a snowstorm. There was irritation, but it rarely rose above the level of exasperated sighs. Most Parisians spent the day talking on their portable phones, commiserating with friends and relatives, looking for alternative routes to work, or just filling time. Parisians are invariably sympathetic toward their protesting or striking compatriots.

We thought that the tolerance was remarkable given how much the French strike—that is, until we realized that the French actually do not strike that much. In an average year, the French miss proportionately *fewer* working days from strikes than Americans do. According to labor statistics compiled by the Organization for Economic Cooperation and Development, France is one of the *least* unionized of all member countries. Only 9 percent of French workers belong to a union, compared to 14 percent in the United States, 24 percent in Japan, 29 percent in Germany, 33 percent in Great Britain, and 37 percent in Canada. In 1996, the French lost 448,000 days of work in strikes—four times more than the Germans, but three times less than the British, and *eleven times* less than Americans. The number of days lost per one thousand workers from 1990 to 1994 shows exactly the same pattern: Japan lost three, Germany twenty-three, France thirty, Britain thirty-seven, and the USA forty-three. On a per-capita basis, American labor strikes two and one-half times more than French labor.

What the French really excel at is protesting. Protests, marches, and demonstrations are an essential element of the French social fabric. Rich or poor, bourgeois or working class, the French have no inhibitions when it comes to taking their views to the street, grabbing a sign, chanting slogans, forming human chains around towns, or cracking fireworks in front of bored riot squads. Protest, to the French, is not a mere expression of frustration. It is an important rite of public life.

There are various factors that explain this phenomenon, but they can all be summed up in one idea. Paris's streets are not just for transport; they are a political forum. In a rigid, centralized state devoid of counterpowers, street protests are one of the few legitimate methods citizens can use to curb the system. They are part of the choreography of power.

Protesting is hardly a modern phenomenon in France. The huge moat on the east side of the Louvre Palace was not dug to protect the king from foreign armies marching on Paris, but to shield him from his own people. Since the Middle Ages, the Paris mobs have triggered countless political crises. That's the main reason the French government has never allowed Paris to have any powers. By doing this, the government adds one institutional barrier to any local attempt to take control of the police and turn them against the State.

Yet the fact that France has one government and one capital makes the work of protesters a lot easier. It means they can easily go for the jugular. All roads and railroads in France lead to Paris. A couple of well-placed trucks are sufficient to block the capital and paralyze all air and ground transport. That fact raises the stakes, so the French government has always been careful to keep some kind of fortress around Paris. All roads within a sixty-kilometer radius of the capital were built to carry tanks in case of an invasion or insurrection. In 1961, when France was again on the verge of civil war over the question of Algeria's independence, sixty tanks were brought in to guard the National Assembly.

Since Paris is the political, economic, and intellectual center of France, it's the obvious choice for almost any protest over any issue. The city guarantees immediate visibility. In federations like the United States or Canada, protest has less impact because power is diffused between one federal government and fifty states, ten provinces, or sixteen länder, and there are hundreds of lower jurisdictions that fraction dissent. Moreover, political and economic powers are rarely concentrated in the same cities in North America. For example, Quebec teachers who go on strike have to choose between Quebec, the capital, and Montreal, the province's largest city and economic power. Similarly, in Massachusetts education is municipal, so only small-scale protests make sense. Similarly, education in the United States is the jurisdiction of the different states or, often, of the towns or counties—which reduces the likelihood of a national teacher's strike to nil.

But in France, there is only one government. This means that when the teachers' union calls a strike, it can rally one million teachers and professors. Twelve million kids will have to stay home, and some twenty million parents will have to find day care on a day's notice or call in sick to take care of *les p'tits* (the young 'uns). Even local protests can turn the country upside down if they are well executed. In the fall of 1998, a student protest over classroom shortages in Toulouse spilled over to the entire system and provoked a gigantic march of one million students in Paris. From the strikers' perspective, this is good penetration in a country of sixty million inhabitants.

Despite Paris's drawing power, there are still a lot of protests everywhere else in France on any given day. But of course, the State is everywhere in the form of *préfectures*, and no matter what the issue, that's where protests tend to be held. We got our first taste of local protest on a trip to Marseilles, three months after we moved to France. When we took the boat to visit an off-shore castle, there were about five hundred people in front of the *préfecture*, on the port, protesting shortages of public housing. When we returned, there was a new crowd in their place. Five hundred bikers were protesting a law that would make driving fifty kilometers over the speed limit a criminal offense.

The *préfet* is a local fuse of the French government. Unions or associations file requests for permits to protest at the city hall of their *commune*. The applications are then transmitted to the *préfecture*. The *préfet* assesses the general climate in his or her *Département* and if it's deemed to be too explosive, forbids the strike. The French call this balance of social peace or unrest in a *Département* the "social climate." *Préfets* have their finger on the social climate day and night. Once a week they report on it to Paris, like a social weather forecast, usually by phone.

Assessing the social climate is not as easy as checking the protest forecast in *Le Parisien*. Local demonstrations can be provoked by events far away from a *Département*. This was the case for the famous French farmers who destroyed the McDonald's in Millau in July 1999. Several weeks before the incident, the World Trade Organization had allowed the U.S. government to impose a surtax on European luxury products in response to Europe's refusal to import American beef. One of the items the American government taxed was Roquefort cheese. The decision infuriated the farmers around Millau, whose sheep supply the milk for Roquefort—or more specifically, it infuriated a group of notoriously militant farmers in Larzac. The *préfet* had seriously misjudged the social climate when he authorized the farmers "symbolic dismantling"; news of the protest spread far beyond Paris.

In a way, *préfets* are asked to predict the unpredictable, because it is very hard to tell what local event will spill over nationally. Who indeed can evaluate the social climate of a whole country? No *préfet* or prime minister could have foreseen the extent of the support the farmers would garner. Bové's crusade against multinational corporations and against junk food was just the consummation of a series of food scares that had taken place in France and Europe that year—mad-cow disease, contamination of chicken with dioxine, and the closing of a Coke plant in Belgium because of alleged poisoning. It's no surprise that Bové's protest against new industrial techniques, like genetically modified organisms, attracted so much attention and got so much support from the media. By the time he was released, Bové had been turned into a national icon. When the farmer was tried for the McDonald's dismantling a year later, one hundred thousand supporters descended on Millau—sending Millau's social climate measure off the scale.

The case of Bové was extreme, but this is the kind of incident a *préfet* is supposed to avoid. It's the *préfet's* job to defuse crises and make sure they don't make waves in Paris. We observed the efforts this requires at close range, in Guadeloupe, where we were guests of our *énarque* friend Gustave.

Gustave had close dealings with the *préfet* and filled us in on the action behind the scenes of the island's social climate. Guadeloupe looks like a tropical paradise, but behind the beach houses the island is actually a social volcano. In 2000, the *préfecture* had to quell 150 strikes (in a population of four hundred thousand), and that was a quiet year. When we got there in May 2000, workers at the island's main port were on strike. For fifteen days, no goods had been shipped in or out. That's a big problem for an island that depends on imports the way Guadeloupe does; it has never been self-sufficient, not even in fish. Normally, labor problems are solved between unions and employers, sometimes with the help of arbitrators. In this case, the *préfet* judged that he couldn't tolerate a full-fledged food crisis on top of the strikes and disruptions that were already on his plate. He monitored the strike talks, and when the parties were ready for his input, he presented a package that was acceptable to everyone. There's nothing in the law that gives *préfets* this role, except the obligation to look out for the *intérêt général*. Preventing the island from starving clearly fell under this category.

Since there's only the one State in France, protesters almost always have a shot at the same target. But that doesn't necessarily make it easier for the State to suppress uprisings. The centralized organization of the State actually makes it easy for protesters to pull off quasi-insurrections.

We saw the balance tip in the winter of 2001 when truckers and taxi unions were protesting high fuel taxes. Their original strategy of just honking horns on the Champs Elysées didn't have much of an impact, so the truckers and taxi drivers decided to fabricate an oil crisis by blockading oil depots throughout the country. It almost worked, foiled only by the quick thinking of half a dozen *préfets* who managed to stave off blockades around a couple of France's main depots, including one near Paris. The rest of the protest went on for a week, and Paris got a bit thirsty for petrol. But the strike ended when some *préfets* managed to open up several more depots and the government made a few concessions on taxes.

Although the rate of unionization is relatively low in France, French unions have a great deal of clout. There are no laws making union membership mandatory in France, but unions are given a monopoly on labor negotiations. Whatever concessions the union of a particular labor group wins (or loses) in negotiations applies to all the workers they represent, whether they are unionized or not. In a way, this makes almost every working individual in France a *de facto* union member. However, because of labor laws, unions often deal not just with one company, but with the employees of an entire industry, which gives them more clout. That gives them more bargaining power because they can threaten to paralyze entire sectors of society.

Unions also get power from practicing *la cogestion* (joint management) with employers both in the private and the public sectors. For instance, the Federation of National Education, one of France's biggest unions, lends about 1,100 of its staff to the Ministry of Education. The union's managerial staff in the Ministry keeps the union well informed about what's going on in the milieu. It's a cozy situation and unions don't want it to change. Shortly after taking office in 1997, Education Minister Claude Allègre declared that "he was the Minister," suggesting that in joint management situations, he was going to keep the upper hand. The union created so much unrest that Allègre was kicked out of Jospin's cabinet in 2000.

When we visited Guadeloupe, we interviewed Gaby Clabier, the secretary general of the islands' main union, the *Union Générale des Travailleurs Guadeloupéens* (General Union of Guadeloupian Workers), which controls 90 percent of the labor in hotels and even has a hand in the management of some of them. The interview took place at his office, in one of the new sectors of Pointe-à-Pitre built in the former swamp, not far from the statue of Hugues, one of the leaders of the abolition struggle in 1802. The office had a typical union atmosphere: full of posters and notices in Creole, people floating in and out, and meetings taking place on corners of tables. We even saw a couple of the mandatory goons of union folklore coming and going. The secretary general was not a goon, but a bespectacled intellectual type. Among the many things he said in the hour we met, one summarized not only his *raison d'être*, but that of all French unions: "Our goal is to win power, not just money!"

Joint-management deals with ministries and power brokering by unions lead to ferocious competition between France's unions. That, in turn, sparks even more strikes and demonstrations. When we visited Larzac and spoke to the friends of José Bové about the symbolic dismantling of the McDonald's, we discovered that the backdrop of the whole story was a quarrel between two farmers' unions. José Bové's left-wing union, the *Confédération Paysanne* (the Peasant's Confederation) was using Bové's popularity to push their own agenda, promoting small-scale farming and protesting the European subsidies that promote large-scale farming and so-called Frankenfood (genetically modified organisms). To do that, the *Confédération Paysanne* had to beat out France's largest and most influential farmers' union, the *Fedération Nationale des Sociétés et Exploitants Agricoles* (National Federation of Farming Companies and Farmers). Much older and much bigger than the *Confederation Paysanne*, the right-wing *FNSEA* enjoys a particular hold on the policies (and subsidy programs) of the Ministry of Agriculture through the *chambres départementales d'agriculture* (departmental farming chambers), which have direct input into agricultural policy. The members of the *Confederation Paysanne* wanted to use Bové's public relations achievements to win more representation in the *chambres agricoles* in the winter of 2001— and they did, gaining 20 percent of the seats. That will translate directly into more clout for small farmers in France's agricultural policy.

Because money is considered vulgar in France, French unions have learned to make demands for money sound like statements of principle. The French public eats it up. Ministry of Finance workers never protest against the closing of a regional office: they organize a march in favor of more public services. In Guadeloupe, the *Union Générale des Travailleurs Guadeloupéens* is particularly adept at portraying demands for more pay and better working conditions as a part of the fight against colonialism. In December 2001, when French *gendarmes* staged an illegal protest to demand higher salaries and more personnel, they presented their cause as a struggle against so-called "insecurity" (a euphemism for violence). The government not only agreed to pay more, but the *gendarmes* were so successful that the issue of insecurity stuck in public opinion and became the main theme of the presidential elections four months later.

French unions are also maestros in the art of logistics. We saw the machinery at work when we followed a *Confédération Paysanne* protest in the fall of 1999 starring, once again, our friend José Bové. That morning, a group of two hundred *Confédération* sympathizers gathered outside of the Châtelet subway entrance in the middle of Paris. They had advertised the protest two weeks earlier, rather obscurely, as a "determinant action" against a French multinational, whose name was not disclosed. The *Confédération* did not have a permit from the *préfet*, who surely would have foiled their plan. The real objective, it turned out, was to occupy the company's head office. And to do that, the farmers had to outwit the police.

It was a remarkably smooth operation. We joined in. Only a few union leaders actually knew the company whose offices we were targeting, in order to prevent a leak to the *Les Renseignements Généraux* (General Intelligence—the national security branch of the police, whose mandate is to document the activities of potentially subversive groups like the *Confédération Paysanne*). That's why the peasants chose the Châtelet metro station as a meeting place: the station is a hub where subway cars converge from all directions. At H-hour, the two hundred protestors, including us, barreled into subway cars heading for *La Défense* in groups of fifty, with no idea where we were headed or who was really leading us. When we reached the end of the line, several farmers herded us out of the metro. But it was a foil. Just as we were about to exit the station they herded us back in, and we took another subway back to the *Arc de Triomphe* station. When we were on the way out the doors of the station, the farmers told us to "run."

Our target was one block from the station: the head office of telecom multinational Vivendi. By the time the two of us arrived, police cars were already howling nearby and riot police with shields and clubs were pouring out of buses parked on the curb in front of the building. We stepped aside (we weren't ready to follow the action to the point of losing our residency permits) and watched some of the latecomers wrestle with riot police, who were trying to block the entrances. Meanwhile, most of the protesters had made it into the building. Some were unrolling banners from the second floor window, where an enormous woman in a red track suit was singing *l'Internationale*, which was composed by two Frenchmen. It was a successful occupation, but no one walking by on the street seemed excited or even startled by the scores of riot police swarming around the building. It was just another day in Paris, just one more illegal protest. (The next chapter describes in more detail the function of unions in the French system.)

The mystique of the French Revolution fuels France's culture of protest. The myth of the Revolution has held an important place in the French psyche and in French folklore for two centuries now. Even the country's *élite* buy into the Revolutionary rhetoric. In modern France, employers' unions take their complaints to the street just as workers and employees do. Although all European capitals have a history of violent protest and food riots that produced grave political crises, the big difference between Paris-style food riots and London-style food riots is that the French upper classes often joined the mobs and took control of them. This was the case in France's most dramatic revolutions: the Fronde (1648–52), the French Revolution (1789), and the Commune of Paris (1871). In each case, mobs were protesting food shortages or stiff taxes and the *élite*, meaning nobles or the bourgeois, either exploited the movement for their own advantage, or just surfed on it.

The enduring power of the Revolutionary mystique is one reason protesters in France enjoy relative impunity. The French government is willing to close its eyes to a remarkable degree of violence and tolerate impressive destruction. French farmers (including the right-wingers) are famous for bombarding shopping malls with apples, or spraying pig shit on *préfectures*. Farmers get away with a lot because in a country that still idealizes its peasant roots, they enjoy a great deal of sympathy. The police almost never arrest farmers. Three months after our arrival, a group raided the office of the Minister of Environment and simply destroyed the premises. Although the suspects were known, no one was even arrested.

When we went to Larzac to meet friends and colleagues of José Bové, they still couldn't get over the fact that they were actually arrested for protesting. The farmers told us they had not done that much damage (although, as noted earlier, estimates situated the damage at $200,000). But the real reason they were surprised was that farmers aren't normally thrown in jail for protesting, even when they do destroy private property. Several of the farmers thought local conservative *notables* and the *FNSEA* (the right-wing farmers' union) were conspiring against them, which may have been true. The speculation was a bit coy on their part, though. It was the arrests, and Bové holding his shackled wrists up for the RV cameras, that turned their protest into a national news item.

Preserving the social climate is so important to the government that *préfets* often choose not to enforce judgments if they think doing so is likely to spark more protests. This is a common situation in disputes over leases in neighborhoods that are considered hot. Because the law is very favorable to tenants, it can take landlords up to two years to get an expulsion order for a tenant who doesn't pay the rent (expulsions are forbidden between October and April). In fact, policemen often advise landlords *not* to file a complaint and encourage them to find a way to expel tenants by other means. *Préfets* sometimes refuse to enforce expulsions for fear of sparking neighborhood revolts on grounds that such violence could "disturb the public order." (In which case, the landlord is entitled to compensation for the nonenforcement of a ruling.) Again, *préfets* make the call by assessing the social climate—the street is powerful in France.

The sympathy for protesting in France goes hand in hand with a general disrespect for the law. The basic French man or woman doesn't consider the law an absolute, but a set of general principles that can be ignored if circumstances justify it. Activities like driving fast, running a red light, driving a motorcycle the wrong way on a one-way street, or parking on the sidewalk are often thought to fall into this category. No one in France gets indignant about these small infractions. Entire ministries have been known to ignore the law when it suits them. The employees of some ministries, such as Foreign Affairs and National Defense, don't have the right to strike, or even to belong to a union. However, that didn't prevent the French *gendarmes* (part of the military) from staging a massive protest over shortages of personnel and resources in December 2001, in full public view. Their demands were met, so now there are even more *gendarmes* to try to force the French to obey the law.

Everyone takes their cue from the highest level. We were in France in March 2002, in the heat of the presidential campaign, when the campaign

244 sixty million frenchmen can't be wrong

debate got to the question of amnesty. For two days, the two main candidates presented their program on who would get amnesty if they were elected—both proposed to give a general amnesty on parking and speeding tickets, and to release a couple thousand convicts who were nearing the end of their sentence. This has been a great classic of the French presidency since de Gaulle, but Chirac had been the first in 1995 to make a distinction between convicts of small crimes and those of severe crimes, who would not receive any amnesty. Not a single paper, not a single reporter or columnist, asked how the two highest representatives of the law could actually encourage people to disobey the very law that is supposed to protect the common good in the first place. We expressed our surprise to our friend Daniel, and he replied that all French people have a repressed—or not so repressed—delinquent side.

French literature and popular culture are full of characters that mock the law and its representatives and ridicule the establishment. The most famous is Guignol, a cocky and cunning puppet created in 1808 by Laurent Mourguet, famous for taking on the *gendarmes* with a stick. Parents bring their kids to watch Guignol shows in parks throughout the country. Attendance has been declining steadily over the last fifty years, but they are still popular. The famous character of Scapin, in Molière's plays, is a servant who humiliates his boss and authority. Beaumarchais's Figaro does the same, as does Hugo's Gavroche, the street kid in *Les Misérables* who is famous for his sassy comebacks to adults and the police. One great standard of French vaudeville is to present cuckolds as the villains and adulterers, and sinners or home wreckers as the heroes. Not to forget Maurice Leblanc's Arsène Lapin, *gentleman cambrioleur* (burglar).

The French value almost any character that mocks established values or breaks the law. It might seem paradoxical that the French glorify the spirit of defiance while at the same time willingly submit themselves to an extremely centralized, authoritarian State run by a technocratic *élite*. Much of the puzzle can be understood through the lens of what is affirmed and what is not. In reality, most French are probably as law-abiding (or not) as most Americans. The difference is that they don't openly affirm the value of the law. Like money, they know it's necessary, they might even like it, but they don't publicly embrace it. Almost everyone we met boasted a little about flaunting the law, even if they didn't break it. Law exists and law is the authority, but no one champions it—unlike the State, which most French revere.

What goes around comes around. Open defiance of the law and disrespect towards its enforcers is what happens in an extremely centralized country where citizens enjoy little real political liberty. And the State puts up with it because such behavior is a recognized check in a heavily centralized democracy. People don't make the law in France. It comes from above, from very far away—from the political class and the Parisian *élite*. So people consider it an act of liberty to defy or break the law in full public view. It's the ultimate challenge to authority. And that's one reason people are so tolerant of strikes.

This attitude has not spelled disaster in modern France so far. In a way, the Republic just gets what it's asking for.

(chapter 18)

Redistributing Wealth

Each July the French press ritually publishes articles on *les exclus des vacances* (the holiday-excluded). These are low-wage earners who get their five weeks of statutory holidays, but can't afford to spend them on the beach or in a *maison de campagne* somewhere in *le pays*. Holidays aren't the only type of exclusion that gets press coverage in France. There are also *les exclus des HLM* (social-housing excluded), people who are not poor enough to qualify for a place in a public-housing project, but can't afford rent in the private market, either.

We read about the *exclus* every day in French newspapers, but it took us a while to understand who they were exactly. The term can refer to a person who has no home, no job, no bank account, and no social protection of any kind. Yet we also heard it used for people who couldn't afford to send their kids to summer camp. We wondered why the French called these people "excluded" and not just unemployed, poor, homeless, or disadvantaged, depending on the case.

History solved the riddle. Until the mid-1960s, a French man or woman could not cash in on social programs like health, retirement, unemployment, or family allowances unless he or she, or a close relative, had a job. This policy obviously barred, or "excluded," those in the utmost need of welfare: unemployed people who didn't have any family support. So those people came to be called *les exclus*. In 1964, one-third of the population was "excluded" from social coverage. By 1978, almost no one was. Since universal health coverage was introduced in 2000, experts estimate that only about 1 percent of French society have no health benefits—compared to 18 percent in the United States.

Considering its original definition, the term *exclus* is applied fairly leniently these days: it is now a label for groups that suffer almost any kind of social disadvantage and shows just how much importance the French place on the system. Social rights are as important to the French as individual liberties are to Americans. Poverty and disadvantage are considered a failing of the system, not of the individual.

The social safety net in France is so huge and complex that it is difficult to discuss as a single system. Some welfare responsibilities clearly fall under the State's jurisdiction, others don't, and some are managed jointly with the private sector through incredibly complex arrangements. France gives citizens coverage for retirement and unemployment, like American Social Security, but it also extends to family assistance (including child allowance, day care, maternity benefits) and health care. Each branch of the program has different degrees of universality and of independence with respect to the State. For instance, health coverage is managed jointly by both unions and employer unions under State guidance, but the State's role has been steadily increasing over the last two decades. In the whole gigantic system of social benefits, there are so many agencies of all types with so many acronyms like URSSAFF, UNEDIC, ASSEDIC, that even insiders have trouble remembering the differences.

For the purposes of this chapter, we'll refer to the whole welfare system as *Sécurité Sociale*.

Commentators are quick to accuse France's welfare system of being unwieldy and costly. They are not entirely wrong; the system is enormous and soaks up a huge proportion of France's gross domestic product—about 14 percent. Yet there are no obvious signs that France is crumbling under the weight of its Social Security net, and from most angles, the system looks well managed. Most of all, it serves the purpose the French want it to serve. It keeps people out of misery and ensures a reasonable degree of equality across the population. The real problem with the system is not the size, *per se*, but the way the State has divided up responsibilities between itself and France's employers. The system keeps unemployment rates high, but not because benefits are too generous. Employers simply foot too much of the bill, with the result that they don't hire any more employees than they absolutely need. In the face of such constraints, government attempts to encourage hiring with regulations like the thirty-five-hour working week end up being futile.

France's welfare system is often labeled "socialist," but in fact, the system is a hybrid between the German joint-management model and British universality. The credit for inventing social welfare goes to the German Otto von Bismarck (1815–98), chancellor of the First Reich. Bismarck was not a democrat: he was the chancellor of an autocratic regime, second only to the kaiser. He happened to be in power when the Industrial Revolution was creating strife throughout Europe. Workers were demanding more rights, staking their claim on the profits of capitalists who exploited them, and revolutionary sentiment was brewing. To stave off a socialist revolution, Bismarck created three insurance plans: one for sickness (1883), one for injuries (1884), and one for old-age pensions (1889). All the countries that followed in Germany's footsteps and created large-scale welfare plans acted for exactly the same reason.

The overall organization of the German joint-management welfare system has hardly changed since it was invented. Unions and employers manage basic welfare services jointly. In practice, that means that employers and employees foot the bill for the whole population's health expenses, as well as their unemployment insurance and retirement pensions, with little assistance from the State. There is no unity in the system, just a multitude of different insurance plans.

The British waited until the beginning of the twentieth century to develop a welfare system, and then built it piecemeal through private initiatives of various kinds. During World War II, they veered off on a radically different direction from the Germans, nationalizing all the existing welfare programs, including retirement pensions and health, family, and unemployment benefits. Funding came out of the overall budget of the State—in other words, from taxes. From the outset, the British government decided how resources were to be allocated throughout the system. Employers and unions have no official input in decision-making.

France actually had the first ever pension schemes: the *Invalides*, a hostel built by Louis XIV and his prime minister, Jean-Baptiste Colbert (1619–83), for disabled soldiers. A century and a half later, revolutionaries embraced social welfare as one of their fundamental principles, but their only concrete accomplishment was to grant some benefits to civil servants and soldiers. The Catholic Church took care of social welfare throughout the nineteenth century. In the 1890s, the French government started creating a welfare system, first by granting free medical assistance to the destitute, the old, and the infirm. But until World War II, their logic remained one of *laissez-faire* (the French invented the expression, after all). By 1945, France spent only 5 percent of their GDP on welfare of any kind. Most of the money still went to civil servants and soldiers.

In 1945, President Charles de Gaulle passed a decree creating *Sécurité Sociale*. De Gaulle favored the German style of joint-management social welfare, but wanted welfare programs to be part of a single, unified national system, like in Britain. In the end, he took the middle road. De Gaulle handed unions and employers the responsibility of creating a national system and instructed them to negotiate the terms of it on their own. However, many of the people running the existing plans for civil servants, merchants, and artisans refused to join in the national system. And the government, in those years of political instability, was never strong enough to force them to do so. In 1964, France's social welfare system was still far from universal. The only joint-management schemes working were for workers in commerce and industry. One-third of the French workforce still didn't have any social protection at all. So in 1967, de Gaulle forced workers and unions to sit down together and create a real national system for retirement, health, and family allowances that would apply to all workers in both the public and private sectors, even in small companies without unions. He made it universal by decreeing that the plans would extend not only to workers' spouses and children, but to parents and relatives up to the second degree, and even to anyone living under the same roof. This managed to cover about 98 percent of the population.

Aside from keeping people out of misery, social welfare brings France one other benefit: social cohesion, which is immeasurable, but vital, given the country's history. De Gaulle, like Bismarck, Roosevelt, and Churchill before him, created *Sécurité Sociale* primarily to ensure social peace. Throughout the 1930s, France had managed to fend off most of the worst effects of the Depression, but workers were poorly paid, and employers were unwilling to redistribute profits in the form of higher wages or more social protection. Ten years later, at the end of World War II, France was exhausted by five years of recession that saw the economy shrink by 80 percent. *Sécurité Sociale* played a vital political role in keeping French labor content during the post-war reconstruction effort because it contributed to raising the standard of living. And the French system ended up having another advantage. Because the rules for coverage are uniform throughout the country, labor is very mobile in France—unlike in Germany, where labor mobility has been hampered by a social welfare system that is extremely fragmented between unions and *länder*.

Sécurité Sociale is universal in principle and in spirit. All French citizens have access to family, retirement, health, and unemployment benefits, one way or another, regardless of their condition. But not everyone gets the same coverage.

Only the family branch of Social Security, which accounts for 10 percent of overall expenditures, can be said to have been truly universal from the start. Family programs apply not merely to people who have jobs, but to anyone with a family. All mothers are eligible for family allowances, and for pre-natal and post-natal care, regardless of their income or employment status. Other family allowances are tailored to income, like supplements for low-income earners, and back-to-school or housing supplements. Day care, summer camps, and even young-workers residences are government funded in France. As a result, a jobless, single mother at the age of twenty, having her first, second, or third child is entitled to aid that amounts, nowadays,

252 sixty million frenchmen can't be wrong

to one thousand dollars per month for three children—enough to keep her out of misery, but barely.

Unemployment insurance benefits are much more restrictive. Until 1988, a childless, unemployed male bachelor living on his own and looking for his first job wasn't entitled to any welfare at all. In 1988, the government created le RMI, revenu minimum d'insertion (minimum welfare), to cover anyone who wasn't entitled to unemployment assistance because they were first-time job seekers or had been unemployed for too long. Recipients had to be twenty-five or older, a calculation based on the assumption that they would be living with their parents until that age, meaning they can benefit from the Social Security coverage of a working parent, sibling, or grandparent if they are living under the same roof. To collect RMI, all you need to do is register yourself as a job seeker at a job center. RMI was one more measure designed to give social protection to those who do not fit any other category. Between 1988 and 2000, the number of RMI collectors in France doubled from half a million to a million.

Pensions and health coverage account for 44 percent and 35 percent of the total Sécurité Sociale budget, respectively, and both were slow in becoming universal. The French government didn't create universal health coverage until 2000. Before that, people who had no coverage through an employer had to fill out forms at their local city hall or prefecture before going to the hospital. There are such wide discrepancies between different pension categories that it's hard to regard that system as wholly fair, let alone universal. The private sector clearly subsidizes the public sector. Employees of the government-owned railway system and gas-and-electric utility can retire at age fifty. At the railroads, 86 percent take advantage of this opportunity, while 60 percent do the same at the gas-and-electric utility. Civil servants need to work thirty-seven years to get 75 percent of their salary (based on what they earned during their last six months of work). A female civil servant who raised three children is entitled to retirement after fifteen years (instead of thirty-seven). Taxpayers foot the bill for this perk. Private-sector employees must work forty years to retire with 50 percent of their salary (based on an average of their best twenty-five years).

The French government has never managed to eliminate these inequalities, which are shocking in a system that professes to be universal. In the fall of 1995, just-elected prime minister Alain Juppé attempted to make the system more uniform by raising the retirement age for civil servants. Public service unions reacted by going on strike, paralyzing transport in and around Paris, shutting down many government services for two weeks. Oddly, the rest of France supported them, even though taxpayers foot the bill for civil servants' sumptuous retirement plans. In Paris people cycled, skated, or walked fifteen, twenty, or even twenty-five kilometers a day to get to work. The government gave in, and the French pension system remains as inequitable as it's always been.

The French system started out as a true hybrid between British universality and German joint management, but the State's role in the joint-management structure has steadily increased. Like in the case of RMI, the State is often forced to barge into joint-management schemes to find ways to compensate for inequalities and deficiencies in the system. At the moment, 60 percent of the indemnities for the unemployed come through various State supplements, not through the official *Sécurité Sociale* scheme. On three occasions, in 1967, 1983, and 1995, the State also had to step in to restore a balance between unions and employers in the joint-management organizations. Unions are very strong in France and often manage to get the upper hand by winning a majority of seats on the organizations' boards.

The government now chips in about one-third of the total *Sécurité Sociale* budget of 250 billion dollars. As the State intervenes more and more in joint-management organizations, the system is really becoming a kind of *ménage à trois*. In 1995, the government ordered that all administrators in the local offices of joint-management organizations had to be State approved. The measure was clearly meant to curb the influence of unions. In 2000, when employers forced unions to accept a new deal on unemployment, the government declared it unacceptable and sent them back to the drawing board.

During a day hike in the Pyrenees mountains that make the Franco-Spanish border, Jean-Benoît sprained his ankle when he slipped on a slab of rock. Fortunately, his friend had a walking stick Jean-Benoît could use to walk down the mountain; otherwise, he would have had to pay for the rescue—it is not a free service in France. Later, the doctor recommended that Jean-Benoît do some physiotherapy, but since this is a para-medical service, the expense has to be preapproved by the insurance service. On the whole, the system paid about $140 (U.S.) for ten sessions, and Jean-Benoît found a physiotherapist who did it for $150 (U.S.), which means he had to pay for the difference. But he could have gone to see a physiother-apist that would have charged twice as much. This is the best summary of how the system works: people manage a check that is allocated, which they are allowed to spend wherever they want.

Not a day goes by in France without a story in the papers of individu-als whose welfare benefits didn't arrive on time, or who were forced into a game of administrative Ping-Pong because of the failings of one service or another. These stories appeal to the keen interest the French have in social justice and equality—to their credit—but they are anecdotes. In reality, a look at the numbers shows the system to be rather efficient, both in terms of what it costs and how well it redistributes wealth.

There is no doubt that *Sécurité Sociale* is extremely costly: the 250-billion-dollar-per-year bill actually exceeds France's total national budget of about 230 billion dollars. In all, the French pay about 45 percent of their GDP in tax and social security contributions, compared to about 33 percent in the United States. But simple accounting methods have to be taken into consideration in this comparison. A person who falls ill in the French system is entitled not only to free health care, but also to half of their salary. These expenses are all accounted for in the overall budget of France's welfare system. Employees of most American companies enjoy exactly the same benefits, but the cost of these benefits is off the gov-ernment's books since they are managed by private insurance schemes. That doesn't mean one country supplies better or more efficient services. It just means that in France, the cost of welfare is visible. *Sécurité Sociale* also picks up the tab for a lot of work that gets done by North America's millions of associations and charities. None of the many articles we read criticizing France's "unwieldy" welfare system ever mentioned these basic factors, or included them in calculations of the overall burden social welfare places on the State.

The observations of our friend Pierre, a French physician studying for a Ph.D. in public health at the University of Montreal, offered another illustration of why it is difficult to compare the cost of welfare in France to North America. Studies comparing the consumption of medicines in industrialized countries have shown the French to be the world's most prolific pill poppers per capita. The problem, our friend pointed out, is that the studies don't specify whether they are counting pills consumed, pills purchased, or pills prescribed. In France, *Sécurité Sociale* refunds all medications prescribed by a doctor, even aspirin. Because of this, the French rarely leave the doctor's office without a prescription. Every trip to the doctor is an opportunity to stock up on over-the-counter drugs. This obviously raises the statistics of consumption, but so does the way medications are sold in France.

In the United States, when a doctor prescribes eleven pills, the pharmacist opens a big pot and counts out eleven pills. This labor-intensive system is profitable because pharmacies are allowed to cushion their profits by selling anything from cosmetics to cookies. In France, pharmacies only sell pharmaceuticals. Pills are sold in prepackaged boxes. So if a doctor prescribes eleven pills, the pharmacist pulls out two packages of ten and actually ends up selling twenty pills, or almost twice as much as the prescription. People put up with this practice because *Sécurité Sociale* foots the bill, refunding medications with no questions asked. French pharmacists are in no hurry to change the system.

When both the cost and the quality of the French health system are considered, it's pretty hard to criticize it. France only spends 9.5 percent of its gross domestic product on health, compared to 13.5 percent in the United States. A 1999 study from the World Health Organization ranked France's system first in the world for allocation of resources and overall coverage. The United States ranked thirty-seventh. The French have a high ratio of beds: 8.5 per one thousand inhabitants—slightly lower than Germany, but twice as high as the United States, the United Kingdom, or Canada. The French administration rigorously enforces standards and controls: it's their forte.

The French keep costs low and quality high by maintaining a good balance between public and private medicine. In Britain, all doctors are civil servants. In France, it varies. Doctors charge patients directly. Because we were not covered by *Sécurité Sociale*, we had to fork over eighteen dollars for every trip to the doctor; our private insurance later refunded the sum. Most of the population simply show their card, and *Sécurité Sociale* foots the bill. Before they go to a doctor, the French must check whether the doctor (or the hospital) is *conventionné* (conventioned), meaning the doctor charges rates that *Sécurité Sociale* covers in full. A doctor who is not *conventionné* can charge whatever he wants, but *Sécurité Sociale* will refund only the amount it accepts to pay. Naturally, specialists charge radically different prices for the same services, depending on the neighborhood where they are practicing.

The same difference can be found between hospitals, which can be either fully public, semi-private, or fully private. About one bed in six in France belongs to a private hospital or clinic. Semi-private hospitals are in fact privately run, but charge rates acceptable to *Sécurité Sociale*. These are highly criticized in France because they are known to add extra fees. Our friend Daniel Roux had to have an emergency operation in a semi-private clinic. As he was waking up from the operation in the observation ward, a nurse came to him and asked him for an extra six hundred dollars in cash for so-called *dépassements* (excess charges).

The French also practice home medicine on a large scale: one-third of medical consultations are done at home by a visiting practitioner. As our friend Pierre told us, in France he was able to see patients in their home environments and often spot problems he wouldn't have seen in his office. He would even check out patients' medicine cabinets to see if there were surplus medications they could use, and he often found some.

Users in France make a lot of public health choices themselves because they are the ones who actually manage the allocation of resources between the private and public sector. For example, *Sécurité Sociale* may establish that it will refund $140 for ten sessions of physiotherapy for a sprained ankle. The patient can find a physiotherapist who charges that sum, or pay extra for one who charges more, either assuming the expense privately, or through a complementary insurance plan. The French refer to the patient's contribution as *le ticket modérateur*. It can cover from 20 percent to 65 percent of the total fee and is usually refunded by a third-party insurance plan that is often part of a joint-management scheme. All in all, private expenditures amount to 23 percent of total costs.

Sécurité Sociale isn't exactly a State-run welfare system, but the French government retains tight control over it and steps in when it needs to. In the 1980s and 1990s, when the numbers of both retirees and unemployed rose in France, there was suddenly less money coming into the system at a time when expenses were rising. Tax transfers were the only way to ensure the survival of the system, so the government stepped in and created a special income surtax, *Contribution Sociale Général* (General Social Contribution). It started at 1 percent of all earnings (including investment earnings) and rose to 7.8 percent by 2001. Thanks to another 0.5 percent surtax, the State also managed to pay *Sécurité Sociale*'s cumulated debt of ten billion dollars between 1991 and 1996. The government also discreetly introduced a series of austerity measures to restore the balance and keep the system running. Before 1986, people could send mail to *Sécurité Sociale* without stamps, free of charge. Stamps aren't much of an expense for individuals to absorb, but the move did free up funds that were then reallocated elsewhere in the system.

Managing such a vast social assistance system means walking a fine line between generosity and stinginess. One of the methods French employers use to cut corners is the well-entrenched practice of topping up salaries with bonuses. French employees receive bonuses for having children, for housing, for having a spouse who lives far away, for working far from home, for subway transport, and more. Some of our friends working in the public sector told us that over half of their overall income came in the form of such bonuses.

The practice is so common that the government itself has difficulty accounting for exactly how much it pays employees. The practice is not a sign of bad management: it's a way for employers to reduce their contributions to the system. Bonuses are not counted as salary in *Sécurité Sociale* calculations. However, employees do lose out in the long run. A friend of ours, who had worked as a press *attaché* for the French government in Lithuania, collected bonuses that amounted to 90 percent of his salary. When his contract ended, he was entitled to 50 percent of his *salary*—that is, half of 10 percent of his paycheck. It's an extreme case, but it's not rare for bonuses to double a salary, which means that benefits for retirement or sickness will end up being lower than expected from a rough calculation of earnings. This is one of the main techniques the State, employers, and unions use to cut costs in the welfare system.

The goal of *Sécurité Sociale* in France is to keep people out of misery, not to make them rich. RMI, which is the basic welfare for the unemployed (and the unemployable), pays $360 per month per person: a pittance. Other benefits can usually be added to this sum, but no matter how you look at it, even one thousand dollars per month is not much for an unemployed mother of three, even when considering all the free services available for the poor. Basic pensions are not high either: the average is around $820 per month for the private sector and $1,300 for the public sector, pretty comparable to France's minimum wage of eight hundred dollars per month. Regulations are also tough on the widows of deceased retirees. If they are younger than fifty-five they get nothing, not even if they are dependents. France's so-called "socialist" system is anything but cozy. So workers are encouraged to improve their retirement earnings by contributing voluntarily in joint-management mutual-funds.

And the contributions employees make are not cheap, either. Low-wage workers are exempt from some contributions, either totally or in part. But that means other workers have to contribute more, directly or through taxes. Some categories of these workers contribute more than others do as well, like private-sector workers who get lower pensions than public sector workers do. Self-employed workers also get a bad deal: they have to pay their contributions to *Sécurité Sociale* even in months when they aren't working, or have no revenue. Students have to make a mandatory $175-per-year contribution. The family remains a strong institution in France and it's no surprise why. People have to stick together.

The main problem with the French system is that it keeps unemployment levels high. Since the 1980s, France has had unemployment rates systematically higher than most of its neighbors. *Sécurité Sociale* asks too much from employers and not enough from workers. Because unions in France are so politically powerful, employers have ended up footing most of the bill for social welfare. That amounts to a tax on wages, so companies and businesses are loath to hire more staff than is absolutely necessary. According to OECD statistics, in 1997 French employers paid two-thirds of overall contributions, and employees paid only one-third—and 1997 was a normal year. In Germany, Great Britain, and the United States, contributions are split almost equally between employers and employees.

But there is a limit to making comparisons on the basis of unemployment rates—it all depends on how you define a job. French labor laws do not encourage part-time work. As a consequence, a 10 percent unemployment rate means that most of the 90 percent who work hold a descent full-time job. In countries with unemployment rates below 5 percent, like the U.S., Great Britain, or the Netherlands, it means that a higher proportion work part-time jobs. This difference in defining jobs explains for the greater part why France has fared so well, all in all, in spite of its heavy taxes, *Sécurité Sociale* levels, and its apparently high unemployment level. Those who did work had, on the whole, better jobs.

In addition to making employers foot the bill for social expenses, the government also expects them to redistribute welfare themselves. Companies of more than fifty employees must pay 2 percent of total wages to the in-house *comité d'entreprise* (workers' council), which uses the money to either build a company cafeteria or distribute *titres-restaurant* (restaurant vouchers) to employees. Sixty-three thousand French restaurants accept these lunch vouchers (there is a sticker in their window saying they do). Companies are also encouraged to give employees *chèques-vacances* (holiday vouchers) worth up to seven hundred dollars per year. These vouchers can be used in 130,000 French travel agencies, hotels, restaurants, resorts, and more. In 1998, 1.3 million French workers received holiday coupons. Two thousand French companies even run eight thousand resorts with a capacity of 240,000 beds just for their employees. And companies give employees other perks like cinema rebates or refunds for subway fares. Companies that don't want the trouble of managing different perks often pay their employees a thirteenth-month bonus.

There is a reason that French employers get away with substituting perks for salary increases. The French don't consider holidays, good meals, and theater tickets to be luxuries so much as basic rights. That explains why the French consider even the holiday-deprived to be in some way "excluded" from society.

chapter 19

Economic Interventionism: The State Will Do

We spent Christmas of 1999 back in the Loire Valley at the Marsaults, the friends we visited the previous Easter. We had planned to leave on the day after Christmas and drive across the country to the town of Sarreguemines, on the German border, where another family of friends was expecting us. Unfortunately, a windstorm swept across the entire country that morning, killing seventy people and leaving a trail of destruction behind it. Normally, we would have passed through Paris, but the trains weren't running that day and the capital was in havoc. As we tried to devise an alternative route, Jean-Marie, our friend's father, disappeared in his office for a couple of minutes. He returned with three detailed driving plans with highway numbers, kilometers, and estimated driving time—the three shortest routes. One was a little longer in actual distance, but quicker in time; one was shorter, but slower; and one was picturesque. Jean-Marie had gotten all this precious information from his Minitel.

Minitel machines are a pure product of the early 1980s. They look like a cross between a cellular phone, a TV, and a computer, and in many ways, they are. Our version was a four-pound, beige plastic box, equipped with a built-in handle, featuring a 5 x 7–inch grayish-glass screen protected by a collapsible brown keyboard and old-fashioned springboard keys. Its earth-tone coloring and Duran Duran allure evoked the years when disco was going belly-up, but neon colors still hadn't hit.

The old-fashioned look is deceptive because Minitel works. Over 40 percent of the French use one of the six million existing machines to learn about the weather, get their bank balances, find the best route to Sarreguemines, register at university, or figure out if one of their suppliers has ever been sued.

Throughout the 1990s, whenever anyone accused the French of "resisting" globalization, the proof supplied was the fact that the French did not use the Internet. It was true. Until 1999, only 10 percent of the French were online—one-third the rate of the British and one-quarter that of the Germans and the Americans. Yet nobody bothered to mention that the French weren't using the Internet because they had Minitel.

In many ways, Minitel *is* Internet technology, working on different principles. France Telecom lends the machine to anyone who asks for them, for free. And anyone can use it. It takes five seconds to plug a Minitel in, turn it on, and get online. There is no downloading time—it's like a telephone. No programming, no interface, no ugly wires, no modem. Tuning into a radio station is more of a hassle than using a Minitel.

For the French, the great symbol of Minitel is not the @ we recognize in email addresses, but the number "36." All Minitel service numbers start with the prefix 36, followed by two other digits from 13 to 19, that give the price range of the service, and then four or more capital letters that stand for the name of the service. 3615 AAVOYANT takes you to an astrology service for forty cents per minute. For half that price, 3615 CHAMONIX allows you to rent a room in a ski resort in Chamonix. 3617 COUVRETOI (cover yourself) sells condoms for ninety cents per minute. 3617 RJLJ gives you the names of bankrupt businesses. There is also a weather report site and a sex chat line known as *Minitel Rose* (Pink Minitel).

Like everywhere else in the world, Internet use has been increasing in France. Yet to everyone's surprise, Minitel use has not proportionally declined. The main reason is that Minitel, ugly though it is, does one thing better than the Internet: electronic transactions, or e-trade in e-parlance. Until 1997, the French produced more electronic trade inside France than the Internet did worldwide. In all, twenty-five thousand Minitel service providers generated an annual business of one billion dollars in data exchange, plus an untold number of private transactions between individuals or companies, estimated to be worth another billion dollars.

No country and no company in the world has developed a more efficient or safer system for trading small consumer transactions. The French never really resisted the Internet; they just did not see the point in switching from a system that already worked for them. France was, and remains, the only country in the world with a national electronic mail system and a national electronic marketplace. In spite of all the fuss made over a web-user being able to surf the world, most Americans on the Internet use American sites. The French also stick to French sites, on Internet and on Minitel.

The untold story of Minitel encompasses all the best and the worst about French State interventionism. While Jean-Benoît was researching the topic, he met the father of Minitel and the great modernizer of French telephones, Gérard Théry. A graduate of *Polytechnique*, the famous *grande école* of engineers, Théry headed the telecom division of the PTT (*Poste, Téléphone, et Télégraphe*) from 1974 to 1981. During this period, he reduced a Soviet-like waiting list of three years to a mere three days by installing 1.5 million new phone lines per year, one hundred times the rate of a decade earlier! As a result, the number of phone lines in France tripled to twenty million in 1981.

Théry and his assistant thought up Minitel during a short flight from London to Paris in 1977. They were returning from a British post office presentation showcasing Prestel, a new interactive technology. Transistors were new then, and all phone companies were showing off their projects to competitors. Théry, like all the others, dreamed of ways to transmit images and text over phone wires. Prestel, which featured a very simple remote control linked by wire to a TV, was the most impressive success of the time in telematics, but Théry could see the flaws. "Who would want to interrupt their TV show to check the weather?" he said. "Besides, a TV was six thousand francs then, and not many French households had TVs." Prestel was too rigid for Théry's taste: its remote control could only scroll preset pages.

True telematics, in his view, required a real keyboard that could start a word search in a database and show the results, but would remain as simple, reliable, and affordable as a telephone. "We needed a machine that cost as little as six hundred francs ($100 U.S.) per unit. We could only get prices that low if we ordered millions of machines and gave them to consumers. A huge national database of phone numbers accessible by Minitel would save us the forty thousand tons of paper it cost to print those damn phone books." The project was not as simple as it sounds, and it took them four years to put it together.

Minitels are cheap because they are not really computers. Minitel machines don't have any processing capacity: the power is all in the computing centers. Just like a phone, they are useless without the network. The idea of giving away millions of low-end computers worth $100 (U.S.) each was not as foolish as it sounds. Polaroid sold cameras at a loss in order to sell more of its costly films. Gillette did the same with razors to sell blades. And nowadays, cellular phone companies give away phones to generate traffic.

Minitel is the pure product of French *dirigisme* (interventionism), but the scheme worked because Théry and his successors were wise enough to leave a lot of room in the system for private entrepreneurs. All national phone services that have tried to develop telematics have made the mistake of trying to control the content and supply services themselves. The French understood right from the start that they should leave the content to external "service providers"—the concept and the term were invented in France. Moreover, the French allowed the "service providers" to control their own content through their own "servers"—another term they created. The phone company kept doing what it did best: transmitting. This is pretty close to the structure of the Internet today.

French technocrats also made the brilliant decision to protect the anonymity of transactions. That suited the French with their highly developed sense of privacy. Minitel never asks for names or requires subscriptions: it works entirely on pay-per-use. Users never give their names to use a service. They simply get online and the rate gets added to their phone bill. The phone company redistributes the proceeds to the service provider minus a cut of about 30 percent. No questions asked: you're in, the meter runs; you're out, it stops.

In spite of this success of economic interventionism, the French never managed to export Minitel. In the 1980s, all advanced countries were reluctant to embrace foreign technology in the strategic field of telecommuniations, but no other country had the capacity or will to create a telematics system equal to Minitel. The British Prestel never sold more than 150,000 machines. And the United States, the key market for exports, was closed. American decision-makers did not like the French idea of a telematics network based on low-end, giveaway machines, primarily because companies like IBM needed to sell lots of home computers for one hundred times the price. Besides, Minitel was not adapted to the regulatory environment: the United States was a patchwork of standards and contradictory regulations that resulted from the dismantling of AT&T in 1973.

Ultimately, Minitel failed as an export and could only work in France. No other phone utility in the world had a centralized, technically advanced system, total control over regulations, a uniformly price-tolerant consumer population, a pay-per-call system for domestic calls, and the financial leverage to distribute millions of machines for free. Although the French failed to export their invention, Minitel did create a lively entrepreneurial sector of service providers. But France became a sort of Lost World of online data processing.

French *dirigisme* (interventionism), like French cuisine, is a well-known feature of the country. However, foreign media rarely address the topic with as much sympathy. The Anglo-American media generally dismiss interventionism as hopelessly outdated. France would fare much better if it would stop tinkering with the private sector, the argument goes. Perhaps. But if interventionism is so bad, why does France have the fourth or the fifth highest Gross Domestic Product in the world—on par with the United Kingdom? For that matter, all modern states have monetary policies, Social Security, minimum wage, state-owned companies, subsidies, credit facilities, and trade barriers—all features of interventionism. So why is everyone so hard on the French?

Many economists fall into the trap of believing that interventionism is an ancient, ingrained pattern in France. There is even a widespread belief that French interventionism dates back to Jean-Baptiste Colbert, the prime minister of Louis XIV. Colbert may indeed have been an interventionist, but it would be a mistake to pretend his example was followed for the next three centuries.

The basis of Colbert's economic vision was actually mercantilism, a loose economic doctrine of the sixteeth, seventeenth, and eighteenth centuries that argued nations could increase their power and wealth through strict governmental regulations of the economy. Since wealth was, even more than today, an indication of power, governments assumed that to increase their power, they had to accumulate as much gold and silver as possible. To do this, they needed to develop agriculture and manufacturing, establish colonies, and fight wars in order to get more gold than they spent.

The most advanced industrial nation of Europe and the biggest naval power of the period was the Netherlands. Obsessed with the idea of beating the Dutch, Great Britain and France each became militant mercantilists, though through different means. British mercantilism was mainly commercial. The British used a wide array of legal tricks to dominate trade, including monopolies, barriers, and quotas. They developed slave colonies to supply them with raw materials and serve as markets for their manufactured goods. But their best trick of all was the Navigation Act of 1651, which required all imports and exports in Britain to be shipped by British sailors on British vessels. With this stranglehold on all goods leaving or entering the country, Britain broke the sea power of the Dutch and became the dominant power in maritime trade for the next two centuries. The British repealed the Navigation Act in 1849, when there was no competition left.

French mercantilism was predominantly industrial. When we arrived in Paris in January 1999, we stayed for a week in a bed-and-breakfast in the thirteenth *arrondissement*, the southern section of the city of Paris. The two main features of the neighborhood are Chinatown, located around the Place d'Italie, and the *Manufacture des Gobelins*, a tapestry factory built in 1662 as part of Colbert's mercantilist program. Although Colbert tried very

hard to develop French colonies and maritime trade, he was more successful in developing industry, to the point of creating an industrial boom that
stunned his contemporaries, partly because France was so far behind at the
time. In addition to the Gobelins factory, Colbert created state-owned fac-
tories to produce soap and guns. In 1664, he created a *Conseil du Commerce*
with orders to foster new industries like knitting, lace-making, and smelt-
ing. He brought foreign tradesmen and their expertise to France: Venetians
to make mirrors, metal casters from Liège, German miners, and Spanish
hatmakers. He granted national and regional monopolies to guarantee
markets.

The industrial structure Colbert created lasted almost to the end of the
eighteenth century. But nobody after Colbert had the same talent or drive.
No one grabbed the torch after him until Napoleon, who created chambers
of commerce and launched industrial exhibitions that would allow industrialists to display new innovations to the wonder of the public. Napoleon's
modernization of the legal system was also a great boon to the business sector. But otherwise, there is little to say about French interventionism for
the two centuries after Colbert. All European states practiced interventionism during this period, the French less than many. The ruling doctrine
in France was that of the physiocrats, a school of economic theorists who
argued agriculture was the only source of wealth and that production must
be allowed to flow freely. The economist Vincent de Gournay (1712–59)
summed this doctrine up with four words, *laissez faire, laissez passer* (let do,
or let go), which is at the source of the expression *laissez-faire*.

Interventionism started to make a comeback in France after World
War I, when the French created the formula of *Société d'Économie Mixte*
(semi-public companies). Still widely used in France, SEMs are joint ventures between private enterprises and the government, usually for the sake
of developing infrastructure like tunnels, highways, bridges, and water-
works, or for the management of systems like railways and channel networks. The idea originated in Belgium and Sweden, and was very popular
in Germany at the turn of the century, under the name *Gemischte
Wirtschaft* (mixed economy). But France turned out to be fertile ground for
the structure because it gave its 36,851 small *communes* responsibility for

major works in road and water distribution. Most *communes* were, and are, still too small to execute large-scale infrastructure projects on their own.

There are no statistics on the exact number of SEMs in France, but most important infrastructure projects are carried using this formula. The French like SEMs because they show that the State is doing its job. SEMs also have the merit of bringing the public eye inside private ventures that are in a position of monopoly, like in the case of water distribution. These schemes have proved very good for private business in France, and are no doubt responsible for many of France's international business successes in highway construction and energy and water distribution.

Some SEMs are really nationalizations in disguise. The SEM structure was used to create Air France in 1935, to nationalize war industries in 1936, to create *Aérospatiale* in 1937, and to create France's national railway company in 1938. In most of these cases, the main motivation for nationalizing was to allow the government to keep control over the massive subsidies that went into developing each sector. In the case of the national railway, it was also a good way to consolidate the activity of seven different rail companies and simplify the circulation of goods and passengers by reducing them to one company.

Mass nationalizations were a post-war phenomenon in France. In 1945, de Gaulle owed a huge political debt to the French communists, the most powerful political party in France and the majority in the National Assembly. De Gaulle wanted to make the communists happy, but keep real power out of their hands. One concession he made was to confiscate the assets of the automobile manufacturer Louis Renault, a well-known collaborator. Other measures looked like concessions to the communists, but actually undermined them. To create *Sécurité Sociale*, de Gaulle nationalized thirty-four private insurance companies, but his real intention was to assuage the working class and stave off a revolution. The communists were satisfied when the coal, aviation, steel, motor production industries, and banks were nationalized, but de Gaulle's chief motivation was economic, not political. All these sectors had suffered from ten years of neglect and underinvestment due to the war and the fear of socialism in the late 1930s. The private sector could not afford to revive these sectors on its own, so the government stepped in.

There was nothing original about the idea of economic interventionism. The British did exactly the same thing at exactly the same time in about the same sectors, with the same fervor and about the same ambition as the French. The model was very much the fashion among post-war democracies, but it worked better in France than in the UK. One reason was that the French liked the idea of a strong and visible State. But more importantly, interventionism was a vehicle of change and modernization in France, not just a set of crutches in order to placate the population following the sacrifices it made during the war (which was the case in Britain). In 1945, the French acted out of necessity, not ideology. Only the State had the power to curb the severe shortcomings of the French business class, like their lack of capital and ambition, so the State adopted the role of economic educator. Economic planning was run by a brilliant generation of technocrats, mostly engineers, who brought France out of its pre-WWII semi-agrarian economy and modernized the country into one of industry and services.

The most idiosyncratic aspect of French interventionism was the open-planning approach that de Gaulle adopted. In the weeks before his January 1946 resignation, he added one more item to the package of reforms he had created: *Le Commissariat Général du Plan* (The Economic Planning Commission). This body was actually the idea of a famous French economist of the time, Jean Monnet. The son of a cognac maker, Monnet became familiar with American institutions from 1917–18, while he was in charge of purchasing war supplies in the United States. After a stint as assistant secretary general for the Society of Nations from 1919–23, Monnet was put in charge of reorganizing the Polish and Romanian economies and in 1939 became head of the Coordinating Committee of the Allied War Effort. Churchill later appointed him to the British Council of War Supplies and actually sent him—a Frenchman—to Washington to work on common defense plans with the Americans.

Monnet joined de Gaulle's National Committee of the Liberation in 1943. It was Monnet who convinced de Gaulle that France's main problem was its antiquated semi-agrarian economy and lack of an openminded business class. Monnet won de Gaulle over to the idea of *la planification;* a system of economic planning that would be very different from the Soviet model. Monnet's idea was that the State should form an economic plan and give the private sector directions without forcing them to follow specific imperatives. *Le Commissariat Général au Plan* would be a number-crunching agency that identified which economic sectors were lagging. It set economic objectives for periods of three to five years. Its members were civil servants working in consultation with business people and union leaders. Each plan the Commission came up with was presented to the National Assembly, who voted on it. Since 1946, France has been through eleven plans.

The planning system worked because it was indicative, as opposed to the Soviets' imperative system. The Commission set objectives in consultation with the business sector and unions to reduce inflation, create jobs, or develop a particular industry. It also established the incentives to be applied, like subsidies, loans, tax credits, tariffs, and quotas. All other developed countries had such plans, but the French system also played an openly political function: the National Assembly voted on the plan. However, if economic realities changed, the government simply dropped the plan. For instance, the Sixth Plan was supposed to produce "strong economic growth through a huge development in heavy industries." But a surprise event, the 1973 oil crisis, changed all this—to drive up prices, petrol-producing countries threatened to starve all modern economies of petrol. Surviving the crisis became the number-one priority, and the idea of producing "strong economic growth through huge development in heavy industries" was simply forgotten. The plans were the product of a State that saw itself as responsible for the industrial education of the nation—to the point of sending executives and union leaders abroad to visit foreign firms.

When de Gaulle came back to power in 1958, French economic planning was being applied more specifically to sectors that were lagging behind. De Gaulle limited his ambitions to nationalizing petrol production, an area where French business had been notoriously weak. He encouraged the Commission to launch specific plans to develop aeronautics, weaponry, computer technology, and telephone services—a sector in which France was sixty years behind most other European countries. Raising France to a higher standard had been the main mandate of Gérard Théry, the father of Minitel. The Commission also attempted to stimulate the stock exchange because they sensed that the French stock market was underdeveloped as a source of capital for French business (businesses at the time relied heavily on loans rather than investment).

The year 1975 was the end of a period the French call *les Trente Glorieuses* (the thirty Glorious Years), in reference to the economic renewal that occurred during the period. Between 1945 and 1975, the proportion of farmers in the work force had decreased from 36 percent to 10 percent, and the proportion of workers in services had risen from 32 to 52 percent. In 1945, there were 650,000 students above grade eight. In 1975, there were seven times as many. In the same period, the number of cars in France increased from one to fifteen million. Only 37 percent of households had cold running water; then 97 percent did, and the proportion of households with a bathroom and shower rose from 5 percent to 70 percent—they were not completely out of the woods yet.

France's economy also changed during this period. The creation of the European Community in 1958 had marked the beginning of the end of *planification nationale* because the EC blocked certain measures, like subsidies, quotas, and tariffs, and linked France's economic future to its neighbors'. Long-term predictions on a national basis were becoming increasingly irrelevant as world economies became more integrated. Sensing change in the wind, de Gaulle had already begun to adapt economic planning to the new era of international competition by focusing on sectors rather than the economy as a whole. The economic troubles that followed the oil crisis and rising inflation in the 1970s challenged many assumptions. Nothing seemed to be working as it had for the French. But of course, in those years, nothing seemed to be working the same way for anyone else, either. In the middle of the 1970s, *la planification* was scaled down. It was nearly abandoned in 1998, and now it serves as a very discreet advisory board performing studies.

The man who gave French interventionism a bad name was socialist president François Mitterrand (1981–95). Mitterrand's approach to interventionism was ideological and wholesale. Shortly after his election in 1981, he nationalized some thirty-nine banks, two finance companies, and five major companies in the industries of glass, aluminum, chemistry, and pharmaceuticals, and electronics and electric material. By the time France began privatizing again in 1986, about 12 percent of the French labor force worked in publicly owned companies. In some sectors, like railways, the State ran monopolies. The State ran half of all air and sea transport, aeronautics, electronics, and broadcasting companies, and owned 33 percent of the auto-mobile industry and a good chunk of the rental market for apartments.

Yet even Mitterrand's interventionism had its practical justification. At the time, governments throughout the world were seeing unemploy-ment rise, in part because of the increasing importance of multinational corporations whose main agenda was profit, not national development. Mitterrand grabbed and nationalized at least one company in every indus-trial sector. The idea was to maintain national employment by protecting parts of these sectors from foreign ownership. He had the same motivation for nationalizing banks: the socialists wanted to control the allocation of capital to protect jobs.

Whatever his motivations, Mitterrand's nationalizations turned out to be badly timed, costly, and futile. All the nationalized companies ended up laying workers off. Unemployment continued to rise along with interest rates, and the combined debts of publicly held companies doubled from one hundred billion to two hundred billion francs. The fiasco seriously undermined France's credibility on the international stage. All modern countries were grappling with the exact same problem at the time, but France alone had chosen wholesale nationalization as the solution.

The Mitterrand era earned France a reputation as a semi-socialist country, when in fact, the economy had been basically free-market driven until then. The public-relations bomb was made worse by the fact that it happened just as national economies were becoming more intertwined and the financial sector and stock exchanges were being used increasingly to fund national debts and finance private companies. The opinion of the international financial sector mattered. Investors at the time nearly black-balled the French.

It took the French twenty years to get over the financial headache Mitterrand caused through his strong interventionism. Starting in 1986, the French government embarked on a very aggressive privatization program. As a result, the public sector now accounts for only 6 percent of the workforce, compared to 12 percent twenty years ago. By 2000, the French government had sold fifty billion dollars worth of State-owned companies, as much as the British government had sold since the 1980s. Still, the French government was less ideologically driven than Britain in reversing privatization. It maintained a share in the companies, like 50 percent of Air France and France Telecom, respectively. The foreign press hailed the French for becoming less interventionist, and the French government gained confidence in the capacities of private business.

But on the whole, the shift came not so much from a declining State role in the economy as recognition that interventionism needed to be limited. The French did not abandon their desire for a strong State that intervenes in the economy when it's necessary. Nor are they ever very likely to.

One reason France sticks to interventionism is that it works rather well. French business leaders don't hunger for world domination, yet they have produced remarkable successes anyway. Total-Fina-Elf managed to raise itself to the world's number four oil company at the turn of the millennium. The French have produced successes in aviation like Airbus, which now receives more orders for airplanes than Boeing. Ariane Space operates the only profitable rocket-launching program in the world. And their extremely efficient high-speed railway system transports millions of people throughout the country with few delays. After lagging behind in telecommunications for sixty years, the French completely overhauled their telephone system in the 1970s and went on to create Minitel, a national online data processing network that is the backbone of the world's only profitable e-commerce industry.

There have been shameful farces, too. One of the chief objectives behind Minitel was creating a springboard for French electronics, but low-end monitors for the mass market were not necessarily the best visiting card, especially because no other country succeeded in creating its own national network in the 1970s and 1980s. No matter how hard they tried, the French have never managed to create a viable electronics industry—although no other European country has, either.

But France's failures certainly can't be explained with sweeping generalizations about the inefficiency of publicly owned companies. France's national electricity and gas utility, EDF-GDF, not only turns profits, but is in the process of buying up privatized utilities in neighboring countries like Britain and Germany. In many ways, rejecting the Internet made business sense because France Telecom was merely trying to protect its turf. The huge investments were not fully repaid before 1999, and France Telecom needed to stick to a one-billion-dollar-a-year cash cow.

Ten years of business journalism have taught us to be careful about claims that privately owned companies are more efficient than publicly owned ones. We bore that in mind when we looked at France's economy. Free-market ideologues have worked hard over the last few decades to convince the public that the private and public sectors are two worlds and two cultures that don't speak the same language. But the view that state and business are separated is misleading, everywhere. A great number of the private-sector companies in all societies have government contracts to thank for their success. And when contracts for public works are managed poorly, it's not always the fault of the public sector. Some publicly owned industrial schemes in France, like the aerospace industry, have turned out to be money pits, but so have a great number of private American air companies, not to mention privatized energy schemes in California, and privatized rail in Britain—which is in a dismal state. At the time we wrote this book, the spectacular bankruptcies of energy broker Enron and telecom giant WorldCom showed that the idea of self-regulation in the private sector was not only ludicrous, but costly to millions of small investors, and damaging to the overall economy.

Are the French really more interventionist than the British, Germans, or even Americans? Even this is debatable. But one thing was clear to us: the French are blunt in affirming the role of the State, whereas other countries understate it. Americans, who value community life and civil society, have always underplayed the role of their government and championed their business sector. The State is seen as playing a support role, doing whatever lower levels of government can't do. That's probably why private companies in America downplay subsidies and don't advertise them. Ronald Reagan's 1980s Star Wars scheme—ostensibly meant to deploy a network of missile-killer satellites around the earth—never worked. But it did succeed in its real purpose: to hand dozens of billions of dollars of research subsidies to United States companies. Star Wars helped American industry develop scores of valuable patents, notably for the computer industry, which fueled the economic boom of the 1990s. George W. Bush came up with the missile shield scheme just at the time when those patents were exhausted and the boom they produced was over. Interestingly, defense contracts are not included in World Trade Organization regulations on subsidies. That makes it hard for any other country to contest this brand of American interventionism.

State interventionism is visible in France because the French don't try to hide it. In France the State is the founding principle of society, not community life. This is one reason the French prefer SEM (*Société d'Économie Mixte*) schemes, where the State's role is visible, over simple old public contracts where the State's role is hidden. A public contract is money contracted out by the state to (theoretically) the lowest bidder, who takes the credit for realizing the contract. In the SEM system, the government chooses a partner to complete a contract. Roughly the same sum of money is spent, but the State gets partial credit for executing the work, not just for funding it. The French find that reassuring.

For all of France's openness about economic interventionism, there are aspects of the program that the French government doesn't advertise. Between 1997 and 1999 socialist prime minister Lionel Jospin accomplished the *tour de force* of selling off nearly as many government assets in two years as his predecessors had in twelve years. But the socialist party downplayed this as much as possible. To hide his tracks, Jospin called the privatizations "normalizations."

In some instances, the State also camouflages economic intervention. In 1999, the socialists delivered on an election promise to reduce the work week from 37.5 to thirty-five hours, supposedly with the goal of creating jobs. But the real purpose of the thirty-five-hour law was to force unions to accept more flexible labor rules. In the French system, management has always wanted to make holidays mandatory for periods when there is less demand for work. Unions have traditionally negotiated fixed holidays according to seasons, which doesn't always coincide with labor demands. The thirty-five-hour week forced a thorough reorganization of work schedules, which unions had refused to concede to before that. In the give-and-take of the negotiations, many employers got concessions from unions that allowed them to set holiday schedules according to their own needs, rather than good weather. And this measure forced unions to be more flexible about shifts. In 1991, only 650,000 people in France worked night shifts: now three million do. The possibility of getting these kinds of concessions from unions was one of the reasons French employers did not protest the thirty-five-hour week as much as they pretended to. The French government, meanwhile, did all it could to downplay the real effect of the measure on French labor.

Economic interventionism also has an important social dimension in France. The way the French see it, the economy should serve the social well-being of the country, not the other way around. Former prime minister Lionel Jospin is famous for having said: "*Oui à l'économie de marché, non à la société de marché*" (Yes to a market economy, no to a market society). In the French mind-set, the State might make mistakes, but so does the market. The French don't trust markets to solve social problems, which they view as political. They do not believe that private profits will trickle down to the rest of society and eventually work to everyone's advantage. That view shouldn't come as a surprise in light of the terrible abuses of power the French have seen, even in recent history. And of course, markets don't guarantee citizens five weeks of holidays per year.

Strangely, we confronted this philosophy when we went to open a bank account in Paris. In France, bank accounts come in packages. Ours included a mandatory savings account, called the *Livret A*, which is a tax-free savings plan similar to a 401-K in the United States or an RRSP in Canada. Both encourage citizens to save, and allow them to place invested assets in a tax-free environment. But the French government goes much further than forc-

ing savings. The *Livret A* gave a 2 percent return on the money, which the
French regarded as fair. The French government then takes that money and
loans it to public housing schemes at a 4 percent interest rate.

We saw this dynamic again when a French film distributor, UGC, created a shock wave by coming up with a subscription scheme. UGC offered
monthly passes for ninety-eight francs that would allow pass holder to see
as many UGC films as they wanted—a good deal since film tickets cost
fifty francs at the time. UGC sold seventeen thousand cards in three
weeks. Their competitors, naturally, were disgruntled, as was the Minister
of Culture, but not because the scheme represented unfair competition. In
France, 11 percent tax is tacked onto the price of movie tickets, the proceeds of which go straight back into the film industry in the form of production subsidies. The French are quite willing to tax themselves to
subsidize their own national film production and support their own culture,
nationally and internationally, and they will stifle competition if necessary
to uphold that principle. After deliberation, the Minister of Culture
decided to let UGC keep selling their membership cards, but she forced
them to apply a time limit to the scheme.

The French, of course, aren't the only ones in the world who believe in
supporting their culture with tax money. But they may be the most vocal
about it. Americans and the British are much less likely to affirm their government's role in encouraging culture even when they do get involved, like
the U.S.'s quota on foreign artists and entertainers. Conversely, even
though the French know deep down that it's all right for private enterprise
to be self-interested, they rarely admit it in public.

In 2000, French tire giant Michelin created a stir when it laid off seven
thousand workers in spite of the fact that it had not lost any money that
year. What the layoff actually amounted to was closing down some plants
and reassigning most workers, but Michelin made the mistake of justifying
the move by saying that international financial markets were asking for
better returns on their investments. The idea that financiers could control
the economy this way provoked an outcry of indignation in France. The
affair climaxed when Prime Minister Lionel Jospin, cornered by a TV
interviewer, said, "The State cannot do everything."

Some people applauded the fact that a socialist prime minister had finally dared state the obvious, but many disagreed. Shortly after Jospin's statement, we noticed an op-ed piece in the daily newspaper *Libération* with the title: "Tell us the State can do everything."

PART THREE:

change

chapter 20

The World According to France

When Peter Martin, the director of the Institute of Current World Affairs, came to visit us at the end of our first year in Paris, he noticed a moving company hoisting furniture into a neighboring apartment on a miniature conveyor belt. It was a curious sight for an American, but easily explained. Moving companies use portable escalators because most elevators, and even stairwells, in Paris are too small to move furniture through. "Imagine an American moving company coming in here. They wouldn't know what to do," he said. "Space restrictions change everything."

Space does change a lot, but there are many other invisible factors in France that change things too. In the first section of this book, we explained how French history, their attachment to the land, ideas about space, privacy, language, notions of *grandeur*, intransigence, and recent historical events like World War II and the War of Algeria all affect the way the French think and live. The weight of history means that the French don't wipe the slate clean to make way for progress the way Americans do. Because of their centuries-old attachment to the land, restriction is their second nature, not expansion. The French have completely different ideas about what's public and what's private, and those ideas influence how they think about money, morality, eating, manners, conversation, and even political accountability. The French glorify what's elevated and grand, not what's common and accessible. They value form as much as content. And finally, they created many of their institutions to try to deal with the after-effects of two major wars. These factors don't add up to a neat picture that diametrically opposes French and Anglo-Americans. They just explain a lot about why the French think and act the way they do. Unless Americans recognize these differences, they will never understand the French.

The chapters in the second section of this book show the concrete differences in how the French organize themselves. English may be the global *lingua franca*, and the Anglo-American social and business models may have become the norm, but they won't slip onto French culture like a glove. France is too different. It is a centralized county with political reflexes that are completely alien to North Americans, including a penchant for authoritarianism and disdain for compromise. France has no local government and no competing political jurisdictions. Its legal system functions on principles, not jurisprudence, and is controlled by politicians, not the other way around. The French don't just glorify their *élite*; French society *needs* a clearly identified *élite*. The whole education system is designed to produce an *élite* to run their institutions. The French strongly believe in the common good and happily grant the State all the powers and privileges it requires to act for the common good. They affirm the State's role in virtually everything—culture, language, welfare, and the economy. The market economy is important in France, but the French don't glorify it.

We began this book by describing France as "something else," and it should be clear now that France is a clock that runs on a different set of gears. But the distinctions between France and North America don't end there. The French also see the world differently—to such an extent that discussions about the famous French "resistance" to globalization become almost pointless. Globalization doesn't mean the same thing to the French as it does to Anglo-Americans for the simple reason that their *world* is not the same.

France's wide global presence is one reason they see the world differently. France has a reputation for being insular, and as we have argued ourselves, the French have a history of being acutely continental in their thinking. Yet much in the way that Alaska, Hawaii, and Puerto Rico are American, France has overseas *Départements* and about a dozen overseas territories, some very large. Aside from Corsica, which is just off the coast in the Mediterranean, the French own French Guiana (in Latin America), Martinique and Guadeloupe (in the Caribbean), the Reunion Islands (Indian Ocean), and St. Pierre-et-Miquelon (in the Gulf of the St. Lawrence). These are not colonies: they are *Départements* like any other, and they even send representatives to the National Assembly. Territories like Polynesia and New Caledonia in the Pacific have retained some of their sovereignty, but belong to a form of French federation, much in the way that Puerto Rico is part of the United States. There are also small territories, including Wallis-and-Futuna in the Pacific and the Kerguelen Islands in the Indian Ocean.

In all, overseas France accounts for 5 percent of the French population and 20 percent of the territory. French vacationers might forget to include Guadeloupe and Martinique when they talk about "France," but they are part of the same country. French citizens visiting overseas territories or *Départements* don't need a passport or a visa; they don't need to exchange their euros and are entitled to the same *Sécurité Sociale* services they would get in Europe. If they have a problem they can go to the *préfecture*. If they want to call home they just go to a France Telecom phone booth. They can mail postcards from the French post office using French stamps, and they can take money out of the bank with smart cards. It's France.

France's overseas departments and territories mean France's neighbors include not only Great Britain, Belgium, Luxembourg, Germany, Italy, and Spain, but also Australia, Brazil, Venezuela, and Canada. Having territory on all sides of the globe means that the French are also economically active the world over. The French have good reasons for holding onto these territories. New Caledonia, next to Australia, is the world's fourth-biggest nickel producer. French Guiana, which shares borders with Brazil, has been the home of France's profitable commercial space program (the *Département*'s proximity to the equator increases the sling-shot effect and allows French rockets to lift more load). The 3,521 islands of French

Polynesia give the French control over a swath of the Pacific Ocean four times the size of Alaska that they use for nuclear testing (the closest neighbor from where they test is five hundred kilometers away). The French also keep a permanent base of sixty-seven people on the desolate islands of Kerguelen, in the Southern Indian ocean, the center of a rich fishing zone.

The French follow international political affairs closely. We were very impressed by the quality of foreign coverage in the French press. Part of the reason for this interest is that many international affairs are also domestic affairs in France. Since 1945, referendums have been held, and elections fought, on issues like the status of Indochina, Algeria, and New Caledonia, and the creation of Europe. France's famous press agency, *Agence France-Press*, supplies the French with an excellent source of news from 110 countries. It was created by de Gaulle when France wasn't yet liberated and it now has two thousand employees, making it the third-biggest press agency in the world behind Reuters and Associated Press. The agency operates in six languages, giving the French a powerful foreign-policy tool, and it was the first big agency to publish in Arabic.

Since their World War II purgatory, the French have learned to live with the idea that they are neither the biggest, nor the strongest, power on earth. But they still believe they are the best. The French don't see themselves as a pawn in the global chessboard, but as one of the players. This conviction gives them a degree of self-assurance that few other countries have—and it's one reason the rooster and the eagle often ruffle each other's feathers. In diplomatic crises, such as the UN resolution over Iraq in 2003, they are often singled out even if they are not the only country holding a contrary position, in part because they like speaking for others. In Washington, the French are seen as provocative, pushy, whimsical, and self-important, and are often derided as a mid-size power, even though they rank fourth in the world for the size of their economy.

The world has Charles de Gaulle to thank for this assertiveness. His actions shaped French foreign policy, diplomacy, foreign aid, and military intervention since World War II. De Gaulle was asserting France's independence even when he was little more than a refugee in London with no legitimate authority. It was certainly this attitude that provoked President Franklin Roosevelt's animosity toward de Gaulle—one of the greatest mysteries of World War II. The French general-president was the first European politician to assert an independent foreign policy from America, and he did so without reserve. "States have no friends. They only have interests," de Gaulle said, quoting former French statesman Charles de Talleyrand.

De Gaulle pursued French interest without flinching from the very start. In 1944, de Gaulle refused to let the Americans take control over currency, transport, the appointment of civil servants, and the war tribunals, like they did in other liberated countries. He sensed that the Americans would use their presence to force their values and customs on France and that the prestige of his country would be eroded by this. Against the will of the Allied high command, de Gaulle ordered the American army to be at the disposition of *préfets*, who were quickly installed in every liberated zone. His decision cost France America's trust. While he was busy establishing France's independence, de Gaulle also fabricated a few myths to bolster French morale and support for his reforms. The main one was that France liberated itself from the Germans. It's partly true—the French army did fight for the Liberation—but French soldiers mainly surfed on the wave of the American, British, and Canadian war efforts.

After de Gaulle returned to power in 1958, he spent the next decade giving the American government cold sweats by pursuing a policy of rapprochement with China and the Soviet Union. From a purely European interest, this policy was understandable, since Russia was a neighbor. The problem was that de Gaulle never consulted his allies before acting. In February 1960, France detonated its first atomic bomb in a test zone in the Algerian desert. In March of 1966, he announced that France was leaving NATO and ordered all U.S. bases to leave. De Gaulle even messed in North American affairs. In July 1967, during a visit to the Montreal Expo, he declared *Vive Le Québec Libre* (Long Live Free Quebec) from the city-hall balcony, lending support to a separatist movement in North America when he would have happily crushed similar movements in Brittany, Corsica, or the Basque region. (Historians are still debating de Gaulle's intentions regarding *le Québec Libre*. Most agree he was hoping to repair the damage done in 1763, when the French simply abandoned their greatest colony to the British without hesitations. But de Gaulle was also taking advantage of an opportunity to express his Anglophobia and take a jab at the Americans, who resented a free Cuba and feared the idea of a free Quebec in the North.)

There has never been another president as provocative as de Gaulle, and his legacy has endured. France has remained independent and assertive on the international stage, at least in comparison to the British, whose foreign policy since World War II has been closely in tune with the U.S. While the French have always been a U.S. ally, it's only when the United States really needed them. For the most part, France has gone its own way in the world, and that shouldn't come as a surprise. Americans often forget that France is a global power with its own space program and nuclear program, its own central intelligence agency, its own marines (the foreign legion), foreign military bases, spy satellites (the only ones in Europe), and even its own mercenary soldiers. In economic, political, diplomatic, and scientific circles, France's presence simply cannot be ignored. The French spend four times as much as Americans on foreign aid per capita (0.38 percent of their Gross Domestic Product, according to OECD figures). They hand out five billion dollars for America's nine billion dollars.

France also gets a lot of international leverage from the *Francophonie*, a French-speaking commonwealth of forty-nine countries. This multilateral agency, which has former United Nations Secretary General Boutros Boutros-Ghali as its head, was created principally to defend and promote French culture. With a budget of two hundred million dollars per year, the *Francophonie* funds hundreds of projects in education, Internet development, and media. One-third of its budget goes to TV-5, an international French-language television network. The *Francophonie* does suffer from permanent underfunding, but it plays an important role in promoting the French language and defending French interests internationally. Along with English, French is the only language spoken on all five continents, and it still has an appeal among foreign *élites* in Latin America, the Middle East, and Africa. Boutros Boutros-Ghali's own family, part of the Egyptian *élite*, schooled their children in French as a way of reducing the British influence on them.

The *Francophonie* wasn't a French idea. In the 1960s, newly independent African countries and Quebec proposed the idea of creating cooperation among French-speaking countries and governments. Initially, France refused the concept out of fear that the French Left would accuse them of neocolonialism. France slowly accepted the project, but their initial reluctance ended up working to their advantage. The fact that these countries have actively solicited France's cooperation has helped France overcome its bad colonial legacy on the international stage. The *Francophonie* countries now form a French-speaking block in the UN, and they did not shy away from using this leverage in the 2002–3 political debate over the invasion of Iraq.

Anti-Americanism, of course, does shape France's world view, particularly in this era of cultural globalization. Yet American commentators often forget that the French are not the only ones who resent the United States. American scholars are just beginning to talk about the way America has extended its power and influence through "soft imperialism," as opposed to classic (military) imperialism, and it seems to be difficult for Americans to grasp the fact that the world has mixed feelings about their cultural imperialism. Americans assume that their technology, culture, and language are spreading across the globe only because the world loves American culture. They forget that the U.S. government and American companies have been hard at work, actively spreading their influence for many decades now.

The French are keenly aware of this effort, perhaps more than many societies. They have been feeling the active push of American culture since the end of World War II. The Blum-Byrnes Accord, signed by France and the United States in 1946, made American aid conditional to the introduction of American products in France. One annex specifically required the French to play American films in their theaters. In the late 1960s, France was hoping to launch telecommunications satellites, but its space program was crumbling. France approached the United States to see if it could use NASA launchers to send up the satellites. The Americans would only agree if France promised never to use their satellites for commercial ends (leaving the field of telecom satellites wide open for the United States). The French refused to accept that kind of cultural imperialism and decided to resuscitate their own space program instead, which they did successfully.

Chancellor Otto von Bismarck once said that the most important phenomenon of the nineteenth century was that America spoke English. At the time, the sun had still not set on Great Britain, the dominant superpower. By the end of World War II, American power had definitely supplanted the British, meaning that two successive empires, Great Britain and the United States, spoke the same language—a historical phenomenon with very few precedents. In 1919, during the negotiations prior to the signing of the Treaty of Versailles, Americans were in a position to demand that the treaty be written in English as well as French, a first in roughly five hundred years of European history. America's true dominance was delayed for the next twenty-five years only because they refused their role as a true global power by withdrawing from the League of Nations and conducting an isolationist policy.

Even during isolationism, America's technological superiority and the English language were spreading American ideas over the planet. The United States is now surfing on this effect to foster myths that consolidate its influence and power even more. One of the biggest myths is that D-Day was an American landing. In reality, the majority of troops were British and Canadian. Another is that the Americans defeated the Germans, while in reality, the Soviets were doing this pretty much on their own by D-Day. During our stay, an interesting controversy erupted in Britain over the release of the film *U-571*, which tells the story of American sailors who captured a German submarine in 1941, a major strategic breakthrough because they got ahold of the very secretive German encryption machines. The film's story is true, with the exception of one major fact: the sailors who captured the submarine were British, not American. The United States wasn't even in the war in 1941. None of these myths are created on the orders of the White House. They are perpetuated by a multiplicity of agents, probably in good faith—who all believe them—with the overall effect of spreading the American world view without shooting a bullet. This is what is meant by soft imperialism.

As a former dominant power of Europe, the French are especially sensitive to American myth-making. One reason they see through the myths is that they created and exported their own once upon a time. These days, the French do not fancy themselves as economic or military rivals of the United States, but they still feel like cultural rivals.

Americans, for their part, have a tendency to blow French anti-Americanism out of proportion. We saw this while we were living on the other side, among many American expatriates. Americans are notoriously sensitive to rejection. On the whole, they genuinely believe that if the world adopts the American ways, it's because the world likes them. This is often true, but not always.

Throughout our stay, we wrestled constantly with the complexities of the anti-American and pro-American sentiments floating around France. At best, it is hard to even define what anti-Americanism *means*. Most of the French simply have mixed feelings about the United States. Some people are extremely welcoming of American ways but detest Americans. Others admire America but hate Americanization. (By the way, Americans have the same mixed feelings about the French.) There are things the French welcome. Many English words are creeping into French vocabulary, and English is actually quite fashionable. Some French use English words to project an air of worldly sophistication. And some French just like American culture. Euro Disney could have been in London or Hanover, but the French wanted it thirty kilometers east of Paris. Even de Gaulle, who was very protective of French culture, accepted the idea that France had to adopt some of the American ways of doing things.

However, there is still an undercurrent of anti-Americanism in French culture. We knew it was there every time we heard the expression "Anglo-Saxon." Typically, if politicians want to kill a bill in the National Assembly, calling it "Anglo-Saxon" does the trick. People talk about "Anglo-Saxon" values, "Anglo-Saxon" multinationals, "Anglo-Saxon" consulting firms, legal practices, films, food, fashion, and more.

American Democrat Jesse Jackson and filmmaker Spike Lee are called "Anglo-Saxon" in France. The expression does not mean WASP. The concept has nothing to do with race or religion. It refers to anything that comes from the United States, Great Britain, Australia, New Zealand, or Canada, but also Germany, Scandinavian countries like Denmark, and even South

Africa. What these countries share is a strong Protestant ethic, with a strong emphasis on community life, individual liberties, and economics.

So why don't the French just say Protestant? That would be admitting they are "Catholic." France is officially secular, and ever since the Church openly opposed democratic regimes from 1789 to 1944, "Catholic" has been a dangerous word. Yet while countries like Italy and Spain are more fervent followers of Catholicism, they never created a State as Catholic as France's, which is heavily centralized, hierarchical, and homogenizing. It is almost as if the French studied the Catholic Church and created their State in its image. While the French sense how different they are from Protestant societies, they skirt religious labels to avoid playing into the hands of true Catholic activists. Inaccurate as it is, "Anglo-Saxon" is a convenient label the French can use to differentiate themselves. (Chapters 9, 10, and 11 discussed the characteristics of the French State in depth.)

France's so-called "resistance to globalization" is largely an extension of their rejection of Anglo-American cultural models. The French do not actively resist economic globalization in any concrete way that we could see. They are extremely active players across the globe—even if the political class curiously avoids the issue. Shortly after we arrived, automobile maker Renault took a controlling share of Nissan. Retailer Carrefour made headlines because of difficulties in the city of Porto Alegre, Brazil, where local authorities feared Carrefour's presence would damage local business. The fact that Carrefour was a common household name in Brazil should come as no surprise: the company does nearly half of its business in fifty countries outside France. They rank number two in world retail behind Wal-Mart, which is three times bigger, but operates in only nine countries outside of the United States. At about the same time, the water-management and telecom multinational Vivendi also took the control of U.S. Filter, Seagram's, and Universal. And of course, France's state-owned electrical utility EDF is now buying up privatized networks and services in Britain and Germany.

Beyond the issues of removing trade barriers and integrating markets, it is very difficult to sum up the French attitude toward globalization. The

French refer to at least three things—the assimilation of all cultures, technological progress, and Americanization—interchangeably as "globalization." And opinions on any one of these topics vary enormously in France.

But the French do have their own way of looking at globalization. If anything, this is what the story of Larzac farmer José Bové really shows. More than two years after the McDonald's sacking, French journalists, economists, and politicians still invoke Bové's name when they talk about genetically modified food, the world economy, the WTO, or resistance to multinationals. Not everyone in France agrees with everything Bové says or does. But almost all the French do relate to the basic vision he articulates. In short, the French want to see political controls applied to economic globalization.

That was the essence of the French farmers' message in August 1999. It was a hard message for anyone outside of France to understand. The farmers actually said they were protesting WTO rules that forced people to accept hormone-injected American beef, multinationals that fed people "frankenfood" and junk food, the European Union that drove family farmers out of business, the neo-colonialism of the international agencies like the World Bank that worsened living condition of the middle class in third-world countries, and the destruction of the environment by unsustainable production. They used globalization as a catch phrase to sum up those elements. Yet Bové is the first to admit there's no turning back globalization. He and his comrades simply don't agree with the model of globalization that is gaining consensus in the international community—the model espoused by the WTO.

Over the last thirty years, financiers and economists have convinced the media and most decision-makers that big government, high taxes, high national debt, and trade barriers or any form of protectionism curb prosperity. They claim that the state should be an arbitrator with a central policy: markets know best. Bové asks, why should globalization be only about free trade? He wants to see globalization made politically accountable. Most French men and women we met favored this idea, at least in principle.

We got a better understanding of the French farmers' campaign when we looked into a French group called *Association pour la Taxation des Transactions Financières pour l'Aide aux Citoyens* (Association for the Taxation of Financial Transactions for the Benefit of Citizens), which was starting to make headlines when we got to France. ATTAC was born in 1998 when the editor-in-chief of *Le Monde* revived an old idea, a one-tenth-of-one-percent tax on financial transactions. It was dubbed the Tobin Tax, after Nobel Prize–winner James Tobin (1981). The newspaper was flooded with enthusiastic responses and the editor-in-chief created ATTAC. This association became twenty-five-thousand members strong and coordinates dozens of similar organizations worldwide.

Given the deleterious nature of financial markets, the Tobin Tax is probably inapplicable, but the idea of taxing financial transactions has begun to gain currency among some Western democracies anyway, notably Finland and Canada. Former Canadian Finance Minister Paul Martin regularly made declarations to the effect that all rich nations should accept the idea of redistributing some of their wealth among poorer nations, much like the Canadian systems of tax transfers from rich provinces to poor provinces. That means that, at the international level, one entity would have the authority to collect the money and redistribute the proceeds.

The French National Assembly debated the Tobin Tax and voted in support of the principle. The views of Bové and ATTAC have support among the French. Broadly speaking, the French are in favor of a controlled globalization. They want a global market with rules, institutions to enforce them, and a global government to make decisions.

Around the same time as the French farmers affair, we discovered a little-known fact about the WTO in some preliminary research for a magazine interview with WTO Director General Mike Moore. The World Trade Organization, like the International Monetary Fund and the World Bank, are not creatures of Wall Street, but agencies of the United Nations. Western governments after 1945 believed that the Second World War had been triggered by the very active protectionism put into place during the 1930s to reduce the economic damage of the Depression. They created the IMF and the World Bank to handle macroeconomics and began negotiating a General Accord on Tariffs and Trade (GATT), which was renamed the World Trade Organization in 1994.

Bové is, of course, very critical of the pro-business agenda of the WTO. Yet what he wants is similar to other UN agencies that set environmental, educational, and labor standards—but for financial transactions. Until now, it has been assumed that self-regulation should be the *modus operandi* of the global marketplace. Bové, ATTAC, and many French people simply reject this assumption. President Chirac made this idea even clearer at the Earth Summit in Johannesburg in September 2003 when, in the presence of one hundred heads of state, he called for the creation of a global "solidarity tax" that would be levied "from the wealth produced by globalization."

Judging from the size of the antiglobalization protests in Seattle, Washington, Quebec City, Davos, and Milan, the French are not the only ones toying with such an idea. But you can bet they will take the heat for it for a long time.

chapter 21

The French Melting Pot

We arrived in Paris shortly after the beginning of Ramadan, the Muslim month of fasting and celebration, and we couldn't have missed it if we had been walking around with bags over our heads. On our first walk through the city, we passed by the Great Mosque of Paris, near the Roman circus, and saw the faithful streaming in and out. *Le Monde* was running a daily special on the "Nights of Ramadan." On our second night in Paris we ended up at a concert listening to some of France's leading Muslim composers and performers.

Though tourists visiting France for the first time might not know it, France is the biggest Muslim nation of Europe, with an estimated five million followers. Islam has been the second religion of France for nearly thirty years. There are twice as many Muslims in France as Protestants (one million) and Jews (seven hundred thousand) combined, and Arabic culture is now definitely part of mainstream French culture.

Even a decade ago this was not the case. On our first visit to France in 1992, we heard the term *Beur*, a slang expression for the children of Arab immigrants, being used to describe a lively subculture known for speaking in a mix of Arabic, French, and *Verlan* (a form of French *Argot* that consists of reverting syllables). But a decade later, names like Djamel, Fharid, Sami, and Khaleb were part of mainstream culture in music, literature, television, and cinema.

Our friends and acquaintances all attributed this "coming out" of Arabic culture to the victory of the French soccer team in the 1998 World Cup. Of all the European teams, France's was exceptional for the mixed origins of its players, many of who were Beur or black (the French use the English word). The World Cup victory was followed by a fantastic explosion of joy on the Champs Elysées, where one million people paraded in celebration (the same celebrations happened all over again when France won the European Cup in 2000). In a popular pun, the patriotic expression *Bleu Blanc Rouge* (Blue White Red: the colors of the French flag) turned into *Black Blanc Beur* (Black White Beur). France's center field player Zinedine Zidane—a Beur of Algerian descent—became a common household name and a role model for hundreds of thousands of French youngsters—Beur, black, and *blanc* alike.

The French refer to this new cultural reality as *métissage* (crossbreeding). At first that expression struck us as strange and slightly offensive: France's population has almost always been ethnically mixed, and normally the French don't lean on people's ethnic origins, especially when they are referring to assimilated French citizens. Many of France's cultural stars, past and present, were immigrants, or children of immigrants. The famous French singer Yves Montand was Italian. The painter Picasso was Spanish, as was writer Albert Camus by his mother. While the Americans were still fighting the war of secession, one famous mulatto, Alexandre Dumas, wrote *The Three Musketeers* and *The Count of Monte Cristo*. In the 1920s, Americans were flocking to Paris to discover jazz music and listen to black artists like Josephine Baker. Actor Michel Coluche was Italian. In 1985, the former president of Senegal, Leopold Sedar Senghor, became a member of the French Academy. And this is not counting the number of artists of North African origin, which is even more impressive.

Beur culture is different, though, partly because of the sheer demographic weight of the North African immigrants. Beurs are provoking a grassroots cultural shift powerful enough to redefine mainstream French culture altogether. One of France's biggest international pop stars of the moment is the *raï* singer Cheb Mami, who recently recorded a duet with pop singer Sting. Like the American rap that originated in urban ghettos,

French rap coming out of the suburban ghettos has quickly gone from marginal to mainstream. One of the most popular French comedies of the last decade, *Taxi*, was about a Beur taxi driver from Marseilles. In 2001, a big hit in movie theaters was *La Vérité Si Je Mens* (*The Truth if I Lie*), the story of five Tunisian Jews working in the Paris garment district who are swindled by a big French multinational. Judging by the number of jokes in the film in *Verlan* and Arabic (and the number of people who laughed at them), it is probably safe to say these languages are entering mainstream vocabulary.

The French have always considered artists and performers as quasi-intellectuals, and Beur artists are clearly adopting this role. The main contenders in the 2001 municipal election in Toulouse were a right-wing slate of Philippe Douste-Blazy and a group of Beur singers from a pop group called Zebda, whose song *Tombez la Chemise* (Drop the Shirt), had been a major hit in the 1990s. The pop group got 45 percent of the vote. They lost that time, but as the French would put it, *ce n'est que partie remise* (we'll see next time).

Despite all the signs that France is absorbing, rather than assimilating, Arabic culture, life is far from rosy for France's immigrant population. Many recent immigrants live in the country's suburban ghettos, known as *cités*, the products of France's disastrous urbanization schemes of the 1960s. *Cités* have made a lost generation out of the children of France's first wave of Muslim immigration.

Cités started out as giant public housing projects built throughout suburban France to answer urgent housing needs in the post-war period. The government meant well, but many of the projects quickly fell into decay thanks to poor design, poor building standards, and poor management. Much like apartment complexes in many North American city centers, France's *cités* ended up housing mostly the poor working class and immigrants. In the aftermath of the 1973 oil crisis, unemployment exploded and hit the least-qualified workers first—immigrants for the most part. This added misery to an already grim picture. Unemployment rates of 25 percent became the norm in the *cités*.

This misery was compounded by the fact that until the 1980s French immigrants had no political representation of any sort, not even advisory committees. As foreigners, they didn't even have the right to create their own associations, to the extent that they could not even organize soccer leagues without the approval of their *préfet*. A subculture naturally developed, reinforcing the ghetto mentality. Chronic unemployment and violence became rampant. Nights of rioting, burning cars, and *rodeos*—a ritual of driving stolen cars around and destroying them—have been the daily lot of residents for many years. Not a week goes by without a severe incident involving the disenchanted youth of the *cités*, whether it's the burning of city buses, gang fighting, assaults, rapes, theft, or other vandalism. In January 2001, two hundred kids from rival bands fought openly at *La Défense*, the hypermodern high-rise office complex west of Paris. When a policeman in Toulouse shot a car thief in a *cité* in 1998, three nights of riots followed.

Friends of ours in Paris, an anarchist musician and a left-leaning *lycée* teacher, moved into an apartment in one such housing complex in the suburban town of Épinay-sur-Seine, just north of our neighborhood in Paris. We visited them half a dozen times while they lived there. The area, like many on the periphery of Paris, had a bad reputation, but the first couple of times we saw it, the actual building seemed fine. A number of young couples like our friends had just moved in. However, while our friends took fewer prejudiced notions into their new life than most French would, in the end their open-minded optimism just wasn't enough. Six months after they moved in, the foyer was covered with *tags* (graffiti), and all the first-floor windows had been broken. Their nights were disrupted by noise, yelling, and explosions. They packed their belongings and moved to Saint-Cloud, a peaceful and prosperous town on the outskirts of Paris.

While researching municipal governments, Jean-Benoît had the opportunity to see *cité* life up close in the town of Meaux, just east of Paris. He was interviewing Jean-François Copé, the young mayor who decided to buck the system and create his own local police to deal with the chronic problems of the *cités*. Copé invited him to tag along on a night patrol with his newly created city police. The center of a region famous for producing

Brie cheese, Meaux is also a Jekyll-and-Hyde community. One-half is a quintessential small French town: old, quaint, small-scale, and densely populated. The other half, where 53 percent of the population lives, is a forest of decaying high-rises. But Meaux is not exceptional: most suburban areas of France have pockets that are modernist nightmares.

Before Copé got his city police up and running, the electors of Meaux tried to solve the problems in the *cités* themselves—so to speak. During the 1995 legislative elections, residents of Meaux cast 23 percent of their vote in favor of Jean-Marie Le Pen, the leader of France's extreme right party, the *Front National*. Le Pen's party had campaigned on the promise to bulldoze all the *cités* in France and send the immigrants back to the third world (ignoring the fact that half of France's immigrant population is European). Although Meaux never elected a *Front National député*, the party's 23 percent take was well above the national average of 15 percent.

Jean-Benoît set out with two policemen on a routine patrol of two of Meaux's *cités*: Beauval and la Pierre-Collinet. About twelve thousand people live in each set of complexes. Beauval, the more prosperous one, consisted of about fifty small apartment buildings. Trees had been planted between the buildings, one obvious effort at humanizing the environment. The police said there were only a few trouble spots left. Indeed, things were pretty quiet that night. The only incident that required police intervention was a case of two ten-year-olds who had thrown stones through the window of Beauval's police station.

La Pierre-Collinet, several kilometers away, was a different story altogether. It had four buildings that were two hundred meters long, twenty floors high, separated by two-hundred-meter stretches of open space. Each building had a ring of graffiti around its first floors. One was in such bad shape that the authorities had decided to demolish it. As the officers cruised by the buildings, something fell on the car roof. Residents whistled and yelled insults from the windows. As one of the officers explained, the police never go inside these kinds of buildings without special protection measures, and never in groups of less than three—progress from the time when no police ever entered them. In any event, he explained, locals tend to settle matters between themselves and rarely call the police, who are widely distrusted in the *cités*. To get a foothold in the neighborhood, the city police of Meaux opened a station in a nearby mall. But a week before Jean-Benoît's visit, a group of young men had rammed a car through the station's steel shutters, sacked the station, and set it on fire.

Relations between police and immigrants in France couldn't be worse. Police have the reputation of, on one hand, not caring about what happens in the ghettos, while constantly harassing the *basané* (literally, "tanned") youth who venture into good neighborhoods. Racial tension isn't the only problem. The kids in the *cités* are known for being extremely defiant of authority. The two policemen Jean-Benoît accompanied, Rachid and Tony, were a Beur and a Guadeloupian, respectively. Both grew up in the suburbs. But that didn't matter to the residents of the *cités*, who saw the officers first and foremost as cops. That evening there was a call from an apartment block in a good neighborhood. A resident was complaining that some *jeunes* (literally "youth," but actually a euphemism for black or Beur youth) were making a lot of noise. Rachid and Tony intercepted four teens coming out of one of the buildings, but whenever the police officers opened their mouths to ask a question, the kids laughed, interrupted them, or just walked away. It was only when one of the officers demanded their ID cards that the youngsters complied.

Police in France also have the reputation of being lenient on whites. Jean-Benoît followed Rachid and Tony to a neighborhood where they had made an arrest the previous evening. It was a peaceful neighborhood of cottages, not high-rises. The object of the visit was to check on a man who had been attacked by a neighborhood thug—a remarkably violent white teenager who was the leader of a gang. During the visit, all the neighbors showed up, chatting with the police over their garden's fence. They all seemed appreciative except one black man, who accused the police of reverse racism.

"You would have come earlier if the kid had been black!" he said.

Tony and Rachid told him, "Well, sir, you're talking to a black and a Rebeu (*Verlan* for Beur). So what you're saying doesn't really make sense."

Racial relations in France are extremely complicated. And racial discrimination is by no means confined to the *cités*. We saw plenty of it in our own working-class neighborhood, which had a strong North African presence. We heard about racism firsthand from the mouths of friends, in particular our local grocer, Ridha, who had immigrated from Tunisia as a teenager and lived in the back room of his store for fifteen years before he could afford to get married and rent an apartment. When he was ready to get a nice apartment, it proved a difficult task, as it is for all North African immigrants in Paris. More than one landlord refused him, telling him they didn't want any "Arabs" in their building.

Strangely, though, it is very difficult to talk about racism, immigration, and integration in France, let alone write about them. There are absolutely no statistics available on these issues. Official documents in France simply have no boxes to check about religion, mother tongue, or ethnic origin. The government cannot legally ask for this information on the national census; they only ask respondents to indicate their citizenship. Once immigrants become French, they are considered French only. As a result, no one can make more than an educated guess about the size of any ethnic or religious group in France, or for that matter, about who lives in the *cités*.

There are reasons for the statistical void. Requiring citizens to declare their ethnic origin would be a transgression of the French doctrine of assimilation, one of the founding principles of the *République*. At the time of the French Revolution, France was an ethnic and linguistic patchwork. The Revolutionaries developed a policy of assimilation to further the goal of centralization and create a single French identity. Their motives were, of course, purely political, and not the slightest bit humanitarian. Still, France is the first country in Europe to define citizenship not by blood, language, or religion, but by residency in a territorial entity and adherence to its values. From the time of the Revolution, Protestants were given equal status, as were Jews and the children of immigrants. They were granted full citizenship at birth.

This principle shows a sharp contrast with Germany, where citizenship was still defined by blood for most of the twentieth century. According to the German law, the German-born son of a Turkish worker who worked all his life in Germany was not entitled to citizenship, but a twelfth generation descendent of a German settler on the shores of the Volga would almost automatically get German citizenship. The Germans only modified this law in 2000—two centuries after the French Revolution.

The French, of course, ignored these principles mightily during World War II, when the fascist regime of Vichy deprived France's three hundred thousand Jews of all their rights and sent seventy-five thousand of them to their death in concentration camps. At the end of the war, the French reverted to the strict principle of assimilation as it was articulated during the Revolution, and made it illegal to keep information on civilian's ethnic origin, religious affiliation, or sexual orientation. This official discretion can go very far, to the point that there is no way to gather statistics about any of these issues in France. In 1999, the government decided to legalize common-law marriages in order to give common-law spouses the same claims on Social Security and inheritance as married people. In the process, homosexual common-law unions were permitted. In 2001, twenty-eight thousand people entered a common-law union, but it is impossible to know how many of those were gay unions because the question is not asked on official documents.

Immigration and integration in France are statistical black holes. It's almost impossible, for instance, to compare France's immigrations patterns to other European countries. There are simply no reliable statistics available to make that possible. Germany claims to have 7.3 million immigrants; France claims to have around 3.5 million. The number is high in Germany because the children of immigrants do not automatically become citizens at birth and usually remain immigrants all their lives. It's almost the opposite situation in France, where children of immigrants become citizens at eighteen as long as they grew up on French territory. Then, when they become citizens, they automatically vanish from statistics.

French statistics only allow us to know this much. In 2000, there were 3.5 million immigrants, 40 percent of who were unqualified workers, and about 20 percent of who were unemployed. This accounts for about 6 percent of the population. Another 1.7 million former immigrants became citizens during their lives. This number is considered a low estimate, though; after they become citizens, many immigrants declare that they were born in France on census forms. That makes another 3 percent of the population. How many of their children and grandchildren are now French? A conservative estimate puts the number of immigrants and second-generation immigrants at about 12 percent of the total population. Other estimates, probably more accurate, claim the proportion is more like 20 percent. Racists say it's 50 percent.

No one in France really knows anything about whether immigrants integrate, or what factors determine whether they do. An exact picture of integration in France simply does not exist. There are no statistics on how many former immigrants acquire citizenship, where they live, how many children they have, what jobs they have, who hires them, how much they are paid, what language they speak, who they marry, or what religion they practice. It's anybody's guess. All opinions are based on anecdotal evidence.

Some sociologists and associations do their best with the lack of official data and have even managed to produce studies on the topic. In the absence of true statistical evidence, they use factors like whether names sound French or not, then generalize their conclusions countrywide. According to some of these studies, one-half of male Beurs—second-generation Arabs—marry non-Muslim women, but only one-quarter of female Beurs marry non-Beurs. Another study claims that the rate of delinquency of African immigrants is higher than the national rate—not surprising because poverty is more common among immigrants than the general population. But the margin of error is enormous, and none of these studies are completely reliable.

This statistical black hole is a double-edged sword. On one hand, it prevents any form of labeling, a situation that immigrants appreciate. On the other hand, it allows racists and xenophobes to fabricate any kind of story they want, to magnify local problems into grand theories and argue that immigrants should be sent back to the third world. In other words, it removes the possibility of deflating the racist rhetoric of France's extreme right with plain facts and figures, and to act on real problems.

France's far-right party, the *Front National*, has made good use of this statistical void. The party is the creation of charismatic leader Jean-Marie Le Pen, a lawyer and *grande-école* graduate, who came in second during the

2002 presidential elections. In 1954–55, Le Pen fought in Indochina as a second lieutenant in the crack airborne troops. In 1956, at twenty-seven, he became the youngest *député* of the National Assembly as a member of the right-wing *Union et Fraternité Française*. The same year, he took a six-month leave to go back to the army. He fought in the 1956 Suez Expedition and worked as an intelligence officer in Algiers. He also became Secretary General of a paramilitary organization called the *Front National Combattant* (the National Fighting Front), which supported a French Algeria. Regarded as subversive, this association was outlawed in 1961. In 1972, Le Pen founded a political party, the *Front National*. Until 1983, the party was extremely marginal, winning only 0.5 percent of the vote in elections, at best. But at the 1983 municipal elections, the party won a surprising 11.3 percent of the vote. It has held onto about the same proportion of the vote since then, with highs of 17 percent and lows of 2 percent at some municipal elections.

It is hard to define a cause for the *Front National*'s sudden rise in popularity in the 1980s. Le Pen is an exceptional orator who appealed (and still does) to various conservative political orientations, including voters who are nostalgic for the Old Regime, fanatical anti-communists, die-hard colonialists, opponents of the parliamentary system, or even old fans of Pétain. What these voters all shared was a strong sense of anti-semitism and xenophobia. Le Pen built on this common denominator and used anti-immigration rhetoric to bind his different supporters. The *Front National* is an authoritarian, reactionary law-and-order party that is opposed to European integration and keenly attached to the idea of a powerful French State.

Circumstances were favorable to Le Pen's rise. When the 1973 oil crisis provoked a recession and unemployment rose in Europe, immigration became a hot issue in France, as in Germany, the United Kingdom, Italy, Belgium, and Sweden. Rising unemployment came just when immigration rates in France were peaking at about four million per year. In an odd leap of logic, conservative demagogues convinced many voters that immigrants were to blame for the job losses (when, in fact, immigrants were generally lowest on the seniority ladder and the first ones to be laid off). But there was already widespread resentment against North Africans in France as a result of decolonization and the independence movement in Algeria in the 1950s and early 1960s. Following in the steps of other European countries, President Valéry Giscard d'Estaing placed severe restrictions on immigration and offered immigrants money to return to their country of origin— like elsewhere, the measures were largely ineffective. It was around that time that Le Pen's popularity suddenly started to rise.

Given the *Front National*'s openly xenophobic platform, it is surprising that it has been allowed to exist at all. The French government actually could have stopped it, but it let the opportunity slip by. When it was first created, and for many years after that, *Front National* was considered marginal and inoffensive; nothing it was doing was illegal. Until the 1980s, the party failed to capture more than 1 percent of the vote, so other parties did not regard it as a threat. In 1983, the *Front National* suddenly gained 10 percent of the vote in the municipal elections, then 11 percent a year later in the European elections. This sudden jump in support comes from the failure of the center-right to win at the presidential and legislative elections of 1981, bringing in the socialist François Mitterrand as president. People of the right took this defeat badly, some of them claiming that the "Soviet tanks were waiting in the North of Paris." Some of the right-wing vote swung into the arms of Jean-Marie Le Pen, whose inflammatory rhetoric suited the most extreme conservatives. And suddenly, Le Pen had acquired too much legitimacy to be stopped.

Mitterrand himself is largely to blame for allowing the *Front National* to gain a luster of legitimacy. As the 1986 legislative elections were approaching, the socialists' position was not very good. Mitterrand did not attack the extreme right because he thought that if he left it alone, it might split the right-wing vote. The socialist-communist vote had been splitting the left-wing vote for thirty years, allowing the constant reelection of Gaullists. To make sure the same thing would happen on the right, Mitterrand changed the election system for the legislative elections from a two-round election by riding to a proportional system. But his strategy backfired: the socialists were ousted and he ended up in *cohabitation* with a right-wing prime minister. The *Front National* won 9.7 percent of the vote, which allowed it to take thirty-five of the 574 seats in the National Assembly. Mitterrand restored the two-round vote by riding in 1988, and the *Front National* won only one seat in the legislative assembly. But the damage was done. Although the *Front National* had never gained more than one National Assembly seat in any other legislative election, the 1986 elections gave them the status of a legitimate political party.

Fortunately, the political damage was contained. The French Right isolated the *Front National* and refused to deal openly with Le Pen. To its credit, the French Right has consistently refused to strike any kind of alliance with the FN, often at the price of the electoral victory. (This is exactly what happened in Austria and Italy in 2000 and 2001, where the right joined forces with the extreme right during legislative elections.) During the 1998 regional elections, some local right-wing politicians did strike local alliances with *Front National* candidates, but national parties of the Right and Left condemned the maneuver, and it hasn't happened since. The Right has been more confident about its position since Jacques Chirac won the presidency in 1995, in spite of Le Pen's 15 percent vote.

In the late 1990s, the *Front National* faired badly during elections, partly because French authorities decided to get tough with Le Pen. In May 1998, Le Pen manhandled a socialist protester at a political meeting in Mantes-la-Jolie, east of Paris—the protester turned out to be the city's mayor. Le Pen was prosecuted and found guilty. He was banned from office and stripped of his seat as regional councilor. In 1999, a number of assault rifles were found in the trunk of his car, and he was dragged before the law again. This constant legal harassment seriously undermined his credibility and provoked a rift in the *Front National*, which split into rival factions just before the European elections of June 1999. The two factions won less than 8.8 percent of the vote together. And at the municipal elections of 2001, the *Front National* won less than 10 percent of the vote.

But at the 2002 presidential elections, Le Pen bounced back with 16.8 percent of the popular vote, much to the shock and embarrassment of the French themselves. International commentators made much of his anti-immigrant discourse, but in fact, Le Pen had campaigned more on a law-and-order platform, selling himself as a hard-nosed right-wing candidate rather than the leader of France's extreme-right. Le Pen's traditional extreme-right oratory resurfaced only during the campaign for the second round, when France's other extreme-right parties rallied to him. In the second round, Le Pen's score only rose a tiny bit to 19 percent. The conclusion to be drawn? Most of his party's 2002 success was the result of Le Pen's persona, not support for the *Front National*. Even the legitimacy Le Pen gained by defeating France's socialist party in the first round was not sufficient to win extra votes among hard-nosed right-wingers. In the legislative elections a month later, support for Le Pen's party dwindled to 12 percent of the vote.

Whether the *Front National*'s success will survive its seventy-four-year-old leader remains to be seen, but one thing is certain: his ideas will always get support. That's partly because like any country, a good 15 percent of the French are reactionary and racist. But there is another fact at work, unique to France.

The *Front National* is the only party in France that has ever campaigned on issues of integration and immigration. Unfortunately, no other party brings these issues up in order to give them a positive spin. This allows the far right to monopolize the issue and lay down the terms in which it is discussed. Although the *Front National* never held a seat in any cabinet, Le Pen's party has been in a position to indirectly influence France's immigration policy and shape public opinion on the question.

A vast majority of the population is actually against Le Pen's ideas, but the political parties that represent them have failed in explaining why they oppose him. Even the politicians who do admit France has problems integrating immigrants tend to shy away from saying what those problems are. As a consequence, no one proposes constructive ways to deal with the integration of immigrants. The only coherent voice on the matter was Jean-Pierre Chevènement, a left-wing politician who expressed worries about integration problems while he was Minister of the Interior from 1997 to 2000. He worked hard to find solutions—his approach was to be tough on crime while working on a rapprochement with France's Muslim community. But the issue of integration is so taboo among the French Left that

Chevènement ended up getting very little political support from his natural allies, to the point that some even accused him of fostering extreme-right ideas. The reason for this taboo is the *République's* official policy of assimilation: everyone is expected to integrate. But any attempt to identify the problem of who does not integrate, where, and why, is perceived as a threat to the assimilation doctrine. That leaves the field open to Le Pen.

For fifteen years now, Le Pen has been the only politician willing to speak openly, though badly, about integration problems. France toughened up immigration laws in the '80s and '90s as a result of Le Pen's influence. In 1986, Jacques Chirac's government stiffened the rules for French citizens who married foreigners, forcing foreign spouses to wait two years for French citizenship instead of one. In 1993, the government removed the right to automatic citizenship at birth for children of immigrants and required children to apply for naturalization between the ages of sixteen and twenty-one. In 1998, the socialist government reverted to a more open policy, granting children of immigrants automatic citizenship at eighteen, or at age thirteen if the child requested it.

The *Front National* has probably not made the French more racist. It's safe to assume that a good 15 percent of the electorate is xenophobic to begin with. All European countries, for that matter, have a far-right party, and the proportion of extremists is probably about the same everywhere.

Racial discrimination is a fact of life in France, as it is in almost all societies. In the second week of our stay, the rental agent for our apartment casually remarked that we had chosen a good neighborhood because it was *le bon 18 ième* (the "good" part of the eighteenth *arrondissement*). The "bad" part of the eighteenth was the East Side, where there is a higher concentration of Africans and Arabs (as the French call North Africans). Of course, people in Toronto said something quite similar about the neighborhood we chose there, where there were a lot of Caribbean immigrants. The difference in France was how open, or even brazen, people were about their prejudices. We were struck by that the night an acquaintance drove us back home from a party and spontaneously launched into a rant about "Arabs" as soon as she saw our neighborhood (that would probably not happen in Toronto).

The people who were not that open about their prejudices simply refused to talk about the issue, probably because talking about race contradicts the values of the Republic by definition. The French have a lot of euphemisms for talking about the problems of race relations without calling them race relations. They speak of *insécurité* (insecurity, meaning violence) in *les cités* (ghettos) on the part of *les jeunes* (Beurs and blacks). Unfortunately, the refusal of well-meaning citizens to discuss immigration and integration just opens the terrain for France's far right.

Starting in the mid-1970s, French authorities realized France had an integration problem, but concretely, nothing was done about integration and racism before the 1990s. One of the reasons it took so long to act was that positive discrimination and affirmative action are taboo concepts in a country whose central doctrine of citizenship is assimilation. That seems to be slowly changing.

During the three years we were in France, we very rarely heard anyone say anything positive about multiculturalism. The Republic has been built on the principle that all citizens are equal before the State. The twentieth century showed the French that the existence of non-governmental associations would do no harm to the *République*. But the State always rejected the idea of political liberty at the local level and looked suspiciously on attempts to develop any form of community life, especially around local cultures (because of the risk that this would justify or legitimize such liberties). Bretons, Corsicans, and Basques were never allowed to create their own associations and neither were immigrant groups. This is a sharp contrast to the German custom of allowing immigrants to vote in municipal elections for parallel immigrants' councils with consultative powers. The French never allowed such councils on the basis that immigrants should have no special status—in other words, no more rights than any other citizen.

The government failed to see how this approach would actually work against the goal of integration. The government allowed the geographic concentration of low-skilled immigrants in the *cités*. The result was that entire towns were made hypersensitive to economic downturns. By refusing immigrants the right to vote even for an advisory city council, and by denying them the right to create their own associations, the government prevented them from having any say in their own affairs. The *préfets* were there to manage the *intérêt général*, but they tended to have less time and interest for non-citizens than for voting citizens. Not surprisingly, residents of suburban ghettos ended up feeling profoundly alienated.

That feeling remains, but the situation has been changing since the 1970s, when it dawned on the French government that protecting cultural minorities did not necessarily contradict the principles of the Republic. At that time the government started to encourage Basques, Corsicans, and Bretons to develop their own cultural associations. Slowly, the idea that immigrants could do the same started to gain ground. In 1974, the new president, Valéry Giscard d'Estaing, created a ministry in charge of integration. Its main job was to apply programs for sending immigrants back to their countries of origin, but at least France had officially recognized the issues of immigration and integration.

In October 1981, François Mitterrand officially allowed immigrants to create their own associations. The number of mosques in France multiplied, from 274 in 1980 to between some twenty-five hundred in 1993. Mitterrand granted the same labor rights to illegal immigrants as legal immigrants already had. The government also recognized that the *cités* needed more resources and began to put more educational staff and schools in them. Throughout the 1990s, the government pushed integration more actively and attempted to improve its relations with France's huge and growing Muslim community.

Since the election of the socialists in 1997, the administration has adopted a number of measures to hire more children of immigrants. The very idea contradicts the principle of assimilation of the *République*, according to which nationals of foreign origin do not even exist, let alone get special treatment from the State. But the French are coming around to the idea of recognizing minorities. In 1998, the National Police started systematically hiring citizens of foreign origin as police auxiliaries. But, since no statistics can be held on the operation, there is no way of measuring its success. On a day-to-day basis, we did observe that about one in four police officers do not look old-stock French, though our method might be futile since half the French look Mediterranean, anyway. A number of police officers are also Guadeloupians and Martiniquans, who have been fully integrated since 1945.

In 2000, the socialists surmounted another taboo when they passed a law that said 50 percent of the candidates of any party, for any elected office, had to be women. Women are not a different race, but they have been curiously absent from public offices in France, more so than in any other European country (about 10 percent of members of the National Assembly are women, compared with an average of 20 percent for Europe and most developed nations). French women got voting power and equal civil rights in 1944, but invisible barriers have clearly stopped them from entering politics. The law on equality of electoral seats was first put to the test in the municipal elections of 2001. We interviewed Yvette Roudy, the *député* who had created the first laws on equality in 1981. We met her at a round table in 2001, and her point of view applied both to women and to immigrants: "I understand that every citizen must be theoretically equal, but I came to understand that if the principle of equality is there to justify the permanent exclusion of some groups, then there must be measures to put an end to this situation." The measure worked. After the municipal elections of 2001, the proportion of women holding elected offices in *communes* rose from 20 to 33 percent.

Like Roudy, many lawmakers in France have recognized that the National Assembly will need to do more for immigrants and their children. One of the reasons for the socialist victory in the 1995 legislative elections, and their other landslide in the 1997 legislative elections, is that they deliberately presented candidates from different ethnic communities and didn't hide it. The move was regarded as a novelty in French politics.

In 2002, Paris created its first Council of Immigrant Representation. This is the surest sign yet that old taboos about assimilation in France are finally breaking down.

chapter 22

New Checks and Balances

When socialist leader François Mitterrand was elected president on May 10, 1981, the late President Charles de Gaulle must have been rolling in his grave. De Gaulle thought Mitterrand was a self-interested careerist. First, because Mitterrand flirted with the fascist regime of Pétain during World War II while de Gaulle was leading the Free French; then, because Mitterrand held five consecutive ministries in a regime that brought France to the verge of civil war in 1958.

The feeling was mutual. Mitterrand had always detested de Gaulle's inflexibility and authoritarian style. He accused de Gaulle of mounting a *coup d'état* when he took power in 1958. Mitterrand also claimed that de Gaulle had designed the election rules to favor the right. He said that de Gaulle had turned the presidency into a virtual monarchy and that France's political system had become an ineffective, semi-presidential, semi-parliamentary hybrid. Mitterrand swore that when he became president, he would rewrite the Constitution and reinvent France's institutions.

To everybody's surprise, Mitterrand did nothing of the sort after his election in 1981. He didn't touch the fundamentals of de Gaulle's Constitution, and he pretty much left de Gaulle's institutions alone, too. Mitterrand modified the rules for the legislative elections in 1986, then returned to de Gaulle's formula in 1988. (For details, see Appendix 1.) The most profound change he made in 1982 was to borrow an old idea of de Gaulle's to create Regions, a new administrative grouping of *Départements*.

Mitterrand's failure to fulfill his election promises turned out to be one of the best things that had ever happened to France—and he will certainly be remembered for this. The man, himself, was hardly a model democratic leader. During his first mandate, he had his secret police tap the phones of some two thousand politicians, business leaders, and opinion-makers. He also undertook several disastrous and costly public works projects, like the new national library and the Paris Opera, which were built mainly to ensure himself a glorious personal legacy. Yet his two elected mandates will be remembered because Mitterrand put de Gaulle's Constitution to the test of transition and allowed it to become universal and quasi-permanent.

The French born after 1958 are the first generation to grow up in a stable political environment with solid democratic institutions. Since the Revolution, France has been through five Republics, two empires, three monarchies, and one fascist dictatorship. The Third Republic lasted sixty-nine years (1871–1940), but the period was marred by such political instability that, by 1940, a sizable proportion of the population wanted nothing more to do with democracy and sat by passively when Parliament granted dictatorial powers to Philippe Pétain.

De Gaulle gave France the solid and durable institutions it would need to become a functioning democracy. The new Constitution, the Fifth Republic, will almost certainly last longer than the previous four. Nobody in France now questions the legitimacy of Parliament, the Senate, the presidency, or the *Conseil Constitutionnel*. Legitimate and effective institutions mean tensions are diffused and quarrels solved without the entire system breaking down, so the threat of civil war and revolution have almost been eliminated. The system has also stood the test of two major political crises—including riots over the independence of Algeria in 1961–62 and student protests in May 1968—and a change of regime in 1981.

De Gaulle himself probably never anticipated how much the 1958 Constitution would change France. Democracy is quickly transforming the French, and the French are quickly adapting the institution to their needs. Durable institutions are turning out to be effective checks against the four

P's of French political life: Paris, the President, Parliament, and Politicians. Since 1982, previously unthinkable political liberties have been introduced into the system through the creation of Regions and the devolution of powers to local administrations. Electors have forced the system to tolerate a prime minister and president from rival parties. The French are starting to demand more accountability from their elected officials. And both Parliament and the government are finding themselves more and more subject to the decisions of the *Conseil Constitutionnel* (the equivalent of the Supreme Court, dealing with electoral and constitutional issues).

The process is not without growing pains. Throughout our stay, we were fascinated with the constant debates in media and government over issues like voter abstention rates, what the French call the "trivialization" of politics, the bickering between the president and the prime minister, the power of the judges, and the so-called "mess" of regionalization. A lot of the time, commentators blamed these trends on globalization or Europe, or even American influence. It took us a while to understand what was really happening: the French are simply suffering the growing pains of democracy coming of age.

France's political culture was built around a strong penchant for absolutism, authoritarianism, centralism, and a considerable dose of intolerance. Democratic institutions are forcing the French to suppress those reflexes. Not everyone is happily obliging. For instance, it's only normal for judges in a democracy to assert their independence, and French judges seem to know that. Yet the political class clearly resents judges encroaching on territory that has long been their prerogative, like deciding on the constitutionality of a law. Few French realize that issues like this are simply part of the give and take of democratic life. The old authoritarian reflexes of the French aren't dying easily, even as a functioning democracy undermines them. From the Right and the Left alike, the French still long for "great men"—the de Gaulles, Napoleons, Richelieus, and Colberts of French history. What they don't seem to understand is that democratic institutions make these kinds of "great men" unnecessary, even undesirable.

One of the most profound changes in French democracy was brought about when Mitterrand introduced Regions in 1982. De Gaulle had tried to create Regions in 1969 through a policy he strangely called *la participation*. To do this, de Gaulle needed to change the Constitution, so he called a referendum. No one understood what de Gaulle meant by "participation," so the population voted against it. De Gaulle took the referendum defeat as a vote of non-confidence and resigned exactly ten minutes after the results came in. Thirteen years later, Mitterrand's reform passed because he avoided a referendum and simply asked France's *Congrès* (senators and *députés* voting together) to rubber-stamp it. Twenty-six Regions were created, made up of about four *Départements* each.

Mitterrand's idea, like de Gaulle's, was to instill fresh ideas and more initiative into the rigid centralized system. When the Regions were formed in 1982, Paris transferred various powers to different levels of local administration. *Communes* were given jurisdiction over town planning. Regions were given authority over development planning. Elected regional councils were also created. The government removed the executive power of the *Département* from the hands of the *préfet* and gave it to an elected president of a *Départemental* council, known as the *conseil général*. To anyone accustomed with the workings of a federalist system, these changes do not sound drastic, but such decentralization was revolutionary in France. Certain *préfets* were reported to have cried when the law was passed, though in reality they didn't lose that much power.

In the end, it might have been the *flou artistique* (deliberate vagueness) of the reform that made it possible. *Régionalisation* is also referred to as Decentralization, Deconcentration, State Reform, or Participation—the terms are used interchangeably. What powers were actually transferred remains unclear, even to the French. The only certain thing is that Regions have input into, and some control over, education, economic, and development planning, and culture.

Régionalisation has turned out to be an effective check against the influence of Paris. It has made it possible to create stronger community life, previously a big taboo in France. Local economies have been allowed to pursue development initiatives on their own, to the point that Lyon recently got its own high-speed train link to Brussels with no stop in Paris, a first. The Regions are proving to have a very strong power of attraction. In the 1970s and '80s, 120,000 Parisians left the Paris Region to move to other parts of France. Those numbers shot up in the 1990s, when 570,000 people moved from Paris to more dynamic centers like Lyon, Nantes, and Toulouse. The government has been encouraging even more local initiative since then. A recent set of laws allows *communes*, *Départements*, and Regions to group themselves together to provide common services, in transport, for instance, or for the management of resources like the sea or waterways. Such pooling of resources was allowed prior to 1982, but not without the *préfet's* approval. Now, mayors can more or less initiate projects on their own.

The main gain of *Régionalisation* has been more political liberty for local politicians. Before 1982, city councils had to get permission from their *préfet* to debate any topic publicly. The *préfet* didn't have to justify a refusal. After council votes, the *préfet* also decided whether decisions accorded with the laws of the Republic or not. But since 1982, city councils are free to debate what they want without preapproval. When in doubt, *préfets* forward city council bylaws to an administrative tribunal that rules on their legality.

France is still nowhere near turning into a federation. Regions are actually the equivalent of a super-municipal government. They have legitimacy and a measure of political liberty, but no autonomy and no sovereignty whatsoever. In practice, this means politicians are freer to do what they want, but their taxing powers are still extremely limited. The *préfets* remain the centers of authority who enjoy considerable discretionary powers as the president's personal representatives, and run the police and the national administration in each *Département*. This mandate of control means they still have input in even the smallest of local affairs.

Regionalization is essentially a form of decentralization *à la carte*: each *commune*, *Département*, and Region chooses the degree of initiative it wants with respect to a *préfet*. Some Regions have been more ambitious in taking on powers than others. For that matter, it will take a long time for decentralization to become ingrained in the mentality of politicians and civil servants. Many *fonctionnaires* still try to manage Regions without

consultation like in the good old days of centralization, and local politicians often go along with this out of laziness or habit: it's easier to follow
orders than to show initiative. But that will change as people come to recognize that France's most dynamic Regions are the ones where regional
councils have asserted their independence the most.

The French criticism of decentralization is interesting. *Régionalisation*
is commonly accused of being "disorderly." At the same time, critics blast
the central government for refusing to let go of powers. There is clearly a
lack of political consensus over the issue. After all, the French have always
thought equality meant uniformity, and the very point of *Régionalisation* is
to get rid of uniformity. Regionalization not only recognizes differences,
but encourages them—the kind of thinking that simply flies in the face of
the founding principles of the République.

The great unknown for the future is whether the newly acquired political liberty will be the Trojan Horse of local autonomy and force France to
become a federation. Nationalists and separatists are demanding more
local autonomy, and there's less and less the French government can do to
stop them. In 1999, the presidents of the three regional councils of
Guadeloupe, Martinique, and French Guiana made a joint declaration
demanding more autonomy for their regional councils. At the time,
France's Minister of Overseas was working on a piece of legislation that
would have granted overseas France the power to negotiate trade deals
with neighboring islands, formerly the exclusive turf of Parisian diplomats.
The legislation proposed merging the departmental and regional assem-
blies into a single congress, like Corsica has had since the 1970s.

Corsica, however, is not a very reassuring model for France's relationship
with its overseas territories and departments. Located off the coast of Italy,
the "Island of Beauty," as it is called, was annexed in 1768. After the
Revolution, it was made a full part of the one-and-indivisible Republic
thanks to the most famous Corsican of history: Napoleon. They adhered to
the highest principles of the République and adopted French as their language. Yet their attachment to Corsica remained strong and many kept
speaking the Corsican language. Corsicans have always had a disproportion-
ately strong presence in the French police and civil service. The French gov-

ernment never managed to control the island and stifle Corsicans' strong national identity and nationalist sentiment. Many French believe that the parallel network of Corsicans inside the police and the administration has prevented Paris from breaking Corsican nationalism. (In 2000, the mayor of Paris, Jean Tibéri, and *Préfet* Philippe Massoni were both Corsican.) Violence has been the daily lot of Corsicans since the 1960s, and it is not waning. Not a week goes by in Corsica without a murder or bombing.

In June 2000, Prime Minister Lionel Jospin drafted a bill offering Corsica the opportunity to create a Corsican Assembly with powers to "adapt the laws of the Republic." Opponents in the rest of France violently disagreed with Jospin's plan on grounds that he was opening the back door to federalism. In January 2002, the *Conseil Constitutionnel* declared the bill anti-constitutional on the grounds that the law must be uniform throughout the Republic. The message was: Corsica will only get special powers when the Constitution allows for them. That, in turn, would open the door for other similar demands coming from Guadeloupe, Martinique, Basque, and Brittany, where nationalist sentiment is also strong. Even Alsatia and Savoy—where there is strong community life but no separatism to speak of—would like the power to adapt laws to their needs.

It is impossible to predict the result of this overture. Judging by the reaction to Jospin's bill, Jacobin sentiment is still strong in France. However, Mitterrand's Regionalization did provide the French one tool for holding Paris' influence in check. And now France is moving toward a permanent state of debate and friction over who should do what.

In the 1980s, French voters accidentally created another check to the quasi-absolute power of the president: *la cohabitation*, referring to the fact that the president and prime minister come from rival parties. In chapter 9, we described how the French complain that cohabitation limits the president's ability to exercise power. Yet electors created the situation themselves. Cohabitation does signal a sort of evolution in France's political culture, even if the French fail to see it themselves.

The *cohabitation* phenomenon was actually the result of the political maneuvering of François Mitterrand. Since de Gaulle, it had been assumed

that the president and the legislature should both be either from the Right
or the Left. There is no rule in the Constitution that requires this: it's a
political tradition, just like the tradition of appointing a prime minister
from the elected majority. In the legislative elections of 1986, when the
French elected a right-wing majority, everyone expected Mitterrand to
interpret this as a vote of non-confidence and resign. Instead, he simply
appointed a right-wing prime minister and assumed the posture of arbitrator (doing his best the whole time to undermine the influence of his right-
wing prime minister, Jacques Chirac). Mitterrand repeated the move in
1993–95. His successor to the presidency, Jacques Chirac, followed in
Mitterrand's footsteps, appointing a left-wing prime minister for
1997–2002. When he was reelected president on May 5, 2002, Jacques
Chirac immediately appointed a right-wing prime minister, Jean Pierre
Raffarin, even though the left-wing majority in the National Assembly was
going to be there for another month. The legislative elections on June 9
and June 16, 2002, were a landslide victory for Chirac.

The phenomenon of cohabitation has shown that the Constitution of
1958 and its institutions are strong enough to survive even while the president and prime minister are in a constant tug-of-war. On the one hand, the
president remains supreme: he can still dissolve the National Assembly, call
elections, and appoint a new prime minister if he wants to. But he can no
longer dictate the French government's actions on a day-to-day basis. So
the prime minister and the president hold each other in check. As a mode
of government, it can be clumsy, especially since both the president and
prime minister are entitled to have input in government affairs and cabinet
meetings. The French are convinced this permanent state of conflict makes
governing the country impossible. Yet *cohabitation* has not prevented the
government from pushing through important reforms, like privatizing
dozens of state-owned companies, shortening the work week to thirty-five
hours, replacing France's official currency, and legalizing gay unions.

The popular reaction to cohabitation is puzzling. The French created
it, yet no one has a good thing to say about it. Predictably, French politicians have blamed voters for lacking "coherence." The people have
found a way to hold their president-monarch in check, yet they believe

cohabitation has made modern-day politics "petty." Cohabitation definitely limits the president's power with respect to the National Assembly, but the French don't seem to recognize this. It is as if, by some sort of mental inertia, they can't stop themselves from hating political compromise, even when they bring it on themselves. In any event, cohabitation is not permanent: in 2002, the French gave Chirac a strong majority and a right-wing National Assembly, which should allow him to rule without serious opposition until May 2007.

There is a third check on power sprouting up in France's political system: the increasing independence of judges. As we explained in chapter 15, the French have traditionally demanded that investigating magistrates "keep them informed" about politically sensitive cases. Politicians even feel it is their prerogative to tell judges how to carry out their investigations. To prevent politicians from interfering with the justice system, investigative magistrates have started taking their cases public, a tactic that has turned France's justice system into a bit of a circus.

In 1997, Lionel Jospin became the first prime minister to order his ministers and *députés* not to meddle in the justice system. Even if Jospin's successors carry his torch, it will still be an uphill battle for judges to stop politicians interfering in their work, thanks to the work of the National Assembly. Following a long spell of investigations into illegal party financing in the 1980s, the National Assembly passed a law in 1991 that granted amnesty on all similar charges against parties. Electors punished the socialists for the move in 1993, reducing their seats in the National Assembly from 260 to fifty-three. Yet the political class continues to resist the independence of judges. During the inquiries into alleged cases of corruption at Paris City Hall, the police refused to assist investigative magistrate Éric Halphen in carrying out a search of the city hall, allegedly because they had orders to "stay out of it." Halphen carried on without their help. A right-wing politician even tried to stop him in his tracks by denouncing Halphen's father-in-law for corruption. The accusation proved false, and Halphen carried on. In 2001, he sent a letter to the president requesting him to testify, but Chirac refused, invoking his presidential immunity. Halphen was taken off the case later that year, and he resigned in the first months of 2002.

The separation of executive, legislative, and judiciary powers has long been considered essential for democracy to function. Public demands for political accountability from politicians are only natural; corruption and embezzlement debase the political system. But French politicians don't see things this way. The French political class denounces the rising independence of judges (in other words, the separation of justice from the other powers) as "anti-democratic," according to the logic that politicians (whom the people elect) lose control. Theoretically, because France's political system already has strong authoritarian and absolutists tendencies, judges should be even *more* militant in demanding accountability. Someone has to reduce the absolute power French politicians have over constitutional matters.

The only other check on the power of national politicians in France is the *Conseil Constitutionnel*, a body de Gaulle created to control elections as well as act as the president's advisory board on constitutional matters. The Constitutional Council's pronouncements often challenge government projects and thwart the intentions of the National Assembly, who have almost absolute authority over law-making (ordinary citizens cannot challenge the constitutionality of laws in France). In 2002, the Constitutional Council deliberated a specific article of Jospin's bill for a Corsican Assembly and ruled the whole thing unconstitutional (on the basis that there is only one law in France). And in December 2001, the *Conseil Constitutionnel* censored an article of law that would have forbidden companies to lay off employees if they downsized just to maintain share values. The *Conseil Constitutionnel* has evolved. In 1982, it ruled a law calling for 25 percent of female representation in Parliament unconstitutional on the grounds that the Constitution declares all citizens equal. Yet eighteen years later, when the socialists came back with a law calling for 50 percent female representation, the *Conseil Constitutionnel* saw no problem with it. So things do change in the Republic, and the judiciary system has made significant headway.

Throughout our stay, French politicians and opinion-makers repeat-edly blamed electors for low turnout at the polls. But a close look shows French democracy to be pretty healthy from this perspective, at least com-pared to other western democracies. The United States abstention rate for presidential elections is nearly 50 percent; in France it's a mere 20 percent. It is 30 percent in legislative elections and 40 percent in local elections. This is a remarkable level of involvement in a country where real political liberty is limited to a happy few *députés*, and where voting is free, unlike Belgium, where voting is mandatory, explaining turnouts of 95 percent at the polls.

In every French election we saw during our stay, politicians complained vociferously about rising abstention rates. The abstention rate at presiden-tial elections rose from 15.7 to 20.3 percent between 1965 and 2002. At the legislative level, the rate used to swing between 20 percent and 30 percent, but seemed to have stabilized at around 30 percent since 1988, although it rose above 35 percent in 2002. The decline in voting is most apparent at the municipal level, where between 1965 and 2001, abstention rates rose from 25 to 38 percent, and at the regional level, where they increased from 22 percent in 1982 to 43 percent in 2001. Referendums are clearly drawing fewer voters out. Until the late 1960s, abstention rates in referendums were only 20 percent. That rose to 40 percent in the 1972 referendum (over whether to allow new members in the European Economic Union), to 63 percent in the 1988 referendum (on the status of New Caledonia), and to 70 percent in the 2000 referendum (on reducing the president's mandate from seven to five years). However, the abstention rate dropped to 30 per-cent for the 1992 referendum on creating the European Union, so clearly voters turn out when they think the question is important.

Comparisons over the long-term, and with the United States, show that the problem of declining turnout remains minor in the case of legisla-tive and presidential elections. Still, politicians and opinion-makers complain unanimously. "It's a threat to democracy," they say. Sure, voter apathy can be dangerous to democracy, but there are no absolute levels that define that. And, at any rate, French democracy seems to be doing just fine in this respect.

It is interesting to speculate about why the issue worries French politicians so much. Politicians also sense that the population is just less interested in politics than they used to be. We see two explanations. The population may be less fixated on legitimacy than its politicians are; people consider a victory without a very strong vote, or strong voter turnout, a victory all the same. And more importantly, the French no longer consider politics a life-and-death struggle. But that should come as no surprise. As the 1981 changeover and three cohabitation periods have shown, French governments—no matter what their political orientation is—are managing the economy and social matters decently and defending the system against threats. The role of *société civile*, the private sector, and associations has increased during the twentieth century and is no doubt stealing some of the limelight from politics. Electors know that the government isn't everything.

To say the least, French electors are much more ideologically flexible than they used to be. From 1997–2002, socialist prime minister Lionel Jospin ran a very conservative left-wing government without making a dent in his popularity in polls. But when Jospin did not make it to the second round of the presidential elections in 2002, the French Left voted for right-of-center Jacques Chirac to eliminate the extreme-right candidate Jean-Marie Le Pen.

France's political class has always portrayed politics as a life-and-death struggle. The decline in voter participation may not be a sign that the French are resigned, or feel they have no choices. They probably just think the system is stable. The French have earned the right to be a little indifferent: that's what political stability is all about. Charles de Gaulle should not roll in his grave over that.

chapter 23

The Meaning of Europe

Sitting at his desk writing an Institute report one Wednesday afternoon, Jean-Benoît was startled by the sound of sirens howling in the streets—not fire-engine sirens, but air-raid sirens, distant and melancholy. He recognized the sound from war movies, but it was the first time he had heard the wail for real. His thoughts spiraled. The Kosovo war was drawing to an end, but anything could have happened. Was there a nuclear attack? His thoughts raced to Julie, who was traveling in the Middle East. He thought about going down the street to the subway for shelter.

When he opened the window to check the reaction in the streets, the sirens were still wailing, but no one was running for shelter. A minute later, the sirens stopped. Apparently, it wasn't the end of the world just yet. So Jean-Benoît resumed his work, only to be interrupted ten minutes later with the same blood-curdling wail of sirens. Again, no one in the street looked concerned.

Several minutes later, our friend Gustave called to discuss some logistical details of the hiking club's outing that weekend. Gustave hadn't left for Guadeloupe yet and was still working at the Ministry of Health in Paris, so Jean-Benoît asked him what was going on. As always, Gustave obliged with a thorough explanation. All fire stations or city halls in France were equipped with sirens, he said, and performed routine tests every first

Wednesday of the month in each of France's 36,851 *communes*. The first
alarm signaled the beginning of an alert, and the second, ten minutes later,
signaled the end. The code varied depending on whether it was a fire- or
air-raid alert, but a continuous wail of thirty seconds signaled the end each
time. Jean-Benoît would grow accustomed to hearing sirens in Paris, but he
never quite got used to the sound, which sent a chill down his spine every
month.

Until recently, war was a defining element of European life. Most
European societies, including France, were built for war, and the idea of
war remains in the fabric of society. Down the street from our place was a
subway station named Guy Môquet, after the name of the seventeen-year-
old activist who was executed by the Germans in 1942. Right up the street,
on Montmartre, stands an old windmill on which the miller was nailed by
the invading Russian troops in 1812. France is full of such stories—and
worse ones. North Americans, who never faced a comparable situation to
what the French experienced during World War II, can hardly imagine the
kinds of terrible choices the French had to make just to survive. Until
recently, many of France's close neighbors were aggressive enemies. Until
1989, Strasbourg was further from Paris than it was from the Soviet tanks
on the other side of the Berlin Wall.

Europe is presently in its sixth decade of peace since World War II, the
longest span of peace in five centuries. The cancellation of France's two-
century old mandatory military service, in 1999, is just the most obvious
sign that the era of garrison-states and arsenal economies is over. France's
neighbors no longer pose a threat. Borders still exist, but they are trans-
parent and controls have all but disappeared. For a continent where border skirmishes had global consequences for five centuries, the impact of
durable peace is hard to grasp.

Since 1951, France and its neighbors have purposefully entangled
their national economies to make war impossible. But peace has had a
price. France has been forced to adopt thousands of European regulations,
which take precedence over France's own. As the almost flawless transition from the French franc to the euro shows, the French are very willing

to compromise and adapt structures to ensure peace and prosperity in Europe.

Everywhere in the world, people are speculating about how globalization will affect their societies. In France, many of the changes attributed to globalization are actually the result of European integration. Peace in Europe has transformed the political, economic, and social landscape of France. There are still important decisions to make in the next decade about Europe's direction and institutions, and no one can predict exactly what form the European Union will take. Yet judging by Europe's evolution so far, two things will happen in France: the French will greatly benefit from the integrated European economy, and Europe will challenge France's long-held prejudices about federalism.

As an old saying puts it, failure is an orphan, but success has many fathers. Europe has so many fathers it is impossible to pinpoint precisely who came up with the idea of unifying the continent. The French can safely lay claim to being among the Union's earliest architects. The Duke of Sully (1560–1641), the prime minister of Henri IV, was dreaming of a unified Europe free of customs and trade obstacles in the sixteenth century. In 1865, France, Italy, Switzerland, and Belgium established a system of parity between their diverse currencies, which they called the *Union Latine*. It remained in force until 1914.

French economist Jean Monnet (1888–1979) can be credited for laying the first practical building block of the present European construction. In 1952, he became president of the European Community of Coal and Steel, a free-trade agreement between France and Germany similar to the North American Auto Pact. Monnet's objective was to entangle European economies in a durable way in order to make war impossible. In 1955, he began lobbying full-time for the creation of the United States of Europe. In 1958, the Treaty of Rome created a common market between six countries—Belgium, France, Germany, Italy, Luxembourg, and the Netherlands. Known as the European Economic Community, the agreement was nothing more than an enlarged customs union with some common institutions. Yet this was in the pure spirit of Monnet's thinking. Monnet wanted a United States of Europe, but he did not believe it could be created out of a single grand plan. He argued that Europe should be built out of practical arrangements between countries that would slowly create authentic solidarity between them. The French would adhere to this thinking for at least the next fifty years.

From the start, the six core countries of the European Economic Community used free trade and market liberalization as tools to build unity among them. They never mistook the means for an end. To begin with, the six core countries gave themselves an executive structure: the European Commission. To create a real economic union, the founding countries of the EEC knew they needed a superior level of jurisdiction above their own national sovereignty.

(Commentators rarely point out the fact that Britain, which had refused to join the Common Market, actually began its own competing European project called EFTA, for European Free Trade Association. It involved Austria, Denmark, Norway, Portugal, Sweden, and Switzerland— and later Iceland, Liechtenstein, and Finland. Eventually most EFTA countries joined the Common Market except for Switzerland, Iceland, and Liechtenstein.)

The six core countries of the EEC had good reasons to concentrate on building stronger federal links before trying to complete economic integration. From the outset, Europe had to overcome two obstacles: deeply entrenched attachment to national sovereignty in each country, and lack of labor mobility. Establishing a superior jurisdiction was the only way to break the resistance many countries had to giving up sovereignty. But even common institutions were not enough to conquer the second practical problem: different languages and welfare systems made the bulk of Europeans captive to their own country. In practical terms, no ordinary German could simply pick up and move to Milan because there was more work there. So European countries had to accept the notion that they would have to pool fiscal resources and transfer them where they were needed, since money is more easily moved than people.

The European Economic Community stirred so much enthusiasm that by the early 1960s many European politicians were already talking about turning Europe into a federation with an elected president. French president

Charles de Gaulle crushed any hope that this would happen quickly, pro-claiming that there would be no European federation for fifty years. De Gaulle could make such a proclamation because European decision-making had to be unanimous. He disagreed with the schedule of integration set out in the Treaty of Rome, in particular with the agreement to switch to a major-ity vote by 1965. In de Gaulle's mind, that change would turn Europe into a federation, and he felt France could not sacrifice its sovereignty so quickly (he certainly wasn't ready to sacrifice any of his own power). So in 1965, France simply refused to sit at the table and vote. It took almost ten years for the EEC to revive its dynamism.

The EEC kicked off again in 1974 with the simultaneous election of two very pro-European heads of state in France and Germany who were also friends: Valéry Giscard d'Estaing and Helmut Schmidt. Britain, which joined in 1974 along with Sweden, Denmark, and Norway, became the main obstacle to European integration. The British had always been reti-cent players in Europe; they wanted fewer institutions integrated to a free-trade agreement. Giscard d'Estaing and Schmidt lobbied for more integration anyway and succeeded. In 1979, member countries agreed on a system for creating parity between their currencies, and they created the European Parliament to ratify decisions of the European Commission. The British refused to be part of any parity system, but the other countries moved forward. It was the first time that the EEC accepted leaving one of its member states behind, although this two-tiered approach later became common.

Fortunately, Valéry Giscard d'Estaing's successor, François Mitterrand, also had very strong pro-European convictions. In 1985, Mitterrand worked hard to get the pro-Europe Delors appointed as the new president of the European Commission. Delors believed that the spirit of the European Community should be rekindled with practical measures, and he set to work fostering closer economic integration. In 1986, the member countries adopted the *Acte Unique*, a program of three hundred amend-ments to the Treaty of Rome, which called for total economic integration and the removal of border controls, and granted Europe jurisdiction over research and development programs, regional affairs, and more. But the

Acte Unique was only one step up the ladder. Delors's cherished project was the creation of a single currency, but the issue provoked bitter discussions among member countries. The Germans were very attached to the Deutschmark, one of the few national symbols they had been allowed to keep during the post-war occupation. Mitterrand, who was in favor of the single currency project, promised the Germans he would support reunification (essentially allowing Germany to become the dominant country in Europe) if Germany would accept a single European currency.

In December 1991, the twelve member countries of the EEC signed the Treaty of Maastricht, creating the European Union. The treaty called for economic integration. It included measures like consumer protection, common environmental standards, free movement of citizens, and transfer payments from the richer to poorer countries. Member countries agreed to create a common foreign policy, to reinforce political and judiciary cooperation, and to put in place a common defense plan. In practice, a French company was no longer required to hold a head office in each of the member countries where it did business.

The centerpiece of the Maastricht treaty was a clear timetable for the monetary union. In 1995, the euro would replace the ECU (European Currency Unit) as Europe's currency of reference. By 1998, member countries had to meet stiff macroeconomic criteria on inflation, deficits, national debit, long-term interest rates, and stability of their national currencies so there would be parity between their different currencies. The actual transition phase to the euro would begin in May 1998, in eleven of the fifteen European countries—Britain, Denmark, and Norway refused to adopt the currency, and Greece would need another year and a half to meet the criteria. The euro became official currency in January 1999, but the old currencies of the euro zone remained in use for a three-year transition period. The population could touch the new bills and coins only in January 2002, and the old national currencies completely disappeared seven weeks later by February 17.

In the spring of 1999, Jean-Benoît attended the Bourget International Air Show, named after an airport northeast of Paris. Among the planes, one model truly impressed him: the extremely ugly Airbus Super Transporter, popularly known as "the Beluga." The cargo plane, designed to transport airplane parts between the main airbus plants in Toulouse, Hamburg, and Chester, has a puffed upper deck that really does make it look like a Beluga whale. It seemed the perfect metaphor for Airbus and for Europe: strange looking, but it flies.

Since the Treaty of Maastricht, Europeans have been openly exploring the idea of putting an end to their nation states and creating a federation. Europe is still far from being a federation, although member countries have given up a lot of their sovereignty. In a way, Europe is the blueprint for a form of much more thorough brand of political globalization than simple free trade à l'Américaine, which is almost essentially economic and supposes the absolute sovereignty of the member countries: the United States, Canada, and Mexico. European integration is the equivalent of a North American free-trade agreement that would require the United States to revoke the second amendment and support their minority languages. The European Union is the first case where a diverse group of countries has voluntarily pooled their sovereignty to create a bigger entity and handed over the traditional prerogatives of their nation states to a higher jurisdiction. By comparison, the unification of three hundred German principalities into a single country in the nineteenth century was done by force; the unification of the thirteen American colonies into the United States was done between very similar parts that spoke the same language. The European challenge is all the more impressive: this incredibly complex union is made up of diverse members who speak eleven distinct languages, not counting the dialects.

Like a bicycle, Europe has to keep moving to stay up. The number of member countries could reach twenty-seven by 2015, and without changes, Europe will become unmanageable. Member countries agree that decision-making by unanimous consent will soon become unwieldy. The Germans, who are now the biggest country in Europe, no longer feel it's fair to have the same voting weight in the European Parliament as Britain and France. At the December 2001 European summit in Nice, Germany was granted more seats, but a new balance will have to be found again before

2004, when ten more countries (among which are Poland, Cyprus, and the Czech Republic) will be admitted to the Union.

In mid-December 2001, the member countries appointed former president Valéry Giscard d'Estaing as president of the Convention on the Future of Europe. With one hundred representatives from member countries and future members, this convention will make recommendations about the future structure of the European Commission. It will deliberate on matters like whether to have an elected, rather than appointed, president, and whether to separate the Commission into an executive office and a senate. The recommendations will be presented to the heads of state of member countries in 2003. By 2004, the European Union should agree on rules of a future federation, the decision-making process of the Commission, and the powers of an elected head.

At the moment, the European Union's member countries have different opinions about the direction Europe should take. Will Europe be a minimalist free market, a true federation, a multi-shaped cooperation of sovereign states? The British favor free trade, the Germans prefer a federation, and the French support the model of a consortium of states. Each approach has clear advantages and pitfalls.

The British free-trade approach would have the advantage of making things simple. Reducing Europe to a mere free-trade organization is tempting given the number of states that will soon be involved—twenty-five by 2004. In the British model, all countries would retain their full sovereignty. However, the idea may already be obsolete. The euro has already linked Europe politically. Although there is not yet a clear leader at the helm, member states have already given up some of their own sovereignty over matters as important as trade negotiations, agricultural policy, and even taxing levels.

The German idea of a federation would have the merit of turning Europe into a real State, while allowing each member country to retain some sovereignty. The main obstacle to this model is Europe's diversity. Federations of societies that don't share a common culture tend to be fragile. Even a European union of fifteen countries speaking eleven different languages would be difficult to manage, and there will soon be almost twice that number. There are examples of successful federations that manage two or three different cultures—like Canada, Belgium, and Switzerland, but a European federation of eleven languages in fifteen former countries would be an entirely different project. In Europe, the combined effect of language and very different Social Security systems confines 99 percent of the population to their own national jurisdiction. As a result, a European federation would offer few benefits to citizens unless the notion of transfer payments was fully accepted. Many member countries are also reluctant to give up their individual privileges. At the moment, France and Great Britain both have a seat on the United Nations' Security Council. If Europe became a federal state, they would have to share one seat with the rest of the continent.

The French idea, which they call a "cooperation of states," is the most realistic model, and is pretty close to the way things are already done in Europe. Each state would retain its sovereignty, but be free to adhere to, or reject, any aspect of the Union. That is the status of the monetary union at the moment. Only twelve of the fifteen European countries have joined the single currency; Britain, Norway, and Denmark refused to join in. The British, meanwhile, strongly favored a common defense plan with France and Germany. The Treaty of Lisbon, signed by member countries in 2000, consecrated this principle of "reinforced cooperation," by which a vanguard of countries can break away from the pack and seek tighter links if they want. Prior to 2000, any other member country could veto such a move. The French model is definitely the way things are already moving, and there is frequent talk of a Franco-German federation within the European Union—a rapprochement that some consider imminent.

France's approach is the most realistic of the three because it recognizes that national identities are difficult to break. Coming from the French, the model has a surprising degree of flexibility and trial-and-error pragmatism. But the model isn't perfect. The risk is having Europe revert to the epoch before the creation of the nation-state, when political life consisted of a maze of complicated feudal and religious allegiances. The project also lacks clarity: both electors and international financiers like to know who is making decisions.

The new union may end up combining features of all three approaches. It is already a British-style free-trade agreement. It is becoming a federation by the mere fact that member states are progressively pooling important elements of their sovereignty and debating how the executive (the European Commission) and the Legislative (the European Parliament) will share powers. Yet, the European Union will probably always be a consortium of states, a loose confederation rather than a tight one. National identities will retain strong legitimacy for generations, and states will continue to seek arrangements with other countries that suit them—as the principle of "reinforced cooperation" has already recognized.

The main challenge the European Union will have to deal with in the coming years is how to give its decisions more legitimacy. The Union is not run by an elected official, a problem the Anglo-American press and opponents of the Union in all countries are quick to note. On the other hand, the European Union is not run either by faceless "eurocrats," as many critics maintain, either, although members of the European Commission, which makes recommendations to the European Council, are not elected. It is the European Council, which makes decisions, that is made up of elected representatives (ministers) from each State. Those decisions are then ratified by the European Parliament, whose members are also elected. The power of the Parliament over the Commission is also growing. When the European Parliament committee investigated cases of fraud involving a French commissioner in 1999, the controversy pushed then-president Jacques Santerre to resign, and the entire Commission followed suit. Parliament has obviously acquired a degree of legitimacy in the public sphere that it does not have on paper.

How Europe will evolve and how it will affect France over the decades to come is really anyone's guess. But one thing is almost certain: Europe will have a bigger impact on France than globalization even will.

French attitudes toward Europe have shifted many times since de Gaulle threw a wrench in the EEC's wheels in the 1960s. In 1992, the French population nearly rejected the common currency scheme by referendum. But since then, they have shown remarkable flexibility and willingness to make sacrifices for European unity—more than their politicians have shown, anyway. Like the infamous Y2K bug, the conversion to the euro in France was a much-anticipated catastrophe that never happened. The French abandoned their eight-century-old currency without remorse. And now the same people who nearly said no to the euro in 1992 are barging ahead in the single European economy and hardly looking back.

The positive effects of the single currency are already beginning to show. In the 1990s, the French economy was submitted to rigorous austerity measures in order to meet the tough single-currency requirements set out by the European Union. To strengthen the franc, the French had to reduce their deficit and adopt a zero inflation policy—pretty strong medicine, which produced high unemployment and a sustained gloom through most of the 1990s. The benefits of the euro became apparent in 1998 when the exchange rates between all eleven currencies were frozen for good. In 1999, during the first year of the euro, unemployment in France fell from double digits to single, leaving the country in positive bliss. Foreign publications began to speak of France as the locomotive of Europe.

The French have also begun to think big. The introduction of the euro means that, for the first time, individual companies are staring at a domestic market of three hundred million people, which is bigger than the U.S. domestic market and considerably richer. Boeing owes much of its past successes not only to the quality of its airplanes, but to generous military contracts (in particular, from the all-powerful U.S. Air Force) and to the sheer size of its domestic market. While Boeing grew, many of Europe's national aviation industries were suffering from the crippling effects of small domestic markets. No matter how hard the Swedes or the Dutch pushed their Saabs and their Fokkers, their national market was simply too small to sustain strong growth and achieve high economies of a large scale. But that problem is no longer there. The European consortium Airbus now receives more orders than Boeing.

The French, whose outlook has always been continental (often to a fault), stand to benefit enormously from a single domestic market large enough to equal their ambitions. However, mentalities are slow to change.

During our stay, the French economy was in a merger craze, but most of the mergers, large or small, took place with other French or American companies. The same was true of the British, the Germans, and the Italians. Two rare examples were British Vodaphone's hostile takeover of the German Mannesman (in telecommunications), and the French Rhône-Poulenc's merger with the German Hoechst (in pharmaceuticals). There were cases of transnational mergers, especially in the luxury and fashion industries, but not many. Just as the European Parliament has not yet spawned truly European parties, the European market has not yet created truly European companies that straddle old borders and bridge linguistic divides on the continent. However, many cross-border mergers happen in obscurity between medium-sized French and German companies, some of which will become the giants of tomorrow.

Also, European directives are having the positive effect of holding French economic interventionism in check. The catastrophic management of Crédit Lyonnais is a case in point. Because of bad investments, particularly in the United States, the bank lost more than one hundred billion francs (sixteen billion dollars) over ten years in the 1980s. The French government covered the deficit until the early 1990s, when the European Commission, under pressure from competing European banks, stepped in. The EC ordered the French government to stop covering the debt and told it to clean up the management of the bank while it was at it. Yes, the French State mismanaged a bank, but more importantly, France obeyed Brussels and curbed its interventionist reflex when it was told to do so.

Some CEOs of French State-owned companies are even following their new master without waiting for orders. European directives called for a deregulated natural gas market, but by 1999 the French government had still not yet passed legislation that would allow for deregulation of the State-owned natural gas company, *Gaz de France*. In an interview, the president of the company simply declared that he would no longer heed national regulations on the matter because European directives clearly had precedence. And that was an *énarque* talking—a Jesuit of the sacred principles of the Republic!

Federalism has always been the f-word of French politics. Most of the French only have a scant understanding of how a federation even works. They think of republics and federations as radically opposed, mutually exclusive forms of political organization. When we told the French that it's possible to be a federation and a republic (the United States and Germany are good examples), many didn't believe us. This allergy to federalism is so pervasive that many French opinion-makers have rejected the idea of a federal Europe out of hand, simply concluding that, "France is not a federation." The ideas of uniformity and equality and centralism are so deeply ingrained in the French mind-set that the French have trouble imagining that they could run their own affairs in their own centralized way while being *part of* a federation.

Yet thanks to the European reality, that attitude is changing. Europe has introduced the notion into the French psyche that federalism could have some benefits. The French State has already agreed to give up national sovereignty and, to a certain extent, hand its destiny to a superior level of government. Authors generally argue, probably rightly, that the French promoted Europe at the beginning because they hoped to control Europe and make it a springboard for their policy of cultural and political *grandeur*. The French know they will never control Europe and that Europe will never be "French," yet they are moving forward with integration anyway.

Europe is not yet a federation, but it has already forced the centralizing French government to loosen its grip on domestic affairs. Until the 1970s, it was dangerous to drive around Brittany with a "BZH" bumper sticker—the abbreviation of Breizh ("Brittany," in Breton). Such an affirmation of regional autonomy *in* a regional language was regarded as seditious and could land the car owner in jail! The 1999 European Charter on Regional and Minority Languages states that minorities should be protected in each country, even to the point of translating official documents into a minority language if necessary. So local groups like Bretons, Basques, and Corsicans use Brussels to gain recognition from France.

Europe, not globalization, is pushing the French to adapt their frame of reference and look outside their own borders for new examples and standards. Cultural minorities aren't alone in using the European Union as leverage against old French reflexes. As we saw at a round table on gender equity at the Canadian Embassy in Paris, women are too. Women have always been feebly represented in the French political system. The handful of French female *députées* at the seminar rejoiced about the fact that they could now use Brussels as leverage against the *machismo* of French politicians.

The French were the inventors of the Right and the Left, but under the effect of Europe, traditional political fault lines are mutating into a federalist-sovereignist split, Canadian style. The cracks in traditional party division first started to show during the 1992 referendum on Europe. Much in the way that some Americans never accepted the very existence of a federal government in the United States, Jacobin politicians, whether from the Right or the Left, all turned out to be sovereignists (defenders of France's sovereignty against Europe). The pro-sovereignty camp typically believes that Europe would be a state in its own right, which would reduce former member states to the status of provinces. France's libertarian thinkers and pragmatists turned out to be federalists (who think Europe should have precedence over its member states). Federalists want Europe to be one state. This new split hasn't destroyed any traditional political parties in France yet, but the issue demonstrates that even France is seeking new categories for a new political reality.

Europe is clearly taking its rightful place in French minds and hearts. The European Court of Justice and the European Human Rights Court have turned the *Conseil d'État* into a lower jurisdiction of administrative law. In 1976, the *Conseil Constitutionnel* ruled that transfers of sovereignty to Europe were unconstitutional, since France's Constitution stipulates that sovereignty is sacred. Technically, that means that most of Europe is unconstitutional by French law. Do the French care? No. They are barging ahead with European integration anyway.

But of course, modern France is only a chapter in the life of a very old people. The French aren't less French, even inside Europe. The European Union is certainly not the end of the French story, but simply another chapter. Nobody knows what Europe will make of the French, or what the

French will make of Europe. The only certainty is that the French have put a peaceful Europe at the top of their political agenda for at least the century to come.

A friend of ours recounted a funny anecdote (he swears it's true) that encapsulates the French outlook on Europe these days. He visited a *fromagerie* (cheese dairy) in the very rural *Département* of La Creuse, east of Limoges. Far from the *artisanal* installation he was expecting, the dairy turned out to be a slick operation. The cheesemaker had invested heavily in modernizing to meet Europe's stringent hygiene standards, and complained bitterly about the cost, which had almost put him out of business.

"And the worse of it is, you know what? he asked our friend. *Le fromage ne prend pas!* (The cheese doesn't set.)"

"Why not?" our friend asked.

"It's too clean." (Cheese needs bacteria to grow).

"So, what are you doing about that?"

The cheesemaker had the answer: "We just open the windows and let the outside air in!"

Yes, Europe is changing the French. But the French are still going about it their own way.

Afterword

As the French would say, *la mémoire est une faculté qui oublie* (memory is a faculty that forgets). We were plowing through the second draft of *Sixty Million Frenchmen Can't Be Wrong* when we recalled a conversation with a Frenchwoman on the airplane on our way to Paris in 1999. A snowstorm had delayed the takeoff, and we were chatting to pass the time. Madame Cirinski, who lived in the Paris region, told us she was returning home after visiting her daughter, a hairdresser in Quebec. She wanted to know what we would be doing in Paris, so we told her we were journalists, and explained the Institute. When she realized that we were heading off to study her country, she made one of the most memorable comments we would hear throughout the course of our travels:

"You know, France is not what it used to be."

During our two and a half years in France, we heard those words from at least a dozen different mouths across the country. Sometimes the expression sounded like nostalgia, sometimes it sounded like racism. Yet despite the motives, there is a certain truth to the words. France really isn't what it used to be. What we have tried to show in this book is that France *never has been* "what it used to be."

We are not saying there's no such thing as France. The country simply changes all the time. It always has.

Yet some things about France are not changing quickly. In the first part of the book, we explored the values that we think are durable features of the French national character: their sense of privacy, their love of *grandeur* and rhetoric, and their political intransigence. To put things in perspective for non-Europeans, we developed the idea that the French are the aborigines of France, and we tried to explain their uncanny attachment to their own land, and how that attachment shapes their outlook. We decided to add the two chapters on World War II and Algeria during our second draft, because we realized that these events have profoundly shaped the way the French think and act. In fact, they are still there, shaping France today.

In our opinion, these values, features, and events, together, form the foundation of the French national character. They will change. They already are changing, and who knows what the future holds? France could go through something as horrible as World War II or the War of Algeria again, and the aftermath could send the country in another direction altogether. What we wanted to show in the second part of the book is that France's democratic institutions are made to accommodate France's national character, or even, as in the case of their political intransigence, contain it. Will France's institutions end up quelling this intransigence? Will the French love of *grandeur* and rhetoric be leveled in the process? Maybe, but it's impossible to predict. Criticism leveled at France's *élite* may eventually bring institutionalized *élitism* to an end, or just force a change of *élites*.

It is also hard to predict whether some new event, invention, or pattern of social interaction will redefine the French sense of privacy, space, and time—more distinct traits buried deep in the French national character. Yet anything is possible: France's *terrien* mentality is very strong, but it is becoming increasingly irrelevant in the post-modern, consumption society France has become, and it may well disappear someday. In the past, France has been able to change overnight to adapt to new circumstances and there is no reason why this cannot happen again. The French dropped their old currency, the franc, without a bit of remorse. In spite of rear-guard battles to defend small-scale agriculture, France rejected the agrarian way of life more than fifty years ago and successfully became an industrial nation. Change is not all bad, but more importantly, in the long run, these changes will be little more than anecdotes in the history of an already ancient people.

In the second part of the book, we explained what we believe are the main factors structuring French society: its democratic institutions, the State machine, and lack of political liberty at the local level. We argue that the French are fixed on language at least partly because language and culture were the main instruments used in State-building in France. Education also plays a special role in French society. It is the net the French cast to find talented people to run their country. No matter what the world thinks about the French law system and French political institutions, they, too, need to be understood in their context: they were made by the French, for the French, to suit the French character and France's political culture. Protest and lack of individual initiative each have their place in the system, too. We tried to poke a few holes in common prejudices about the "welfare system," which is more corporatist than socialist, and economic interventionism, which is neither new, nor as inefficient as it is accused of being.

In the third section of the book, we wanted to show the forces that are changing French society. First, we thought it was important to show what kind of global player France is, and to put France's "resistance" to globalization in perspective. In our opinion, the French are not really resisting globalization at all. Immigration, democracy, and Europe are much more important forces of change, anyway. The arrival of millions of immigrants and their children is provoking the same kinds of tensions and demanding the same kinds of adjustments in France as it is in most Western societies. France is slowly realizing that its principle of assimilation may actually be preventing integration. Meanwhile, the French themselves forget that a working democracy is a recent phenomenon, and they will have to adapt their political traditions to suit it. Finally, Europe, which started out as a very progressive common market in 1958, is progressively stripping France of some attributes of its sovereignty. Commentators often fail to consider how these factors—which are almost totally unrelated to globalization—are changing the French.

That brought us to the question of how Europe will affect the structures the French gave themselves. Will the French keep their elected-monarch president? Will they ever conceive of political life outside of a highly centralized system? As Europe turns into a federation, will the French State be diminished and lose its role as a stabilizing force in France? The answer, again, is maybe.

And of course, it's not the first, or the last, time France will adapt to revolutionary new developments. Like all advanced societies, France has already been transformed by democracy, capitalism, the industrial revolution, women's liberation, outlawing capital punishment, double-entry accounting, the end of the gold standard, the printing press, the Internet, and the combustion engine. These powerful changes met hardly any obstacle: their impact only varied depending on the values they met. Ideas and influences started circulating long before the term "globalization" was ever used.

Although it was our intention to do more than explain the news in France, *Sixty Million Frenchmen Can't Be Wrong* will be a book of its time, like all others. It would take a diviner to predict what France will look like in fifty years, let alone a hundred. But one thing is certain: France is not what it used to be. France has never been what it used to be, and it never will. So we might as well enjoy it while it lasts.

— Montreal, July 4, 2002

France's Changing Regimes

France has had twelve regimes since 1789. Some beginning and ending dates are approximate.

Constitutional Monarchy: 1791–92. The legislature is created. The king, legally a citizen like all others, is recognized as the symbol of the State.

1st Republic: 1792–1804. Parliament tries to run the country without a king. Anarchy follows. Napoleon heads a *coup d'état* and is appointed Consul in 1799.

1st Empire: 1804–15. Napoleon crowns himself emperor in 1804 and rules by decree. Rule ends in military defeat and Napoleon is in exile by 1814.

Restauration. 1815–30. Foreign powers install Louis XVIII on the French throne. The two chambers are more Royalist than the king is. The regime veers towards absolutism and ends in a revolution.

Monarchy of July: 1830–48. Constitutional monarchy. Louis-Philippe I, though liberal at first, becomes more authoritarian. Ends in a Revolution.

2nd Republic: 1848–52. No more king. The legislature has strong powers. The president, Louis-Napoleon, is appointed president-prince in 1852.

2nd Empire: 1852–70. The president-prince becomes Emperor Napoleon III. Rules by decree. His reign ends with defeat by the Prussians.

3rd Republic: 1871–1940. This long-lived Republic starts as a quasi-monarchy, but the Republic is finally proclaimed in 1875 by a majority of one vote. The new Constitution gives no power to the president, and no one has authority to arbitrate conflict between the legislature and the cabinet. The cabinet resigns each time the legislature votes against them for the smallest matter. Instability becomes the norm, and the government changes 120 times during this period.

État Français: 1940–44. Fascist dictatorship. As a result of military defeat by the German army, Parliament abolishes itself and hands all power to Maréchal Philippe Pétain. He runs the southern half of the country from the city of Vichy, hence the name the Vichy government.

Provisional Government of the French Republic: 1944–46. Created by decree and headed by Charles de Gaulle. Partly succeeded in renewing institutions, but failed to bring forward a new Constitution.

4th Republic: 1946–58. Similar Constitution as the 3rd Republic, and it works no better, with twenty different governments in twelve years. Ends with threats of a military coup.

5th Republic: Since 1959. De Gaulle bullies the National Assembly into giving him full powers to reestablish order. He redrafts a new Constitution. The president becomes the effective head of state, with special powers over the Parliament and the Constitution.

ENA Postings

This is the translation of the prime minister's decree of September 2000 on the postings offered to the 110 students of ÉNA graduating in April 2001.

The vocabulary used is French and does not translate very well. The term administrateur civil, *which applies to half of the postings, refers to that of a high-ranking official acting as an aid to a minister, reporting to the minister's office. The term* deuxième classe, *which we translated as second-class, should be thought of as junior, as opposed to senior. The army uses the same vocabulary, which highlights the military origins of France's civil service.*

Conseil d'État (Council of State): 5 junior officials, 2nd-class
Cour des Comptes: 5 junior officials, 2nd-class
Ministry of Finance: 5 assistant inspectors
Administrative Tribunals and Appeal Courts: 11 councilors
Regional Revenue Court: 7 councilors
Foreign Affairs: 7 councilors
Foreign Affairs: 1 commercial attaché
Administration Inspection: 2 assistant inspectors
Social Affairs, Inspection Services: 4 assistant inspectors
Prime Minister's Office, General Secretaria of Government: 2 *administrateurs civils,* 2nd-class
Prime Minister's Office, National Defense Secretariat: 2 administrateurs civils, 2nd-class
Ministry of Finance: 14 administrateurs civils, 2nd-class
Ministry of Labour: 13 administrateurs civils, 2nd-class
Ministry of Justice: 1 administrateur civil, 2nd-class
Ministry of the Interior: 12 administrateurs civils, 2nd-class
Ministry of National Education: 6 administrateurs civils, 2nd-class
Ministry of Defense: 1 administrateur civil, 2nd-class
Ministry of Equipment and Transport: 2 administrateurs civils, 2nd-class
Ministry of Culture: 1 administrateur civil, 2nd-class
Ministry of Agriculture and Fishing: 1 administrateur civil, 2nd-class
City of Paris: 4 administrateurs

Index

About the Authors

Canadian journalists Jean-Benoît Nadeau and Julie Barlow have spent the last decade working extensively in both of their country's official languages.

Born in Sherbrooke, Quebec, in 1964, Jean-Benoît Nadeau holds a bachelor's degree in political science and history from McGill University. A journalist since 1987, he has written for *L'actualité*, *Saturday Night Magazine*, *National Post Business*, and *Quebec Science*. The holder of seventeen journalism awards, he was granted a two-year fellowship in 1998 by the New Hampshire–based Institute for Current World Affairs to study why the French resist globalization. In 2001, he published a humorous travelogue, *Les français aussi ont un accent* (Payot, Paris). He has also traveled in Mexico, the UK, New Zealand, and Algeria.

Born in Ancaster, Ontario, in 1968, Julie Barlow holds an honour's degree in political science from McGill University and a master's in English Literature from Concordia University. Over the last decade, she has written for *Saturday Night Magazine*, *Report on Business Magazine*, *L'actualité*, and other Canadian magazines. In 1998, she worked as Editor-in-Chief of English-language projects at Montreal-based publisher Ma Carrière. In 2003, she published *Same Words, Different Language* (Piatkus, London) with international gender expert Barbara Annis. She has traveled extensively throughout Europe, North Africa, Israel, Turkey, the Caucasus, Mexico, the UK, and New Zealand.

The couple is now based in Montreal, where they are living happily in French and English while producing their next book, *The Story of French*.